Dear Diary I'm Wasted

Alexander Strenger

Cover design by Eric Wagner

Website design by Harry Wolff

www.deardiaryimwasted.com

ISBN-13 978-1466242531

ISBN-10 1466242531

Library of Congress Registration Number TXu-1-747-859

TO MEI,
stay in school. don't
do drugs

signature

DEDICATION

To Mom and Dad for allowing me to stay in the house. Without your support this book would have never been finished. I love you guys.

CONTENTS

1   The Creation of a Monster   1

2   Bitches, Bitches, Ho's, and Bitches   37

3   Just Watch It All Unravel   133

4   Putting The Pieces Back Together   232

5   Fuck It All   327

6   Party's Over   383

7   A New Beginning   390

school, I lead a very sheltered life. I grew up in Riverdale, a small town in

the Bronx about an hour away from Manhattan by public transportation.

For most of my childhood and adolescence, Manhattan seemed like an

eternity away, since I had absolutely no clue how to navigate around the

city.

From the age of nine up until I went to college, I attended the

Summit School, a K-12 school in Jamaica Estates, Queens, with no more

than 300 kids. The school provided bus service to and from my house,

meaning that I had very little contact with people other than my parents

or classmates.

Chris and Toby were two of my best friends from high school. We

met as freshmen playing basketball at lunch and were instantly

inseparable. I was never more comfortable around anybody else and felt

completely uninhibited when the three of us were together.

Chris and Toby always seemed to have a story to tell. Most of

these stories were about their various sexual conquests and hearing

about their exploits with different girls left me in awe of them. The thing

about Toby and Chris was that they were not exceptionally good-looking

people. Toby was tall and lanky, with thick wild curly hair, a gigantic nose, and humungous beaver teeth that jutted out like the feathers from a peacock. To get a clearer picture of what Toby looked like, you would have to imagine the byproduct of Big Bird and Waldo (from where's Waldo) having sex and making a baby.

Chris, on the other hand was short, stocky, and prematurely balding. He was half Korean and looked like Oddjob from one of the old James Bond movies. Toby and Chris looked like Goblins. Yet they were getting laid left and right. At the time, I couldn't understand how two people, with faces to scare away little children, were getting so much pussy, especially since they treated girls like they were sub-human. Both of them cheated on every girlfriend they had, degraded girls to their face, blatantly ignored girls who liked them, and would lie about anything and everything under the sun in order to get laid. Yet the worse they treated these girls, the more in love the girls fell with them. Their success rate with chicks was mind boggling to me. And as a result, I saw Chris and Toby as role models for how to interact with the opposite sex.

My life was boring as hell and I craved excitement. I needed to be cool more than anything else in the world and wanted nothing more than to have awesome stories like Chris and Toby. The problem was that I was terrible with girls. Even though I was tall, in shape, and athletic, women were just not attracted to me. I was painfully awkward around the opposite sex and I attribute this primarily to where I went to school. Only 20% of the people at Summit were girls and 90% of them looked like creatures from a sci-fi horror movie. Because pretty girls were so few and far between, anytime I saw a girl who was remotely attractive, I would freeze up and stare at her as though she were some kind of goddess.

The television became my guide for interacting with the female species and I thought that girls acted the same in person as they did on t.v or in the movies. My sister would watch these chick flick drama shows on channel 11, depicting how young adults behaved in relationships. Boy Meets World, Gilmore Girls, Friends and every show on TGIF became my video strategy guide for talking to girls. This could have been why I didn't have stories of my own to share like Chris and Toby.

When I was a junior in high school, I saw "Catch Me If You Can" starring Leonardo Di Caprio, and a light bulb went off over my head. In case you never saw it, the movie was about this guy who stole millions of dollars from the U.S government, by writing bad checks, all while pretending to be, a doctor, lawyer, and airline pilot, when in fact, he was nothing more than a kid. I was fascinated by the possibility of transforming myself into another human being and escaping my boring reality.

I had an SAT tutor at Columbia University, who I was introduced to through Toby's mom. Her name was Sheila and we used to meet twice a week to go over the verbal section, as well as different strategies for taking the exam. Seeing Shiela used to be the highlight of my week, because I felt like a Columbia student whenever I saw her. I was in heaven, surrounded by beautiful College girls, and used to walk around campus for hours, fantasizing about fucking each and every one of them.

After almost a half a year of staring in awe and ogling at these girls, I finally worked up the courage to talk to one of them. I was feeling extra confident, because I had gotten head from some random girl while on vacation with Chris and his family last week. (Granted, she was 14 years old and bi-polar. But hey, it's still better than jerking off, right?) Anyway, Sheila and I had just finished our lesson when I walked up to this girl named Marissa and bummed a cigarette off of her. As we shared one of her Marlboro Red's outside the library, I showered this girl with an unbelievable stream of bullshit that was too ridiculous for words. I told her I was an incoming freshman from California who dreamed of becoming a doctor, when in reality I nearly failed every one of my science classes and didn't know what the 4 chambers of the heart were called. Marissa was impressed and asked for my number, saying that she was due for a "check-up". I couldn't wait to grant her wish and gave the girl 500 cc's of man juice all over her face and chest the next day. Marissa couldn't get enough, begging me to keep in touch with her, saying that she planned on coming up to school for freshman orientation week so I could have "someone to examine".

Orientation came and it was time to unleash my secret identity. I was no longer a shy, sheltered 16-year old kid from Riverdale, but rather a smooth talking Ivy League freshman from San Diego with a budding modeling career. Surrounded by thousands of hot college girls wearing nothing but tank tops and mini skirts, I felt like a kid in a candy store, only the candy had tits and I wanted to put my dick inside it.

Marissa called me so I went up to her room, where she licked my sausage up and down as though it were a Nathan's hotdog. We watched a movie afterwards, before she went uptown to see her grandmother, leaving me to wander around campus by myself.

Sitting outside Alfred Lerner hall, smoking a cigarette and feeling on top of the world, I was approached by some guy named Joey who asked to bum a stoge off of me. We each had a Camel Light and spent the next two hours having an intense discussion on the nutritional benefits of eating pussy. Joey then invited me to a party that PKE (his frat) was hosting.

I met Joey outside the PKE house at 11 p.m. He gave me a beer and introduced me to a bunch of the brothers. We spent the night playing beer pong, flip cup, and taking bong hits. As the night progressed, I realized that the more wasted I got, the more comfortable I became around girls. When the night began, I was perched up against a wall drinking alone, afraid to interact with anybody. Yet by the time the night was over I was a fucking superstar. That's right, in my mind I was the life of the party and felt as though I could do no wrong when it came to talking with the opposite sex.

I wound up making out with this girl Loretta outside the house. Unfortunately, Marissa was at the same party and caught me red handed hooking up with her. She walked up behind me, tapped me on the shoulder, and promptly kicked me square in the nuts right when I turned around. As I lay in a fetal position clutching my sweet precious balls, Marissa began repeatedly punching me in the head, before Joey and a few other brothers pulled her off of me. Joey asked me what happened so I told him that she gave me head earlier in the day. All of us cracked up laughing, before smoking a blunt on Joey's couch and passing out.

Two days later, I hung out with this girl Ariel, who's number I got at the party. We went to her room, smoked a bowl, and spent the afternoon fooling around in bed. At night, Ariel and I went back to the PKE house for another party, where I took bong hits with Joey, who "convinced" me to pledge next semester.

High and drunk, Ariel and I start making out on the stairs before going back to her room. Unfortunately, the night didn't quite exactly end in sex. See, my dick was hard and I had the condom on. But when it came time to "get it in", I was too fucked up to find the hole. She asked if it was my first time and the embarrassment I felt was indescribable. Needless to say, that was the last I heard from Ariel.

***

Believe it or not, I wasn't a virgin. I had sex once before, about a year prior to that incident. I was working at a day camp in the Riverdale Y, where every girl thought I was a weirdo with a staring problem. There was, however, one girl who took an interest in me. Her name was Jackie and she was a 22-year old teaching assistant living in Rockland County. Jackie wasn't the hottest girl at the camp; as a matter of fact she looked like the female version of Peter Griffin from Family Guy. Yet, what she lacked in looks, she more than made up for in sexual eagerness.

It was a week after camp ended and Jackie invited me to her house in Rockland County. She picked me up at the Riverdale Y and played with my nuts while driving over the Tappan Zee Bridge. When we got to her place, Jackie ripped off my pants and gave me head as though she invented the concept of sucking dick.

Jackie made me return the favor. I had no idea what I was doing, but she already knew how inexperienced I was and gave me a lesson I'd never forget, teaching me the proper way to kiss her, finger her, suck on her tits, and eat her out. After getting her off, she told me to put on a condom. As you can imagine, I had no idea what the hell I was doing and my dick kept accidentally sliding out of her after almost every thrust.

My first sexual experience officially became a disaster when I noticed some red bumps on her pussy. Since this was the first time I ever saw a vagina that wasn't on the Internet or in a magazine, I thought that she had herpes and started freaking out. I took the condom off and made her drive me home, only to find out later that they were nothing more than shaving bumps. Oops!

***

Back at Columbia, I took this girl Julie to the movies the day after blowing it with Ariel. After the movie, we walked to Lincoln Center and sat down by a fountain. She had her head rested on my shoulder and asked me to tell her something, so I asked what her biggest fear was. I don't remember what she said, because I was too wrapped up in hooking up with her to care, but I looked her in the eyes and told her that my biggest fear was winding up a lonely old man that nobody cared about. I than leaned in to kiss her and we made out under the stars, before going back to her room and having sex for 25 seconds.

I'll never forget Orientation week for as long as I live. For an entire week, I had escaped my boring reality and became the ideal version of myself, someone who was smooth, suave, and charming, rather than a socially awkward 16-year old. I felt as though I was starring in my own personal movie and it was akin to having an out of body experience. Being able to transform myself into another person was amazing, more powerful than any sensation I had ever experienced, and it made me feel like I was walking on a cloud.

Living A Lie

I got a fake ID during my senior year of high school and began going out to bars on weekends. A man named Dave Roth introduced me to the bar scene. Dave was a personal trainer, who once harbored dreams of playing professional basketball. However, his dreams got derailed during his sophomore year of college when his parents got sick, forcing him to quit the team in order to take care of them. I had known Dave for years and decided to hire him as my trainer because I wanted to play college basketball.

Dave decided to take me out for my 18th birthday. We went to this bar called Evelyn's on the upper west side. From the moment I walked into the bar, a new world opened up to me. I felt a combination of nervous excitement as the bouncer checked my ID and let me through the door. Having my ID examined by someone who could confiscate it at any minute was nerve racking to say the least. I had spent close to $100

on getting a fake ID and would have felt crushed and dejected had it been

taken away on my first night out. My heart was racing a mile a minute

and my hands were trembling. Dave sensed this and calmed me down,

explaining that I would be fine as long as I presented myself like a regular.

He was right and the bouncer let me in without so much as a second

glance at my ID.

As I made my way to the dance floor, I saw a bunch of beautiful

girls grinding up on and making out with whomever they pleased. I felt as

though I were in a giant orgy and was overwhelmed with the amount of

pussy in front of me. Dave saw that I was nervous and put his hand on my

shoulder, before buying me a drink. While we sat at the bar, Dave told

me the most important advice about talking to women I had ever

received, and that was to be as relaxed as possible and not fear rejection.

Dave then began hooking up with some girl who looked like a

hybrid of Rosie O'Donnell and Miss Piggy, leaving me alone to ponder his

words. As I sat at the bar contemplating Dave's words of wisdom, I all of a

sudden remembered what worked at Columbia. "Getting girls ain't rocket

science; in fact it's quite simple. Just get drunk and make up nonsense about yourself. Than you'll be fine. Besides, its not like I can do any worse than Dave." I thought to myself, as I looked in the mirror, realizing that his training had put me in the best shape of my life and that girls were going to like me no matter what came out of my mouth. So with that said, I walked onto the dance floor feeling like a mixture of The Fonz, James Bond, Batman, and Shaft. Speaking of Shaft, some girl wound up giving me a handjob on the couch a few minutes before closing time. I don't recall how it happened, what I said to her, or how she looked. All I can say was that episodes of this nature became common occurrences whenever I went to Evelyn's.

Out of all the no names and no faces at Evelyn's, one stood out. Her name was Christina and she was a 24-year-old Princeton Graduate, who I would not have met if it weren't for a very bad date I had.

A 32-year old accountant gave me her number a week earlier. We agreed to see M. Night Shyamalan's "The Village." She paid for my ticket so I figured that she wanted me to split her vagina in half, but then pushed my hand away when I tried to put my arm around her in the theatre. I had better things to do with myself than hang out with a girl who wasn't going to give me any pussy. And besides, the movie sucked anyway. So I left the theatre and called Chris to get drunk. We met at his apartment and spent the next couple of hours taking shots of Tequila on his balcony before going to Evelyn's.

I used my credit card at a bar for the first time that night. When the bar tender said I had to order a $10.00 minimum, I thought he meant for me to order 2 drinks at once. Here I was, cluelessly walking around the bar, carrying two drinks in my hand like an idiot, when all of a sudden, this beautiful woman with long brown hair, brown eyes, olive skin, and an hour glass figure asked me why I was double fisting. She then introduced herself and I just stood there with my mouth open like a moron because I didn't know what double fisting was, before stammering out an awkward response that caused her to walk away. That girls name was Christina.

Thinking I blew it, I went outside to have a cigarette, when lo and behold whom did I run into but Christina herself? We started talking and it turned out that Christina had just gotten her B.A. from Princeton and was taking a publishing course at Columbia over the summer.

Christina was this jaw droopingly gorgeous girl, with her soft skin, warm expression, and smile that could light up a room. The more she talked, the more beautiful she became. So there was absolutely no way in hell I could tell her the truth about myself. Had she known I was 18, she would have instantly walked away. And that couldn't happen, because Christina had way too much to offer for me to just let her go.

The only way for me to have stood a chance at being with her was to create a totally secret identity, and create a secret identity I did. Because I took an intro to psyc course at NYU the previous summer and had an NYU ID, I told her that I was 23 and starting graduate school at NYU for psychology. I also told her that I was sharing a duplex apartment on 96th street and Broadway with Chris, who was living off his imaginary trust fund, in order to explain how a college student with no job could afford such plush living conditions.

After briefly getting to know each other, we headed to the dance floor and almost immediately began making out. Christina and I had a magnetic attraction, unable to keep our hands off each other, and it wasn't long before we took a cab to her dorm on 116th and Broadway.

Thank god we didn't have sex!! At the time, I had about 5-minutes of sexual experience and would have been awful in bed, ruining any chance of developing a relationship with her. Christina and I clicked on so many levels, not just physically, emotionally too. It was like we were kindred spirits. I wanted to spend every waking moment of every day with her, despite having only known the girl for less than an hour. So when she laid her head on my chest, draping her body around me like a blanket before falling asleep, I made up my mind that we were going to be together.

***

Unfortunately, it was 3 weeks until I saw Christina again, since she had to see her family in Connecticut. During those three weeks I got myself a girlfriend, and that's when I began to fully comprehend how good it felt to be inside of a pussy.

I was a week into my freshman year at Concordia College and had just finished playing basketball, when this guy named Jim invited me to get drunk in his room. After about 8 or 9 shots, we decided to wander around the dorms and make ridiculous comments to girls who passed by. I walked up to this plain looking brunette, while carrying a Maxim magazine, and said: "oh my god, it's you", as I pointed at the cover. She giggled and introduced herself. Her name was Lauren and she was a freshman like me. There was a party on campus so we went there together, before leaving and spending the rest of the night making out under a tree.

The following night we were in bed, about to have sex, when Lauren stopped me. I asked her what was wrong, and she told me that she didn't want to have sex unless she was in a relationship. Well, I wanted a girlfriend because my friends had girlfriends, guys with girlfriends had more sex, and guys with girlfriends seemed pretty happy on t.v, so I told Lauren that I wanted nothing more than to be with her. I then put on a condom and ripped her vagina in two for 45 whole seconds, before ejaculating and falling asleep.

Just for the record, going out with Lauren proved to be the biggest mistake of my college career. There was nothing special about her. She wasn't pretty, funny, nice, or charming, but since I went to high school with a bunch of sea monsters, I thought Lauren was the most beautiful girl on the planet.

Lauren and I went out for a week, and she was my world during those seven "magical" days we spent together. I treated her like a princess, bending over backward to her every whim. Whatever Lauren wanted, Lauren got, and I did whatever was in my power to make her happy: be it taking her to dinner, watching a chick flick, comforting her when she was upset, hanging out with her friends, and listening to her talk about absolutely nothing important for hours on end.

While we went out, people thought I was on the basketball team, because I was working out with them on a daily basis. It didn't matter that Concordia was a small Division II school with less than 2,000 students, the fact that I played basketball still allowed me to literally have my pick of girls to choose from. Instead of taking advantage of such a wonderful opportunity, I decided to be a faithful boyfriend; faithful to the point where I refused to even interact with other girls so that Lauren wouldn't get jealous.

Now what did Lauren do? Well, she stopped wanting to have sex, ignored my phone calls, yelled at me for absolutely no reason, and hit on other guys in front of me. Before I go any further, let me reiterate that I was a retard and still wanted to be with her despite how much of a bitch she was. Lauren grew less interested with each nice thing I did for her, until she finally broke up with me.

I was inconsolable for 35 minutes and decided to get drunk. There was a party on campus and I felt that fucking another girl would be the best way to get my mind off of her. Lauren had other plans, as her

friends swarmed me like a pack of wolves right when I left my dorm. They

dragged me into the hallway and yelled at me, saying that they were

going to call the cops if I ever put my hands on Lauren again. Confused

and bewildered, I asked them what the fuck they were talking about.

Apparently, Lauren made up a fictitious story where she accused me of

trying to rape her. I couldn't believe what I was hearing, especially since

Lauren wanted to fuck the first night we met, and the only reason we

didn't was because none of us had a condom. After listening to her

friends spew out a waterfall of bullshit for what seemed like an eternity, I

than proceed to tell them my side of the story, aka the truth.

I told them that I'd never lay my hand on a woman in that way,

that I never did a single thing to disrespect her, and that she just broke up

with me for being too nice to her. They seemed skeptical, so I showed

them the text message Lauren sent, about how good my cock felt inside

her. That wasn't enough to convince these girls, so I made them call

Lauren and put her on speakerphone, in order to hear the truth once and

for all. This bitch vehemently stuck to her story, until I chimed in, asking

why she would send a rapist text messages about wanting his cock inside her. Lauren than finally broke down, admitting that she made up the story out of guilt for having had sex with me too quickly.

Despite being a complete piece of garbage, I am really glad that I met Lauren, because she taught me what not to do in a relationship: that the better you treat women the worse they will treat you. I was a model boyfriend to her, doing everything "I was supposed to do" in a relationship, and what did I get other than mistreated and ignored? I looked at guys like Chris and Toby, complete and total assholes who girls constantly complained about. Yet, these same girls were fucking guys like that left and right, while also treating them like kings. That's when it hit me. Being a cocky, lying, manipulative, cheating scumbag, who cared only about himself, was the key to getting girls.

A Love Story

I saw Christina the following weekend and my mind was consumed with lust. Like I said earlier, going out with Lauren put me on to how good being inside a pussy felt, and by the time I saw Christina my penis was like a deranged animal ready to pounce on anything that moved.

Pound that shit out!!! That's the key to making a girl fall in love with you, which is what I did, impaling Christina like a "Stanley Power Drill" for over an hour, before finally erupting inside her like a volcano.

"So this is what it feels like to be a man?" I thought, in a state of blissful contentment, as Christina lay cuddled up against me, while I smoked a cigarette in bed. Life was good. I just had earth-shattering sex for the first time in my life, with a woman I cared about no less. This was almost perfect.

Christina and I spent the first of many weekends together. We quickly developed a really intimate relationship, and would literally spend days on end in bed together. In addition to the physical chemistry we shared, there was this instant emotional comfort that existed between us, and I felt as though we could have an entire conversation without even speaking a word.

Christina was amazing. She didn't care if I was her boyfriend, never made me take her out, always offered to pay when we went out, and was genuinely appreciative of everything I did for her, regardless of how small it was. This girl was an angel, an angel that possessed the gift of unconditional love both in her ability to give and receive it.

The more involved we got, the more immersed I became in my own lie. I began to actually feel like an NYU graduate student and even made up a class schedule for myself. On Monday and Friday I took Advanced Psychological Statistics from 5:00 pm-7:00 pm, and on Tuesday and Thursday I took Therapeutic Treatment of Patients from 6:00 pm-8:00 pm. I even went so far as to send Christina papers that other people wrote for these classes so that she could fix the grammatical mistakes.

Christina almost uncovered me when the bouncer at Brother Jimmy's (a bar on the upper east side) rejected my ID. She began to grow suspicious that I wasn't who I said I was, and asked me a series of interrogating questions, such as: "How old are you? Why did the bouncer just reject you? Let me see your ID? Why does your ID say you're from Michigan?"

I was on the hot seat and had to think fast. In a moment of panic, I made up one of the most ridiculous, nonsensical, off the wall stories ever contrived. "Chris got really drunk last week and punched that same bouncer in the face, because he threw us out for being too loud. The bouncer must have recognized me and used the fact that I look young to deny me entrance into the bar." Christina thought this was the dumbest thing she had ever heard and made me take my ID out. "You're not from Michigan. This shit is fake! How stupid do you think I am?" Christina screamed.

"Baby, I can explain that," I said to her. And then proceeded to tell Christina that the reason I had a Michigan ID was because my grandmother lived in Michigan and suffered a stroke, so I had to spend the past year and a half taking care of her. I lost my New York ID, but since I've lived in Michigan for over a year I was able to qualify for residency and just used my Michigan ID wherever I went.

Christina was still skeptical and asked to see my NYU ID, which I actually had, since I took Intro to Psychology as an AP course while still in high school. Last year, I had a huge Jew fro and looked like a 1970s porn star, so my ID picture made me look a lot younger than I was. Cristina believed me after looking at my ID and began to calm down, so I jokingly asked if she wanted to see my birth certificate. She laughed and I seized the moment, holding both of her hands and looking her dead in the eye, saying that I'd never lie to her.

Christina wanted to believe me so she let it go. This girl wasn't stupid and could have easily figured out that I was feeding her a monsoon of nonsense, yet she chose to overlook it instead. Our relationship was based on an illusion but we ignored it, because the illusion made both of us happy. I told her that I was a Psych Grad student and played the role to perfection, acting like a mature adult instead of an 18-year old kid. Christina was so beautiful in every way possible, from her smile, to her voice, to her personality, and she belonged with someone successful, not some immature freshman in college. In her mind I was someone she could be proud of dating, someone she could show off to her friends and introduce to her parents, and I just didn't have the heart to let her down by exposing myself as a child. Telling Christina the truth would have made her feel like an idiot, and this girl did not deserve to be played.

There finally came a point in our relationship where I had to be a man and own up to what I really was. It had been less than two months and we were already getting serious, spending weekends together and talking almost every day. Even though we barely knew each other, both of us could see a future together, which was why she invited me to Connecticut to meet her friends and family.

This was crazy! I couldn't believe how far along I was in this lie. A part of me wanted to see if I could con her friends and family into believing that I was in graduate school. But the logical part knew that was an awful idea, as meeting her parents based on a lie would have instantly destroyed whatever small chance we had of being together after she uncovered the truth.

This was wrong. The lies. The charade. Everything. Christina didn't deserve this. She didn't deserve to be strung along like a puppet. No, she deserved to be with a man that would unconditionally love and honor her, not some little boy playing make-believe for his own amusement. I cared about this girl a lot, way too much to continue deceiving her, and the more I manipulated her the more consumed with guilt I became. My conscience was gnawing at me for living a lie and I had to come clean. We had been together for less than 2 months, so at least by confessing now, Christina would be able to move on without getting her heart broken too badly.

I came over to her house the week before Halloween, bearing gifts in the form of

roses and beer, hoping to ease the blow of what I was about to confess. We were lying in bed together and I started shaking, knowing that the truth was about to come out. Christina looked at me with pressing concern, saying: "What's wrong sweetie?"

Me: "Baby, there's something I need to tell you". I stammered.

Christina: "You don't have an STD do you?" Christina said, half joking, half serious.

Me: "Nooo. Fuck. Are you kidding me?" I said, laughing; yet still scared to death about what I was about to say.

Christina: " Then it can't be that bad. Now what is it babe? You can tell me anything. You know that right?"

Me: "You know I care about you and would never want to hurt you, right?"

Christina: "Yeah, I know. Now what is it baby?" Christina said. Flashing a warm, concerned smile in my direction.

Me: "Remember how I told you about being a 23 year old graduate student living on the upper west side?" (aka, everything she knew about me)

Christina: "Yeah." Her facial expression changing from concerned, to puzzled, to just plan nervous, hoping in vain that I wasn't going to say what she thought.

Me: My hands were trembling uncontrollably at this point. "Well I don't know how to say this, except that nothing I told you was true and I'll be 23 in 5 years." I stuttered.

Christina: "Wait, whaaat? So you're only 18? You have to be fucking kidding me!" Christina shrieked, glaring at me with those piercing brown eyes that looked ready to kill.

Christina: "Oh my god, I can't fucking believe this shit!! How could you lie to me like that for almost 2 months? I wanted you to meet my parents for Christ sakes!!! Do you not have a conscience?" Christina's crying hysterically at this point.

Me: I'm speechless. No amount of words could justify what I've done to her. I felt awful, no better than the scum of the earth.

Christina: "So are you gonna say something or just sit there looking like a retard?"

Me: "Baby, I don't have anything to say. I've told you nothing but lies and you have no reason to trust me. I just wanted to be with you and was scared to tell the truth, cause then you wouldn't like me anymore. Everything I told you about how I felt was real, and I don't wanna be with anybody else." Now I was beginning to cry.

Christina: "Stop!!! Just stop it!! I can't! This won't work. I know you care about me, and I care about you too. But this is crazy. We're at different points in life and there's no way I can do this. Look, I just need time to think. This is all too much for me to process right now." Tears were now streaming down her face and she was sobbing uncontrollably.

Christina: "Wait. What am I even saying? You can't do this!! There's nothing to think about. You're just a kid and this will never work!!!"

Both of us were crying and had nothing to say. We lay in bed facing away from each other for what seemed like an eternity, before she finally wrapped her arms around me, pressing her entire body against mine. She squeezed me so tightly and I could feel her tears on my back. Turning around, I placed both my arms around her and told Christina that I loved her. She loved me too, and began kissing up and down my body, before climbing on top of me as we made love for what appeared to be the last time.

The next day Christina wrote me an email, pouring out her entire heart to me, tearfully explaining why we needed to end the relationship.

Dear Sasha,

Gosh, where to begin.... there's a lot that I want to say, and I'm already getting emotional. I hope you're doing all right, I cried a lot yesterday but today doesn't seem quite as bad, maybe it's the sunny weather. We were together for less than two months, and yet I can't believe how much I learned and gained from you during that time. I feel like we had something really pure and special,

something rare and hard to find in a world that

can be so ugly and cruel and depressing at

times. I'm sorry that what we had was

founded on lies from the start, but I

understand why you did what you did.

I already miss you a lot. I miss having

you here in my bed, cuddling and tickling and

baby talk and watching movies. My roommate

mentioned you last night to her dad and I just

couldn't say anything. I haven't told her

anything yet. I miss your beautiful eyes and

the caring things you said to me. I'm crying

right now, this is just so hard but we both need to be strong and know that regardless of whether or not we ever get back together, both of us have beautiful, exciting experiences ahead of us. The circumstances right now are just too much for me to deal with, and I really need to start focusing on getting a job and starting a career. You said you'll probably apply yourself to schoolwork. I think that's a good idea. I know that there will be plenty of girls who will want to date you, and I want you to have a great and full romantic life, but I hope you won't forget me...

Okay now I'm sobbing. I hope if there's anything you learned from this experience, it's that lying really doesn't get you anywhere in the end, and that you don't NEED to pretend to be someone else because you are so wonderful just as you are. Even if I'm the only one who tells you that, believe it anyway. I'm better than all of those other losers, anyway. ;P

I'm pretty sure you're the only guy I've ever liked who I felt genuinely saw me and appreciated me for who I am on the inside, instead of focusing on all of my surface attributes. I want to thank you for that. I know that you were being truthful about your feelings, and on that level, if you take away all of the superficial things, I think we really are kindred spirits in a way. Maybe we just had bad timing...

I want to simplify my life right now and find a way to stand on my own. I don't think I'll be happier, in fact I think I'll be a lot less happy, but it's something I feel I need to do. At least we'll always have our memories, and maybe we'll talk from time to time. I was almost considering still bringing you to Greenwich this weekend for one last fun memory, but it just might make everything even more painful, I don't know.

I have a feeling that we'll be in touch in the future even if we don't see each other again anytime soon, but I did want to say thank you for everything you gave me and thank you for finally being honest with me. I saw how hard it was for you, but it was the right thing to do in the end. Love cannot truly exist when it's built on lies. But take what you gained from this experience and keep it with you for when you're feeling down, and in the good times use it to spread joy to others. Don't be afraid to feel. Don't be afraid to make mistakes.

Know that you'll have a place in my heart even

if we're not together.

This is already hard enough so I'll stop

dragging it out. Feel free to call me, IM me,

email me whenever you want. Take care of

yourself and love yourself for who you are. I

wish you all the best in life, and more. You're

the baby.

Love,

Christina

I was crushed after reading that email and couldn't picture life without her. Telling Christina the truth was the right thing to do, but it didn't make me feel any less awful about the situation. My conscience wasn't cleared and the burden of guilt was not lifted off my shoulders. Telling her the truth did nothing other than make me depressed. For days, weeks, and months on end, all I felt was sadness, loneliness and emptiness, because Christina and I were no longer together.

PART 2

BITCHES, BITCHES, HO'S, AND

BITCHES

Going into the city to see Christina 3 times a week took a tremendous toll on my grades. In high school, I used to be a really hard working student, but that all changed once I started getting pussy on a regular basis. My grades went to shit and I had to drop two classes just to keep from failing out. Before starting Concordia, I was accepted into SUNY Binghamton for the Spring 2005 semester, provided I maintained at least a 2.8 GPA in the fall. Even after dropping two classes and losing my status as a full time student, I only managed a 2.83 GPA, barely getting into Binghamton by the skin of my teeth.

I got to Binghamton at the end of January and moved into O'Connor Hall, which is in the Dickinson Community. Dickinson was composed primarily of minorities and computer nerds. My roommate was this kid named Kevin Williams and I thought he was black, because of his last name, the box of Dutches on his bed, the 40oz bottles of St Ides on the windowsill, and the fact that I was in Dickinson. When I met him, I realized that ones race couldn't be predetermined by what's in their room, as Kevin turned out to be a tall, skinny, white Italian kid with a blond blowout from New Jersey.

Kevin and I got to know each other by sharing a Corona, when he offered to take me out. We went to Sports Bar, the main bar off of the corner of State Street in downtown Binghamton. Sports Bar was huge, two underground rooms, a slew of televisions, a pool table in front, beer pong tables and a dance floor out back. Kevin told me that the bar was usually packed with people, packed to the point that you usually had to claw through throngs of drunken Binghamton students simply to get a drink, but since we were in the middle of a blizzard, the bar was dead and it was just the two of us.

The 5 feet of snow outside may have stopped everyone else from going out, but not Kevin and I, as we got fucked up beyond belief. We shared at least five pitchers between us, not to mention the random shots we bought, and by the end of the night both of us would have made deans list if projectile vomiting were a major.

2/3/05

So far I hooked up with 2 girls although its not even been two weeks. Saturday night I hooked up with this moose who gave good head. She was a freshman from Syracuse and she gave good head. Yeah, so she said she didn't want to go that far so I felt her tits up and fingered her pussy and before I knew it I was fingering that bitch and she was giving me head. Anyway, I hooked up with this long island bitch tonight and she seemed into me. A couple more dates and I will be hitting that good. She seems to like me and I think she is pretty cool

That night marked the first entry in my drunken journal, as well as the first time I hooked up with Nicole. Nicole was beautiful. She had curly auburn hair that went just past her shoulders, milky white skin, soft full lips, curvaceous child bearing hips, and a smile that could turn any man into jelly.

We met at transfer orientation, a couple of days before I met Kevin, and sat next to each other during one of the meetings. I was eating sushi and trying my best not to go to sleep, while she was maniacally taking notes. After the meeting finally ended, Nicole tapped me on the shoulder and asked if I had a nice nap. I asked her what she meant, because I was paying perfect attention to every detail. She laughed and we talked for a while, before exchanging phone numbers and going our separate ways.

Nicole came to my room a few days later, but nothing happened. It was clear that she liked me, when she placed her head on my chest while we were watching a movie. However, that's all she would do, as I couldn't even kiss her. I thought to myself "what a cock tease, why are you in my room if I'm not getting any?"

Not only that, this girl was a ditz and a half, who sounded like a replicate of Cher from Clueless (only with a thick Long Island accent), as every other word that came out of her mouth was either "like" or "as if". We were even arguing about reality tv-which is already pretty fucking stupid as is. Just when I thought our conversation couldn't get any dumber, Nicole proudly claimed: "I'm a better argumenter than you." Wow. Her dad must've donated a wing to the school, because that's the only way this retard could have ever gotten into Binghamton.

Nicole was dumb enough to burn cereal, but she was hot. So I kept talking to her. She would instant message me 5 times a day and talk to me as though I were her boyfriend, even though we hadn't so much as made out. I figured that if I was going to waste my time talking to this imbecile over instant messenger, than she should at least play with my nuts for a little bit. So I invited her over.

She came to my room that night and I gave her a back massage while we watched t.v. I began softly kissing her neck as I massaged her and Nicole was visibly turned on. However, she still wouldn't let me hook up with her. This did not deter me, as I was a man on a mission, so I began talking dirty to her, insinuating how wet she was. Nicole finally gave in, and as we made out I felt like a fucking God, because that's when I realized I had a gift. My confidence with women skyrocketed.

Feeling happy as a schoolboy, I called Kevin and convinced him to go out with me. We went to some party at the Asian Frat house and drank until we were no longer able to pat our heads and rub our stomachs at the same time. I don't remember a single thing from that night, except for almost regurgitating my large intestine, but when I woke up the next morning and opened my computer, there was a literary masterpiece staring me right in the face. What I saw in front of me was special, and I set out to write a journal entry every time I got drunk.

On a side note, the Moose was some girl I met at a frat party the previous weekend. She looked like one of the Hungry Hungry Hippos but I was too wasted to care. Besides, it was over a month since I'd gotten any kind of ass whatsoever. And well to quote Dave Chappelle "a mouth is a mouth."

2/4/05

Yo I saw this girl Julia but nothing happened. All I did was drink but I drank a lot. There was beer and wine and 151 and I drank it all. Julia wasn't hot but she looked kinda hot after I was been drinking. We went to the RAT and I saw all thses hoese runnin around and I said to myself fuck Julia so I dissapperaed. Than I met Gina and we hooked up on the dance floor. She said she was wet so I said yo let go to my room and fix that sitiaution. I ate that bitch out and she was convulsing like a retard. Than she gave me the brains and 5 minutes later I hit her off wit some sausage milk. Girl #3 sonnnn. Yo if sucking dick were an Olympic sport, shed be in the Olympics.

Ok, so here's the story of how I met Gina. It all started when I met Julia at an off campus frat party last week. I don't remember what I said or how she looked, all I remember was having this girl's number in my phone when I woke up. So I decided to call her.

We agreed to hang out and she invited me to pre-game at her dorm in College in the Woods (CIW). When I got to her room, my stomach began to churn, as Julia had to have been one of the ugliest girls I had ever seen. She looked like Chewbacca from Star Wars, and the only way I could make it through the night was to drink until she was hot. This was no easy task, and I wound up taking four shots of Bacardi 151, five shots of Grey Goose, and drinking three Keystone Lights before heading to the RAT. By now Julia looked like Selma Hayek, and I was on the dance floor grinding against her like a rabid dog that hadn't been fixed.

That was until I had to pee. While I was waiting online to use the bathroom, this girl Gina came up and started talking to me. My mind went blank after that and the next thing I remember was making out with Gina, while she told me how wet she was. Well, the only cure for a wet pussy was a hearty serving of penis cake, so I brought her home and whipped out my thing right when I closed the door to my room.

From the moment those luscious lips touched my cock I was in heaven, because this girl could flat out suck a dick, and it didn't take long for me to give her a sample of my cream filling. Gina sucked dick like a

trained professional, and what do you call a professional cocksucker?

Who cares!

From the moment I walked into the RAT, I was in love. The RAT

was a total shit hole that made certain whorehouses look like respectable

establishments. Nothing more than a basement that literally let anybody

in, I could walk up to the bouncer with an ID that said my name was Paco

Dominguez and be let through the door without so much as a bat of an

eyelash (provided that Paco was 21 of course). On weekends, they had $5

open bar from 8:30-11:30 pm, which resulted in hundreds of freshman

girls, who by the end of the night were so fucked up that they couldn't

shake their asses without falling on them. If Evelyn's was an orgy, than

the RAT was a good old fashioned fuck fest, and getting a girl at the RAT

was easier than taking a shit.

2/5/05

I got friends but nobody likes me. People like me but they don't know

me. I am nothing more than a cartoon character put here for everyone

elses amusement. You like to go out with me and laugh at my jokes and

think im the man cause I fuck these girls and think my journals funny but you don't give a fuck about me. I'm a clown, a clown put here to entertain everyone and once im no longr amusing nobody gives a shit about me and it will be like I don't exist. My college career is gonna be predicated on me being a reckless assshole. Do I really want that? I miss Christina, she was the only one who truly gave a shit about me. I'd give all this up for her in a second. I loved her, really I did she was like my everything. My lifes nothing witout her in it and I would sacrifice my life, my health and everything that keeps my heart beeting just to have one more moment with her. Man I'd turn down Jenna Jameson to be with her. That's love right their.

*You know what, when she thought I was in grad school, she actually took **ME** more seriously. She felt special where as when I told her the truth she felt stupid. At first I kept the lie up because I thought it would make her happy. Well, not happy but it would help her feel more secure knowing that she was dating a grad student who genuinely loved her instead of a college freshman who didn't know what love is.*

*She is the only person who really understood **ME** and appreciated my good qualities as a human being. Even if it was all based on a lie at least* *someone actually appreciated **ME**. That is the closest I will ever come to being understood.*

I made a new friend at the gym last week. He was this huge frat guy in Alpha Kappa Lamda who went by the name of Rambo. Rambo's frat was having a "big" party and he invited me to come.

Talk about an exaggeration. This party was freakin wack!! A total sausage fest, I would have had better luck getting laid in prison. Well, at least the brothers were cool. They fed me shots and asked me to pledge next semester.

I felt better when I saw a few kids from my building. I played beer pong with this kid Juan, who lived across the hall from me, and we got obliterated before going to the RAT.

Out of all the people I could've stumbled into blackout drunk, why did it have to be **THE MOOSE?** As soon as she saw me, her 300 lb plus frame waddled over to me and she jammed her tongue down my throat, devouring me as though I were a Big Mac. This was embarrassing. Everyone at the bar was giving me weird looks for dancing with a Rhinoceros, but there was nothing I could do about it, because her fat ass was literally preventing me from moving anywhere.

I needed to escape and had to think fast, before Jabba the Huts

twin sister ate me alive. That's when a light bulb went off in my head.

"Fat chicks can't say no to food." I thought, and immediately asked if she

wanted to eat. Before I had a chance to say cheeseburger, the Moose

was gone, bulldozing her way up the stairs in order to get to "Rocky's",

the pizza place next door to the RAT, where I saw her inhale slice after

slice like Kobayashi at the Nathan's Hot Dog Eating Contest, as I got into a

cab with Juan and went home.

Juan and I went back to my room to play videogames. Kevin woke up

while we were playing Street Fighter II and flew into a rage, telling me

that I was an inconsiderate piece of shit, and to only wake him up at 4 am

if I have a bitch in the room.

***

The way I met Juan was pretty funny. Kevin and I were playing

pool in the basement of our building during the first week of school, when

this short, stocky Puerto Rican kid with black hair named Juan offered to

play doubles with us, pitting him and his roommate against Kevin and I.

We won the first game, causing me to get cocky, so I put $5 on the next

game and lost. Then all of us went to his room, where I found out that his roommate had FIFA 96 for Sega Genesis. Because I had the original FIFA

as a kid, I thought I was good at the game and bet another $5 that I could

beat him. Little did I know, this kid never left his room and played FIFA 96

all day long. Needless to say, he whooped my ass. The score was 4-0

before the first half even ended so I gave up and went back to my room,

where I lost $10 more playing NBA JAM. So that's how I met Juan, losing

$20 betting on meaningless shit.

2/11/05

Yo I'm not even that drunk right now but I got some brains. I brought

Gina back and I'm in blowjob heavan. How am I getting all this pussy?

That's crazy. I don't even care if I'm the birthday clown.

Gina came over during the week and once again gave me amazing

head. This girl was a world-class cocksucker. She would put porn stars to

shame and I know this because I watch a lot of porn.

2/12/05

Let's put another notch to my championship belt. So tonight I hooked

up with another one. Her name was Mary and the head was pretty good.

But yo, this shit was a bit hard to get. Like I was hooking up with this ho on the dance floor and I know I was doing my shit. Kissing that bitches

neck and everything and I said lets get the fuck out of here and she said

she doesn't wanna leave her friends. So I said fuck your friends bitch come

back with me, I'll show you a better time. And finally the bitch conceded.

So we got a cab and went back home. So I go to this girls room and I'm

hooking up with her and I take her shirt off and start biting this bitches

nipples and before I know it I'm getting my cock sucked again. What is

this girl #3 who went down on my shit? Yeah, that's right! I am getting

more brains than a zombie kiddd   Yo, so finally I got that nut out of me

and I'm like daymm. This bitch tried to kiss me and I'm like nah girl you

have penis breath. And you know I'm not down with that cock breath if

you know what I'm saying. But anyway etiquette 101 got to return that

favor so I started going down on that bitch and I was like you like that ho.

She was kind of getting upset and tried to say she finished early but I knew

the bitch was full of shit. I'm like listen baby I'm sorry if I hurt your feelings

I won't call you bitch. HO! And I fingered her until it looked like she was

having a seizure and I knew I was done with that bitch for now. So I went

home and I got that girls number and maybe I'll call her if I got nothing to

do.

I am so lost getting back to my room so I get a cab and he asked me if I got laid tonight and I'm like nah I just got dome but a nut is a nut you feel me. And he is like yea and than we both talked about how we like going down on girls cause pussys got those essential minerals. He gave me a stoge and I paid him 2 dollars even though it was only one. Being drunk and having my nut just gotten off I was in a good mood. Now I am back here writing a passage in my drunken journal. Listen, on the real I better start fucking more bitches and using some condoms cause I don't want my shit to fall off. I think condom sex is a bit safer if you know what I mean.

You know what, I am thinking on this 5 am on Saturday night that I am actually coming into my own with the ladies. I mean I could conceivably hook up with a different girl every week. Listen, I better not fuck up because if I fail out, I don't get this ridiculous bitch streak. Even so, there is actually a nice girl amongst them. Her name is Gina. At first I thought she was a big slut because she gave madd good head but than I realized that she learned from boyfriends. On the real, she seems like a good person and I don't feel like talking shit about her anymore. I mean, maybe if I trusted her more I would see her exclusively but even than I don't think I can. I owe my true feelings to Christina. She is the girl that I'm meant to be with. All these other girls are just some stupid game in which I have to act like a cocky asshole in order to win. I just want to be happy, winning is a bit trivial but if I never achieve happiness which is very conceivable than at least let me win. Christina was the only girl I felt that I could really be myself around. We just clicked. It just happened, we felt like best friends and I would have done anything for her. She was actually worth sacrificing the fun I am having right now for exclusivity. A soul mate is worth more than some nut from some bitch. Listen, I would have died for her and I still will because her life is worth a lot more than mine. She is a far better person than I ever hope to amount to. I would protect her with my life because she deserves no less. She possibly deserves even more. Never, have I met a better human being than Christina. Even people in my family fail or come dangerously close to measuring up to Christina. I love her and if she wanted to try and make this work than I would stop all the shit that I'm doing in an instant and take her seriously. Her happiness was mine and mine was hers and we truly deeply loved each other.

Mary and I met at 2:30 am, blackout drunk at the RAT. Mary had really big tits and was a special girl. So special that she would acquire multiple nicknames over her career as a journal entry.

All jokes aside, its kind of disturbing that girls were getting turned on by the way I treated them. I was the ultimate dick to Mary, calling this girl a bitch to her face and not taking any of her feelings into account, and what did I get none other than a blowjob? Now what do you think would have happened if I was nice to her, but more importantly what the fuck does that say about women?

2/15/05

Ok so let me give you guys my bitch nicknames. So there is the Moose from the Cuse (don't remember her name), the Long Island Cock tease (Nicole), the Long Island Cock Sucker (Gina), and Penis Breath (Mary). So the Moose broke me out of my slump and the Cock tease gave me my confidence while the Cock Sucker was a result of my newfound confidence and Penis Breath is just another Ho. Get what I'm saying. So cock-tease wants a relationship and I may give it to her but I definitely won't give it to her now. I know girls like that and they want the prospective relationship over an actual relationship. It can't be too easy you know what I mean. Than they will get too bored and lose interest just like Lauren. Lauren was the first girl that made me realize my bitch getting potential. Let me tell you guys, it's all been uphill from there.

Sometimes I just wanna be me. All I do is spit game and spew out nonsense. I guess that's the price you pay for pussy.

Back in the day, I was noble but now I am an asshole. All I want is to satisfy myself and nothing more. I mean back than I would probably die for Christina and now I feel like a totally different person. I just wish that I could have what I had than now. I had something pure and special and now it is gone to be replaced by meaningless pussy that could just as easily disappear. So I got a rotation of bitches, big fucking deal. Christina was my soul mate whom I would die for.

Gee, I look at my life and I think wow, I am worthless. I mean even in my drunken state I have nothing to stand on my own about. I am going to seriously hit the weights and by the semesters end I'll be looking like an action figure. STEROIDS, HULK SMASHHH!!!!

In spite of the confident image I try to project onto other people, I am just a scared little kid. That is it. I am so afraid; I just want to be held if only for a few minutes. In a way, I miss my mom and my dad and my sister. I miss being an athlete and the hope of playing in college. I miss working out for the possibility of playing at a higher level. I miss having a purpose in life. Hope is one of mans most powerful feelings and I had an abundance of that which made me feel strong but now I feel like nothing.

That is because I am nothing.

Senior year of highschool, we were playing Lowell in the first game of the season. I had a relatively disappointing game but we kept it very close throughout. So we were up by one with a few seconds left when their star player hit a shot that looked like the game winner. They inbound the ball to me and I try to put up a desperation shot. However, the Lowell players foul me thinking they are down instead of up. I step to the line for a one and one. The Lowell coach calls timeout to ice me. After the timeout I hit the first of two freethrows and I am fucking pumped. You mother fuckers can't ice me I call out to the Lowell bench after I tie the game with 2 seconds left. Anyway I miss the second freethrow our power forward taps the ball back to me and I hit a floater following my own miss as time runs out and we win by two. I was mobbed by players and fans. Finally I was a hero. My former coach congratulated me for having the mental strength to hit the game winner in spite of having a sub par game. I was than a happy man.

In all my days of being unsure of myself I am now able to get the ladies. That means that either I don't care or I got my game back. I guess that will help when getting wit a football player. The most powerful sex

organ for a woman is her brain so I hope she sees hat is important.

The Alpha guys invited me to a stripper show. They brought a

couple of strippers to the house and gave everybody a bunch of $1 bills to

throw at the girls. You'd think this is really disrespectful to women, but

these bitches ran the show. They beat the shit out of the brothers with

paddles, trampled on their chest with high heels, and put bags of ice

cubes in their balls. One of them even sat on some dudes face after

taking a shit in her pants.

Despite having a rotation of girls, I was lonelier than ever. Getting

all this pussy was costing me a part of my soul and I felt like nothing more

than an image on display. Here I was acting like a cocky asshole who

didn't give a shit about anything, but this was not the kind of man I

wanted to be. When I looked in the mirror, there was a degenerate

scumbag staring back at me, and I didn't like what I saw.

2/18/05

You have no idea how fucking pissed off I am. This girl said she was

going back with me and I actually thought she was a nice girl but instead

she ditched me and danced with some friend of hers and when I found her she told me she was just gonna go back with some of her friends. I waited a half an hour for this stupid bitch and for no avail. Whatever, I really don't need her. As of now she is nothing to me. I don't care how good the head was because I can good head anytime I fucking want. This just made me realize that very few girls are actually worth treating with respect. There will never be a girl at this school who will be regarded to me as a person. From now on they are bitches and ho's and nothing more because these women do not act like human beings. No fucking girl is worth my time if I am not getting a nut out because they are all very low class people. This is why they need to be put in their fucking place. I was actually feeling bad about the shit I was saying in my journal but not anymore. Tonight actually justified all the shit I said. I will call this girl Mary aka. Penis breath and treat her like the piece of shit she is. I will not dedicate time to any of these girls unless I am busting a nut.

Who fucking cares that I hooked up with two girls tonight. The girl I was supposed to get back with played me like a fiddle. That is the ultimate embarrassment. You know what, I am going to stop writing and just go to sleep in order to prevent myself from getting even more worked up.

I went to open bar at the RAT with Kevin and a bunch of his friends. My alcohol tolerance had significantly increased, because after 12 mixed drinks, I was still behaving like a functional adult. Gina was supposed to meet me but she was coming later. So I hit on a bunch of girls in order to occupy myself.

Meet Tara. Tara had the body of a goddess and the face of a cabbage patch doll. I approached her, grinding my dick against her ass like a classy gentleman, when poof, next thing you know we're making out. Shortly thereafter, I asked her to go home with me, but she said no, because her best friend from home (Sam) came up to visit.

After losing Tara, I ran into my friend Kelly from class. Her friends from home came up and I ended up hooking up with one of them. She wanted to go home with me but Kelly was being a cock-blocking cunt and didn't let her, saying she was too drunk to think for herself.

By now it didn't matter, because Gina had finally gotten to the bar. After hooking up for a few minutes, we agree to go back to my room together, but she changed her mind when I got my jacket, choosing instead to stay with her friends. Whatever bitch!

The next day I called Tara and we agreed to hang out that night. I convinced Kevin to play wingman and all of us ended up taking shots of his Bacardi Gold before going to the RAT. Tara and Sam offered me money for the drinks, but I turned it down, acting as though it were my Liquor.

We made it to open bar and got wrecked. Picking up where we left off, Tara and I started making out on the dance floor. She tells me I'm really cute and that we should hang out more. "I agree. Lets hangout in your room."

We got back to her room a little after 3 am and started hooking up under the covers. Kevin and Sam were cuddling on the other bed so we tried to be as discrete as possible, succeeding up until I sprayed my man seed all over her comforter.

Tara was furious, screaming at me on the top of her lungs for "making a mess" on her comforter. Needless to say, our cover was blown, just like my load.

Kevin and I were laughing hysterically. Even Sam was laughing, while Tara was on her knees angrily cleaning up after me, as though episodes of this nature were a routine occurrence.

Tara was pissed, Kevin and Sam were uncomfortable, and I was proudly lying in bed without a care in the world because I had just busted a nut. Kevin excused himself to go home shortly after Tara finished cleaning. And it wasn't long before Tara looked at me and said: "I think it's best if you go too."

I felt like the man when I got back to my room. Kevin was in awe of what he'd just witnessed, and couldn't stop talking about it. The two of us were playing NBA Jam, drunk off our asses, laughing hysterically at what I had just pulled off, before going to sleep. Gina could go ahead and suck my cock!![1]

Tara and I ended up hooking up for about a month and a half, with Tara wanting to date me the entire time. That was never going to happen, since she was just some random girl at the RAT who I had to put on an image for. I could never be my natural self around Tara and felt as though behaving like a cocky asshole was the only way she'd ever like me.

Exuding this image of brazen cockiness was fucking stressful, especially when it's bullshit. If we wound up together, I'd have to act like

---

[1] Correction. I wish Gina would go ahead and suck my cock.

that all the time, which was something I couldn't handle. I knew that Tara would've lost interest and treated me like garbage once my image wore off, so I treated her like a piece of shit as a defense mechanism in order to protect myself from getting hurt.

It didn't matter that Tara and I were completely wrong for each other, because her body was fucking amazing, and I was going to milk this relationship for as long as I could. Tara refused to fuck or give head unless we were in a relationship, which was awful, but her hand jobs were amazing and more than made up for that. This girl used to sit on top of me and jerk me off against her ass like in porno videos, causing my body to go into an unbridled frenzy of lust. I couldn't get enough of Tara and she used to drain my cock dry whenever I saw her.

Tara pampered the shit out of me throughout our "relationship". All she wanted to do was take care of me and would cook, clean my room, and fold my clothes on a regular basis without asking for anything in return. Tara even clipped my toenails a few times, earning her the nickname Captain Toenails.

A part of me was beginning to feel bad about how I treated women, but a much larger part felt that it was well deserved. Lets face facts, the girls at the RAT were a bunch of dumb sluts that just wanted to get drunk and suck cock. It's not like they deserved respect. No, they were bad people. Shallow pieces of garbage who liked being mistreated. And these bitches would've walked all over me had I so much as attempted to treat them decently.

A stoned entry dated 2/21/05

Look at me, I am selling myself out. It's just not me, but maybe by selling myself out I realize what I am all along. A selfish prick, that is what you are. You are king asshole. It is like I think I am going to die so I act recklessly. I have no faith in myself because all I want is cheap thrills because you are afraid to get anything else by the time you graduate so you feel like you need to get all the pussy in the world before it is too late.

. Is to say fuck it the answer? Maybe it is when I say fuck it to the people and just concentrate for myself. I am going to do well because I want these toys, these homes, these girls, I want the pleasure and that is a shallow motivation for success but motivation nonetheless.

Its like the pleasures of sex overwhelm you. I want to stay ignorant. The pleasures give us that bravado and its all about the masculine image. It's the initial attraction and through the power of my deceptive appearance and arrogant sense of confidence, people are drawn to me.

. It is becoming socially acceptable for me to live like this. They see this and they say future. Smart kid, good school, goes out and drinks, gets madd girls, combines potential with sexual confidence and girls are now drawn to you. You are actually doing the right thing. You're just the man right now.

What I'm doing is bad because I'm projecting my insecurities onto other people and thus causing people to be insecure. I'm perpetuating a vicious cycle and it should stop. I wanna spread joy to the world and lead a positive existence. In order to do this I need to create a different cycle and start treating people better. The problem is that acting like an inconsiderate asshole is so much easier and more fun.

Yo I'm getting madd girls acting like a douche bag so why should I change it? After all if it aint broke, don't fix it. Look maybe what I'm doing is immoral but I just need female love and this is the only way I know how to get it. As much shit as I talk about bitches, the truth is I'm lost without women. Its like I need my mom around because I like when girls take care of me but I don't want it to actually be my mom cause I like getting pussy too.

I need to be a good guy and tomorrow I'm gonna get tested. Please if your listening let this shit come out negative. I promise I'll start using more condoms and I wont go in a bitch raw unless I know her really well. Man I'm buggin out, I gotta stop smoking weed.

Mary and I fucked for the first time that night. We smoked a blunt afterwards. I hadn't smoked in over a month and was tripping balls. Kevin and I played NBA Jam after she left and he kept laughing at how stoned I was. Everything was going great. I was high off my ass, playing NBA Jam with my roommate after having just laid the pipe, when all of a sudden I began freaking out. My palms grew sweaty and a million little thoughts began swirling through my mind like a vortex. At that moment, my false image caught up to me and all of my bottled up insecurities had emerged from the shadows, bombarding me from all angles. I was overwhelmed, both mentally and emotionally at the fact that I was living a lie, so I sat at my computer and typed out a bunch of shit in an attempt to gain a better understanding of myself.

Wow. I had some serious issues and the weed I just smoked brought them all to light. I tried so hard to disguise my true feelings by hiding behind a false mask of confidence and bravado, but beneath that mask I was merely a lost, frightened, child.

2/25/05

You know what, there is really nothing to write. In truth, I have to start writing seriously. A drunk journal is only good if you only have sober entries when your not drunk. I have only written drunk as of late and I have to write sober in order to be funny when drunk. I could go out but I feel bad about it. In retrospect, there is really no point. The thing is I am addicted to going out. Can I stop? Nobody likes me except for my journal. Without this I am nothing. Few people know of the journal, therefore I am nothing. I am nothing to nobody. Leys say that it is killim

I got a job making sandwiches at the Dickinson dining hall. That was a disaster since I don't know how to make a sandwich. Everybody was laughing at me and I was so incompetent that people deliberately stood on my line in order to watch me fuck up.

After an exhausting day at work, I had to get wasted. All of my friends were staying in so I decided to go out alone. Some girl from my job recognized me and used my ineptitude at work as an excuse to hit on me. 8 drinks and 30 minutes later, both of us were feverishly making out on the dance floor. Then, right of the blue, this girl tells me she has to leave and find her boyfriend. Classy.

After that I just got into a cab and went home, where I smoked a blunt with Kevin and showed him my journal. I than wrote a mass of unintelligible nonsense before going to sleep.

3/4/05

Yo son, I'm in double figures. I pulled more bitches than Tim Thomas's scoring average as a Knick. Damn, what a bitch ass muthafucka son. I hate Tim Thomas and I wish he would die. Fuck Tim Thomas, he should be playing prison basketball. How could you trade Van Horn for Thoms. I mean yea Van Horn is soft but he can shoot Thomas is soft and is a streak shooter. That is bull shit.

Lets get back on topic. So I am at girl number 10. God do I love college. I want to stay in college for ever and ever and ever. I did a good deed today by giving a down and out friend some hope. I love getting pussy. I love it. Even if it is just making out with a bitch I like it. It is what gives my life meaning. Without a bitch I am a bitch.

But yo, this girl was actually pretty cool. She is so cool that she may not even get a nickname. I mean she was a pretty dope girl almost so much that I didn't want to hook up with her because I would actually have wanted to be her friend. I mean yo, she likes cartoons how dope is that and she is normal. The bitch isn't crazy and she is pretty cute. Hopefully we'll continue to chill. She is a fun drunk.

It's weird, as I was hooking up with this girl, all I kept thinking about was Christinatina. I think I am at the point that I would rather have one Christina instead of a barrage of girls at my disposal. She is more important. That girl Diane would be more like a friend but hooking up with her is a nice bonus. Fo show. I was pleaseantly surprised. I thought she would be just another dumb LI girl but she liked cartoons. That is dope. I could see it now, just chilling and watching Adult Swim while getting brains and smoking a blunt. That would be dope. My transformation has been unbelievable. I actually get normal girls instead of really easy or really drunk girls. I hooked up with Diane and I actually had to work for it. I was madd chill and got a few drinks and soon she was all mine. Hopefully we will chill again.

I am just a jew who lost his cockiness. I mean yea I am confident but not cocky. I need to by an asshole to make money off that journal. I mean, where are the moose jokes? Yo where are they? Why is my friend Ray 20 and a virgin? How come he hasn't kissed a girl? Why does he still think pussy is some kind of cat? That is sad. I treat these girls like shit for him. Girls are nothing serious and I realize that through my awkward phase and Ray. That kid is a life time awkward phase. Fuck, why can't this kid just swing a bitch. Why?

Earlier in the day I wrote Toby (my down and out friend) a letter. Toby had a severe mental breakdown and was sent away to a therapeutic boarding school in Utah. This kid had it all, millions of dollars, a Lexus, parents that loved him, and a barrage of girls as his disposal, but he threw it all away. Toby was one of my best friends and it really upset me to see his life go to shit, so I wrote him a letter, telling him to keep his head up and that everything's going to be ok.

As for Diane, we met at the student union a couple of weeks ago, where she claimed to have recognized me from transfer orientation. She invited me downtown and that's how we ended up hooking up at the RAT.

Diane was fucking cool! Smart, funny, and down to earth, I really wanted to see her again. Unfortunately it never happened, because she got back together with her ex boyfriend a week later.

3/10/05

Today was a little different from the other drunken days I wrote about. First off, I actually didn't go out. That is really a first. We just chilled in this kids room and drank and than we went to this girls room and drank some more. The kid was madd cool and the girl was really nice. Than I boogie boarded down the stairs and came out in one piece. Baller stattuss sonn!! You know, this nights madd different cause I was just straight chillen. No bitches no problem. People asked about the fournal and as of now that shit is sealed side from those who already know. This isn't a public spectacle until it makes that cizash.

Yo, don't mind this paragraph this is a Tim Thomas chapter. I really hate that mutherfucker with a passion. As a matter of fact I hate everyone in the Knicks organization with the last name Thomas. Tim is an overpaid asshole, Kurt is a bum, and Isaiah is running the team into the ground. I mean the fact that you acquired Tim Thomas means you should be shot. Speaking of which somebody should kill that douche bag in order to get the team out of that salary cap trouble. Matter of fact, they should

kill his whole family so none of them could profit off his ass. I mean if the

whole Thomas clan dies than the salary cap is really freed up for the

Knicks. That is what a true Knicks fan would do. Only a real fan would go

to prison and get their asshole ripped open in 2 in order to lower the salary

cap. But matter of fact, it may not even be worth it just because Isaiah

would just acuire another soft athletic bum with a disproportiantally high

salary. I can't stand Marbury either, he is a dick. He makes every team

lose just because of his presence. He aint no leader. He just a liability but

you know what, he would actually be an asset if he were the secondary

option rather than the primary one. Enough about Setph, lets talk about

Timmy. He is such a fucking bum. I will describe in absolute detail how I

would kill him. First, I would stab him in the eye with a fork. Than, I would

take a knife and chop his nose off. After that, I will take a chainsaw and

saw his fucking legs off so he can never play basketball and poison my

beloved Knicks again. Than I would take a rocket launcher and shoot his

arms off so he can never play wheelchair basketball again and poison the

wheelchair Knicks. I will also make a point to chop the guys penis off so

that he can never create another Tim Thomas to poison yet another NBA

franchise. To top it all off, I will rip his heart out with my bear hands and *bomb his family mansion so that none of them collect off his contract and the salary cap is once again free. Go KNICKS.*

I am a dork. It is so cool yet so ridiculous that I actually keep this journal. I mean actually writing when drunk off my ass instead of passing out takes a lot of discipline. More discipline than Tim Thomas. Wow, I really hate him. Actually the best thing that would happen to the KNICKS would not be his death but for him to go to prison. Then the cap would really be free. Why didn't he rape some bitch in Eagle County Colorado? Why? They should hold the trial in NY so that the all the KNICK fan jury can convict his ass and better their franchise. Yo! Isaiah is such a dick. He is just dumb. I mean getting Steph and removing that dead weight was good but than he just OD'd on that power trip. He shouldn't have got Tim. I think Isaiah just needs a good butt raping. Why did I say that? Could be the alcohol. Peace!!!

Man, I say some crazy shit when I'm drunk and not getting pussy. Nothing eventful or substantial happened that night. There was no logic or reason behind what I wrote. I was just drunk and wanted to write about Tim Thomas.

The Start Of A Rollercoaster

3/11/05

I'm going to take a break from all this shit for a long time and get my priorities in order. No more going out and drinking. From now on its just weights and school. I just wasn't into it tonight. You really can't half ass this shit. Either you want it or you don't and I really didn't. When you care more about writing a journal entry than fucking a bitch than maybe you really need a break. I am actually looking forward to my break which I will flush the poisons of alcohol out of my body. I will be a physical machine and mental machine. This is for real. A part of me wants to just leave Binghamton and work on my game like an animal to get another shot at playing ball at a small D2 or 3 school but a more logical part knows that it is just a fantasy. Everything just made more sense when sports factored into the equation. I am so empty without the thought of playing basketball. That is all I really want to do is get athletic and play.

Fucking Nicole! You stupid ass long Island Cocktease bitch. Your breed needs to be extinct. Its bad enough you don't wanna hook up with me but do you really have to cockblock me when your friend wants some dick? What the fuck is wrong wih you bitch yelling at me in front of everyone at the RAT? I should've cock smacked you right in da face. Man

you don't even drink, what the fuck were you doing in the RAT anyway?

Maybe I really should just stay with Captain Toenails. Who knows,

maybe having some stability wouldn't be that bad. And peep this she is a

nice jewish girl. Christina is really the girl I want but realistically nothing

long term will ever envelop with her. I just cannot commit to Tara until

after I see Christina. It's not going to happen. Besides, Tara does seem

really nice. I would actually keep her the entire semester. My desire to

pick up girls isn't there anymore. That is why I need a break from this

journal. It will be nice to not worry about this shit for a while. I just

wanna be a little kid again and play basketball and videogames. I am

going to be alone this week and really find my center before break.

That was the first weekend I didn't hook up with a girl. Coming

home from the bars knowing I'd be sleeping alone made me realize how

empty I felt. I was all alone. and thought for a brief moment about being

with Tara, because than I wouldn't be as lonely.

I ran into Nicole for the first time in almost a month. We hooked

up once more, after I wrote my first journal entry, and my prophecy about

hitting that good almost came true.

***

Nicole and I were making out in my room. And her body was going crazy. She was softly moaning and her nipples were getting hard through her shirt, so I slid my hand underneath and began gently caressing her breasts. Nicole was in heaven, amazed that my hand could give her body that much pleasure, yet she refused to take her shirt off. Her mind and body were in flux, each telling her something different, and it was up to me make Nicole listen to her body. With each passing kiss, nibble, and caress, Nicole succumbed more and more to her primitive desires until she could hold out no longer, unhooking her bra and letting it fall to the floor.

Step 1 was now complete and I began softly kissing up and down her stomach, occasionally teasing her nipples with the tip of my tongue. Nicole could barely contain herself, and was moaning so loudly that she had to bite down on my pillow in order to prevent the entire floor from hearing her.

Her pants slid down effortlessly and I placed my tongue on her clit, ever so slightly swirling it around her labia, before sliding my index finger inside her. At this point, Nicole was beside herself with pleasure, and it didn't take long to send her over the edge. After only a few gentle thrusts and licks, her body violently spasmed, and Nicole had one of, if not the most intense orgasms I had ever witnessed, cumming so hard that my index finger almost broke from the force of her contractions.

Nicole was spent and looked as though she had been ravished by a pack of lions, while I lay in bed marveling at my own handiwork. I felt like a sexual god, a modern day rendition of Adonis, until Nicole all of a sudden began crying hysterically.

This was the first time I had ever seen a girl cry after sex. And I began to panic. "What the fuck is going on right now?" I thought, as Nicole sobbed uncontrollably. "Just 2 minutes ago, this girl looked like she was being electrocuted. And now she won't stop crying. What the fuck? This shit makes no fucking sense to me! Man, all I wanted was to make Nicole happy; not see her like this. What the fuck did I just do? Shit!! Maybe I should've listened to her when she said no the first time. Snap of it Sash! It doesn't matter anymore. What's done is done. Now there's a crying bitch in your room. And you need to calm her down and take care of this situation immediately!"

"Baby what's wrong?" I asked, after my internal monologue had subsided. "Nothing" Nicole replied. "Are you sure?" I asked, not believing her for a minute, as girls don't all of a sudden start crying hysterically, especially when nothings wrong. "Well it's just that things were going a little too fast and I just couldn't handle it." I put my arm around Nicole in an attempt to comfort her. "Baby, I'll never ever make you do anything you don't want to do. I'll do everything at your own pace. We'll take it as slow as you want. I promise!" An awkward pause ensued. "Do you hear me?" I said to Nicole, hoping she'd feel better. Nicole mumbled a yes and I offered to take her home.

Nicole had calmed down by the time we had reached her suite in Mountainview, a plush new community at the very end of campus resembling a hotel more than a dormitory, and invited me inside to meet her suitemates. After quickly introducing myself, the two of us went into her room and started hooking up again as though nothing had happened earlier, only this time Nicole refused to remove her clothes. It didn't matter. We did the exact same thing as before, except now I made her cum through her jeans.

Nicole was unable to resist my sexuality and I thought I had this girl on lock. This, however, proved not to be the case, as trying to see her again proved more difficult than pulling teeth and doing astrophysics simultaneously, shown from our AIM conversation two days later.

KNICK10217: what r u doing tomorrow

qtsummerprincess: packing

KNICK10217: ok

KNICK10217: swing by when u finish

qtsummerprincess: ummm i dunno about that lol

KNICK10217: whats that suppossed to mean lol

qtsummerprincess: i know if i come over we're not gonna have tea and cookies lol

KNICK10217: we may don't underestimate me

qtsummerprincess: i know how you work lol

KNICK10217: lol im complicated

qtsummerprincess: you're not complicated! you sweet talk nice girls like me to get what you want

KNICK10217: lol is it working

qtsummerprincess: not anymoree

KNICK10217: haha ill see u at 10:15

qtsummerprincess: i'm serious im not coming

KNICK10217: y

qtsummerprincess: sorry i dont wanna be used

KNICK10217: what r u talking about

qtsummerprincess: i come to your room and we do whatever and that's it..that's called using

KNICK10217: listen i would rather talk to u about this in person

qtsummerprincess: oh pleaseeee...u just want me in your bed so u can tell me nice things so i think you're the nicest guy alive

KNICK10217: ok whats wrong

qtsummerprincess: nothing's wrong i'm just being honest

KNICK10217: baby im not using u, thats the honest truth, just come by and we'll talk about it, we don't even have to do anything if u dont want to but i really would rather talk to u about this in person instead of through a screen

qtsummerprincess: okay see when you say stuff like that it's hard to believe because the other night when u acted upset when we stopped u put on this sad face so i would feel bad

qtsummerprincess: and u were like i'm gonna be a gentleman and walk you to your room but you just wanted a change of scenery

KNICK10217: thats not true at all i was actually gonna leave but u invited me into ur room

qtsummerprincess: yeah but you didn't hesitate to continue in my room

KNICK10217: of course im not gonna hesitate but that doesn't mean that i wanted a change of scenery, i actually just wanted to spend time with u

qtsummerprincess: well that's a little hard to believe

KNICK10217: explain

qtsummerprincess: you're a womanizer-from day one all you did was try to hook up with me

KNICK10217: that doesnt mean that i still didnt want to spend time with u in the process

qtsummerprincess: i dunno you're a nice guy but i think you wanna enjoy yourself at college and that's fine but i dont know if that's what i want

KNICK10217: look, im not gonna spend any more time talking online about this

KNICK10217: if u want to stop by go ahead u know my number and u know where i live but i honestly wont make u do anything u dont want to do, i just really feel as though it would be better if we talked about this in person

qtsummerprincess: i don't know...i just feel like you'll say nice things to me and tt'hen you'll be like okay let's makeout cause i just buttered you up

KNICK10217: please just come by im being dead in serious in what im saying

qtsummerprincess: alright fine

KNICK10217: cool so ill see u tomorrow

Absolutely nothing happened when she came to my room. Trying to hook up with Nicole was an exercise in futility, as she wouldn't even let me put my arm around her. I was at a loss for words. And it boggled my mind how she wouldn't let me so much as touch her, after I had made this girl explode like a volcano a few days earlier. Whatever. Fuck that bitch!! She played more games than my Playstation. And I was sick of it.

***

Nicole wanted to be friends. But I wasn't ready to be friends with girls. When I was in 8th grade, there was this girl named Sandra, who I used to ride the school bus with. Sandra was about 5'2 and 120 lbs, with creamy white skin, beautiful blond curly hair, a radiant smile, and a nice set of tits (well at least for 8th grade). Aside from being drop dead gorgeous, she was also charming, funny, and intelligent.

We were best friends for over a year and I was obsessed with her the entire time, unknown to her. That was until she confessed her feelings for me.

It was the day before Halloween and we were sitting next to each other on the bus, when Sandra said that she liked me. I didn't know what to do. I should've kissed her. I should've held her hand. I should've done something. But I didn't. Instead, I sat there dumbfounded with my mouth open.

I was so happy that day. Nothing could go wrong. The girl I had loved for over a year had loved me back. Man I felt good.

I called Sandra that night and officially asked her to be my girlfriend. Then I heard what seemed like the most powerful word in the English language. "NO."

To this day, I have no idea what made Sandra change her mind and refuse to go out with me. All I know is that the dynamic of our relationship began to change.

Sandra and I remained friends because we attended the same school and rode the bus together, but our friendship was not the same. I wanted to get over her. Really, I did. But my feelings wouldn't go away, no matter how hard I tried to move on.

If that weren't bad enough, Sandra did whatever was in her power to remind me that I wasn't and never will be good enough for her. Whether it was having a bad game, doing poorly on a test, or getting rejected by another girl, she never failed to remind me of my shortcomings as a human being. Sandra's taunts made me feel ugly, stupid, and weak, making it was clear that I was nothing more than a loser to her.

Now with that said, I have never been able to have a true friendship with a girl, because that's what I subconsciously associate female friendship with. Hanging out with Nicole without hooking up would have messed with my confidence, made me feel like a tool, and ultimately resulted in my pussy total substantially diminishing, which couldn't happen, because getting pussy was the basis of my identity as a man. Therefore, I had nothing to gain from being friends with Nicole. So I promptly cut her out of my life.

***

At this point, I had pretty much forgotten that Nicole existed, when out of the blue, she walked up to me in the RAT and gave me a huge hug, her face lighting up like a Menorah. However, she refused to dance when I asked her so I walked away, unfazed and ready to approach the next girl. Just as I was walking away, one of her friends popped in and dragged me onto the dance floor.

Here I was dancing with this girl, about to hook up with her, when lo and behold, Nicole came out of nowhere and dragged her friend away from me. She was livid and spent the entire night following me around the bar carrying on like a psychopath, saying that I was the lowest form of life on earth and yelling at me until her face turned beat red.

The next day, Nicole apologized for the way she acted and we started talking again. Correction, she did most of the talking, instant messaging me five times a day like I was her boyfriend.

Nicole had really strong feelings for me. It was painfully obvious. Why else would this girl spend so much time talking to a guy that, as far as she was concerned, treated her like nothing more than a sex object?

Nicole may have thought I was using her for sex, but it wasn't true. I liked spending time with the girl. Don't ask me why. I just did.

She may not have been very smart, but lets face facts, neither was I. She may have been difficult and more trouble than she was worth, but I didn't care. It didn't even matter that she wanted to take it slow, because I could still fuck other girls on the side until she was ready. Besides, maybe, just maybe, this girl actually respected herself.

Nicole was a child, an immature pain in the ass, but so was I. Yet despite her flaws, I knew deep down Nicole was a warm, sweet, caring girl, which was all I really wanted. I just didn't know how to express my true feelings, and thought that giving Nicole multiple orgasms was the only she'd ever like me.

Nicole was fucked up in the head, but that's what made us so alike. Scared, insecure, and emotionally vulnerable. That's what drew me to her, because she was just like me.

The more we talked, the more I wanted her back. I knew I was going against my better judgment. But fuck it. I needed to have her in my life, which was why I instant messaged her the day before going home for spring break.

KNICK10217: hey beautiful
qtsummerprincess: hey
KNICK10217: how was ur day

qtsummerprincess: ehhh pretty sucky, u??

KNICK10217: would a back massage make u feel better

qtsummerprincess: haha NO

KNICK10217: wow u must really be upset

qtsummerprincess: yeah pretty upset lol

KNICK10217: and i thought i made an offer u couldnt refuse

qtsummerprincess: haha u thought wrong :-p

KNICK10217: im never wrong

qtsummerprincess: i wouldnt be too sure about that lol

KNICK10217: i mean i know you probably get better massages by your professional masseuse in ur mansion but i mean i do my best

qtsummerprincess: haha IM NOT RICH!

KNICK10217: ok ms dickinson

qtsummerprincess: if i was rich i wouldnt be going to school here lol

KNICK10217: no thats y u go to school here cause daddy has a wing

qtsummerprincess: i dont recall dickinson being a russian last name!

KNICK10217: its short for dickinsonovich

qtsummerprincess: hah now why would he shorten it!

KNICK10217: to sound american thats what they did to immigrants when they got off the boat

qtsummerprincess: shush

qtsummerprincess: then how come my last name isnt dickinson!

KNICK10217: and cmon would u really take a wing named dickinsonovich seriously

qtsummerprincess: haha i would!

KNICK10217: yea just like u would wanna come to my room and get a back massage

qtsummerprincess: no that would be a bad move on my part lol...did we not learn our lesson from the whole nicky mad at sasha saga!

KNICK10217: cmon now thats no way to talk to someone who is doing u a service

KNICK10217: getting back massages from me is a privalege

qtsummerprincess: i guess im just very unprivileged

KNICK10217: i gues so

qtsummerprincess: i'll survive

qtsummerprincess: what happened to not being a womanizer lol

KNICK10217: maybe ur the only woman i want have some self confidence

qtsummerprincess: shut the fuck up! I know ur hooking up w other girls! Haha im not stupid.

KNICK10217: yeah I am, but I'm just trying to find the right one

qtsummerprincess: what makes u think im the right one

qtsummerprincess: obviously the other girls has the same qualities as me so what makes u so sure that im the "right one"

KNICK10217: i never said u were i said maybe u were

qtsummerprincess: yes but maybe im not lol...i dont think its a good idea to start this up again cause honestly, it only made us fight

KNICK10217: we never fought lol

qtsummerprincess: yes we did..do u recall u coming to my room and me being mad..and the whole shpeel at the rat lol

KNICK10217: but that was when we stopped

qtsummerprincess: so? honestly us hooking up didnt make either of us happy let's face it

KNICK10217: nah it was when we stopped that the fighting began

qtsummerprincess: yeah but the fighting began b/c of us hooking up

KNICK10217: Wow!! all that for a back massage

qtsummerprincess: lol sure turn it all on me!!!

KNICK10217: not another fight, see if we were to hook up again we would take out our aggression in the sex saving us from these little fights

qtsummerprincess: haha...thats just what i wanna get myself into..not lol

qtsummerprincess: what was i thinking...i thought we were gonna be "cool" about the situation

KNICK10217: we are cool lol

qtsummerprincess: we're cool until u start offering me back massages lol...it all goes downhill from there

KNICK10217: r u saying im a bad kisser lol

qtsummerprincess: no lol...im saying that if we hook up its just gonna cause problems and i know we both dont want that

qtsummerprincess: sasha, why would u even want to hook up with me after u thinking I play more games than ur "PlayStation" and how i thought u were trying to get further with me

KNICK10217: have u looked at yourself in the mirror

qtsummerprincess: sometimes looks arent enough..if i were u, id be fed up with me

KNICK10217: lol, the stuff we fought over could easily be worked out

qtsummerprincess: how so

KNICK10217: cause it was kid stuff

qtsummerprincess: i'd say you flirting with my friend in front of me isnt kid stuff lol

KNICK10217: i wasnt doing it to piss u off its thats any consolation

KNICK10217: i really was just genuinly being friendly

qtsummerprincess: why would u want to piss me off lol

qtsummerprincess: how sweet of u!

KNICK10217: well i thought u thought i was flirting w her to get u jealous and that was far from the case

qtsummerprincess: no i just thought u were flirting with her because thats how u r lol

KNICK10217: oh ok lol

qtsummerprincess: i dont understand you lol, i dont understand boys in general

qtsummerprincess: honestly ur a good looking guy im sure u can find other girls..im obviously causing trouble lol

KNICK10217: yea i know all this lol

qtsummerprincess: lol so there ya go

KNICK10217: hahaha ur bored w me aren't u those back massages just weren't doing the trick

qtsummerprincess: lol shut up you know thats not it

KNICK10217: ill become a masseuse to win u back lol

qtsummerprincess: lol im not win back-able

qtsummerprincess: ur so stubborn!

KNICK10217: so r u

qtsummerprincess: yeah thats true lol

KNICK10217: i mean cmon u should be in my room getting a back massage by now

qtsummerprincess: nuh uh, im not getting sucked into this again, lol

KNICK10217: i know what you want and its a back massage from sasha lol

qtsummerprincess: u dont know what i want! lol u dont know anything about me except my fave color which my best friend didnt know which is sooo weird

KNICK10217: hahahaha that was hilarious

qtsummerprincess: it wasnt! lol

KNICK10217: no listen it was

KNICK10217: i was asking her questions about u that i didnt know the answer too and pulling the answers out my ass which she believed

KNICK10217: if u listened to the conversation and weren't mad i guarantee u would have laughed too

qtsummerprincess: lol probably, i didnt wanna "interrupt"

KNICK10217: i mean cmon i made up a favorite food for u lol

qtsummerprincess: haha what was it

KNICK10217: i think i said strawberry cheesecake w whip cream but my memory is a bit hazy

qtsummerprincess: shut up!! no u didn't. that's my favorite dessert lol

KNICK10217: see i do know u haha

qtsummerprincess: yeah but thats cause u guessed lol

qtsummerprincess: sasha its not gonna work out ..we're not compatible. all we do is fight

KNICK10217: we never gave it a chance

qtsummerprincess: is it really worth it?? i think its gonna end up just like it did last time

KNICK10217: no it will be different i promise

qtsummerprincess: oh please...how will it be different? u didnt change, neither did i. how the fuck is it gonna be any different?

KNICK10217: ill treat u with more respect

qtsummerprincess: i don't knowww

qtsummerprincess: why do u want this to work out? afew nights ago u didnt even care

KNICK10217: listen in all honesty the only reason i was a dick to u is cause i thought u would get bored w me otherwise cause thats how most of the other girls i dealt with are but obviously ur different which is y u may be worth keeping around

qtsummerprincess: how would u being an asshole make me un-bored?? lol

KNICK10217: cause most girls like to be treated like shit lol

qtsummerprincess: well that's stupid lol

KNICK10217: yea i agree

KNICK10217: girls shouldnt like being treated like shit but a lot of them do so i adjusted to their demands

qtsummerprincess: well u shouldnt change just to please someone else

KNICK10217: i know y girls like the ass hole shit it lies in the fact that it is masked as confidence and if the guy acts cocky there must be something for him to be confident about

qtsummerprincess: not necessarily...they could be trying to compensate

qtsummerprincess: or it could seem like that

KNICK10217: possibly but there are more reasons

qtsummerprincess: cockyness is a major turn off in all honesty

qtsummerprincess: honestly tho, how do i really know how many other girls uve been saying this to...u did admit that ur hooking up with other girls **KNICK10217:** most girls who look as good as u are used to getting their ass kissed by guys who want to sleep with them. if you all of a sudden are an asshole and dont try to kiss their ass they just like it cause the guy isnt that easy

KNICK10217: thats stupid, u think all these other girls are worth all this effort? If im saying all this shit to other girls, would I even have the time to have this conversation with u?

qtsummerprincess: maybe thats a sign that u shouldnt go for looks lol

qtsummerprincess: possibly...i dont know

KNICK10217: everybody goes for looks lol but thats not the point here

qtsummerprincess: looks may be the intial attraction but its the personality that really keeps u interested...how do u know im not actually a total bitch

KNICK10217: i dont but i wanna find out and look i feel as though i could actually trust u

qtsummerprincess: aw, i'm glad for that

qtsummerprincess: y?

KNICK10217: look at the effort i had to put in order to hook up with you and look at the effort im putting in now in trying to not let this slip away. So lets say that we end up dating, obviously not now but 1, 2 or 3 months down the road. I know that you would be faithful and that is something i really value and appreciate.

qtsummerprincess: aww thats really sweet sasha

KNICK10217: i mean the fact that i have to put all this effort in means that u are obviously very careful about who you let in and people who think that way are usually really good to those they let in

qtsummerprincess: yeah cause once im treated badly...toodles, but im really trusting that ur being honest with this

qtsummerprincess: okay i think we should just take relax til after the vaca...u might change ur mind or u might find someone at home who is completely awesome...and then we'll see...okay?

KNICK10217: yea i definitely agree. i dont wanna rush into nething believe me

qtsummerprincess: yeaa same here

KNICK10217: well im going to bed

qtsummerprincess: yeah me too

qtsummerprincess: goodnight :)

KNICK10217: night

I never thought this would happen, but there was a girl other than

Christina whom I was developing feelings for.

***

We got back in touch through this new invention called facebook and have been communicating with each other on a daily basis ever since.

I saw her over spring break and things quickly picked up from where they left off. The dynamic of our relationship hadn't changed, and we spent the week in bed together: having sex, cuddling, and watching movies. However, something was different. Yeah, I still felt extremely close to her, as though we shared an unbreakable bond. And yeah, I felt more comfortable around her than anyone else I knew. But sometimes these feelings just aren't enough.

Christina hadn't fully gotten over the lies I told her, nor did she want to enter into a relationship with an 18-year old kid. Both of us knew that we had something special. Yet we also realized that an exclusive relationship would never work at this point. For me, it wasn't even about the lies or age difference, but rather the fact that I was simply enjoying college too much. Don't get me wrong, I still loved her, but there were just so many girls out there for me to meet, and I wasn't sure if she was the right one anymore.

***

Nicole and I hooked up again when I got back to Binghamton. However, things were very different. We talked a lot over break and had a real conversation about where we were in life. Nicole was a virgin and explained that before meeting me, she had never done anything with another guy other than kiss him, and didn't know how to react to what happened in my room. Combine that with the fact that she was in a new environment, away from home for the first time, and it was clear that she was emotionally overwhelmed. I told her about what I was going through, that I was emotionally overwhelmed as well. I told her about my high school and explained how scary it was to go from knowing everybody in your class, to attending a university with over 10,000 students and being nothing more than a number.

Nicole thought I was a huge player, but I explained to her that I had very little experience with girls up until this semester. I told her about Lauren (the psychotic bitch from Concordia) and Christina, about how I didn't like the person I was becoming because I felt as though I had to behave like an asshole in order to get girls to like me. Nicole was very understanding and said that she wanted nothing from me, other than to be nice to her and treat her with respect.

I no longer needed to put on an image, because the way I presented myself on the surface didn't matter to her. She wouldn't judge me, so I felt comfortable exposing my vulnerability. It no longer mattered that she wanted to take it slow, and we would spend night after night in each other's room doing nothing but cuddling. Even though we weren't fucking, there was nothing I looked forward to more than lying in bed with her, because being with Nicole made me feel safe.

4/15/05

Yo, I have reconvened the journal. The break was nice but I really didn't take that long of a break. I mean St. Patti's day I got hammered so much so that I didn't even remember having sex with Mary until I saw the condom in the garbage can the next morning. Last week I got madd drunk and woke up on Rambo's couch lying in a pool of my own vomit. I had over 15 drinks last night on an empty stomach, woke up with my clothes covered in blood and had no idea how I got home. Tonight I had at least 11 beers and I'm almost sober. What The Fuck? This is ridiculous, why am I writing an entry on the day that I'm least drunk?

Well it looks like I may have found a nice girlfriend. The Cocktease won out but seriously she is nice. I can trust her and trust is one of the most important things in a relationship. The main reason I treated a lot of these girls like shit was simply due to the fact that I didn't trust them. She would be a nice girl to date and I feel somewhat of a connection. When I date a girl I don't fuck around. I literally could basically have any bitch I want but I ignored them because Nicole is really the only girl I want at Bing. In a sense, I feel bad about the Christina thing but in retrospect it will ultimately not work out. This college thing is just one big giant social progression. Sometimes I may be upset but when you really look at it my life is too privileged for words. Jesus, I keep a drunken journal for Christ sake. A peasant in Pakistan would kill his Grandmother to have the leisure time for a drunk journal.

Funny story time, I go out and we go out with this kid who's rockin some serious anti game. I mean yo the last titties he sucked on had milk in them. So we make a mission to swing bitches in his direction. We tried everything from it was his birthday to him having a 12 inch penis but yo some just people don't kow whats really good. How you not gonna talk to a bitch wen I;m throwing these hoes in your direction and you need a net to catch them. What kind of girl doesn't wanna be with someone who looks like Wesley Pipes from the waist down? Shits mind boggling sonn. Dude you need to be fucking these bitches or else you'll marry the 1st girl you have sex with and than your pussy whipped for life. Grow out of that awkward stage or else you're gonna get straight up abused. On second thought, maybe I am that drunk.

I went to TEP's Decades dance with Juan, along with a few of the guys from our floor. This kid named James Rothstein came with us and I decided to dedicate my night towards getting him laid. James had never been with a girl in his life and had absolutely no self-confidence whatsoever, so I decided to do a good deed and introduce him to as many girls as humanly possible.

For all purposes, Nicole and I were practically together, so I felt no need to hook up with anybody. I could have cared less about what any of these girls thought of me, because Nicole was the only girl who's opinion mattered. Having that mindset caused my inhibitions to go out the window, and I spent the entire night making ridiculous statements about James's penis to anybody who would listen.

Nicole came over the next night and I decided to take our relationship to the next level. I ate that pussy like a cantaloupe, making Nicole cum multiple times, because I cared about her feelings as a woman.

Here we were in our underwear, her body draped around mine like a blanket, when I physically suggested that she return the favor. Nicole refused and I was in complete disbelief. Here I was, getting her off on a regular basis, asking for nothing in return, and I was flabbergasted that she wouldn't want to satisfy me as well. If that wasn't bad enough, she had the nerve to ask if we could ever hang out without fooling around. How could she recite such blasphemy? Did she think there were other girls aside from her that I just lay in bed and cuddled with? Get the fuck out of here!!!

I was flat out shocked by Nicole's behavior. What kind of selfish bitch doesn't want to please the guy she's with? I could've been getting laid left and right, but was turning down each and every opportunity to bang other girls, for what? To be with some cunt who gets mad at me for sexually satisfying her. Fuck that!! Nicole didn't appreciate me. So I stopped seeing her and started fucking Mary again.

4/20/05

Fuck you Nicole!! I don't need ya ass anymore u stupid ass bitch I got wat I need in Mary's big fat juicy titteis in my face. Yo im drunk and high as shit right now and I just tore that ass up. I taxed that ass like da

Government. Big Daddy Kane Sonnnnn!! You can suck my dick, oh wait you don't do that. I forgot.

Juan and I went to JT's for 10-cent Tuesday's. The concept of 10-cent Tuesday is pretty self-explanatory; a cup of beer costs 10-cents. Both of us got shit-faced drunk and I ended up taking Mary back to my room and fucking her.

Juan and I began spending a lot of time together. We lived across the hall from each other and would hang out for at least a few hours everyday. Whenever one of us got back from class or the gym, we would almost immediately go into each other's rooms to play videogames, watch a movie, and drink a few beers. When the weather got nice, Juan and I would spend hours playing basketball on the court next to our dorm or throwing a football outside our building.

Juan was the man to go out with. The thing I liked most about him was that he didn't give a flying fuck about whether or not he got laid, and was bound to have a good time so long as we were drunk. That could have been why I almost never got any ass when we went out together (unless I stumbled into Mary). But you know what, I didn't care! I had enough girls already. And truth be told, I was becoming overwhelmed with the amount of pussy I was getting to begin with. I needed a break from these hoes and it was nice to just go out and simply be a guy.

4/29/05

So, in all honesty I am a changed man. It doesn't really matter right now anymore, maybe that's cause I got enough bitches already. I mean I dunno I was having madd good sex with the penis breath bitch when all of a sudden my shit went soft. Why? I dunno but now I just don't want sex for some reason. If anything I want companionship. If I had Christina right now I would be the happiest man in the world. She is so beautiful I just don't want to think about anybody else. I've been an asshole. After all the shit I talk about her, I am still messing w other girls and since they could be with other people fucking I don't know I am just too drunk for this shit.

I went home for Passover break thinking that Nicole and I were through. We were still fighting and hadn't spoken since the night she refused to "return the favor."

Who cares? I had Mary's huge tits, it's not like I needed that bitch anyway. At least that's how I felt before going soft in the middle of fucking her.

"What the hell?" I thought, petrified, as my penis wilted away like a dying rose. "This isn't normal. I'm an 18-year old kid. Shit like this shouldn't happen for at least another 30 years. Ok. Maybe it was the fact that I spent the entire day looking at porn. But still, I'm fucking scared."

This had never happened to me before and I was terrified. My sexual confidence was at its peak, but after that incident it began to plummet. I felt like a shell of a man, emotionally unstable and alone. Now that I'd lost my sexual confidence, I realized that I had nothing. That the foundation I lay out for myself was built on a house of cards, a house of cards that was all but ready to come down.

All-Nighters And Adderall Benders

4/30/05

Maybe the journal was about my adjustment to college. I don't know what to do, without the desire of the general what do I really have? I want it but I don't it doesn't really matter. In reality, maybe I am just a really sensitive kid who just wants a hug or something. Maybe??? Who knows? I guess its kinda nice not really having the desire to pull and just going out and getting wasted instead. It's rewarding in its own right I mean I am just going out and getting piss drunk out of my mind with not a care in the world. I am a drunk college student and it keeps me going.

The exhaustion I feel as a result of this semester is unreal. Maybe a hug is

all I really want you know but I'm not sure what I really want. Gotta pull

through. Look how far you've gotten. Seal the deal on your success that's

all you can say.

This past semester was as exhausting as it was fun. I was about to

make it through my first year of college and was only 3 finals and 2 papers

away from doing so. Despite my extracurricular activities, I somehow

managed to keep up with my work. However, in order to successfully

make it through the semester, I had to turn my studying up a notch and

block out all the emotional stress I was under.

Thank god for Adderall!! I have ADD, or ADHD. Whatever. I'm

not really sure what I have. All I know is that I have a learning disability

preventing me from staying focused for long periods of time, and these

pills were the reason I had made it through school so far.

I did not belong in Binghamton. At least not academically! The

high school I went to specialized in dealing with learning disabled

students. Small classes, teachers who spoon-fed you information, extra

time on tests, you name it-The Summit School (my high school) provided it. Not only that, but if you missed a homework assignment they gave you lunch detention and only penalized you half a grade once you completed it.

Failing at Summit was next to impossible. Shit, getting anything under a B- was almost unheard of. Combine that with double time on standardized tests and 1280 SAT scores, courtesy of sneaking in a dictionary into the exam and taking bathroom breaks to look up words I didn't know, and here I was at one of the best schools in the country.

Nobody thought I would make it in Binghamton. My parents told me that I wouldn't last one semester, my teachers didn't think I could succeed at a large University, and my friends all laughed at me when I told them about my acceptance into Binghamton.

I had to prove them all wrong and was on the cusp of doing so. All I needed to do now was make it through finals week in order to successfully pass my classes.

I'll never forget my first all-nighter. I was taking this class called "Human Rights In A Global Context" and was assigned to write an annotated bibliography on female genital mutilation, a practice where a woman's clitoris is removed so that she can no longer take pleasure from sex. Female castration, that's some nauseating shit to think about right there. If I Sasha Strenger, the guy who's writing a book that will set the women's movement back to 1853, am disgusted by this, than female genital mutilation is one fucked up procedure.

So yeah, I spent 16 hours straight working on this paper, staying up all night popping Adderall like candy, drinking coffee, and smoking cigarettes, before finishing my paper at 1:15 pm, an hour before class.

I had been up for almost two days straight and was finally about to go to sleep. However, other plans were in store for me, as my friend Casey from class invited me to play beer pong right when I was about to drift off into dreamland. I just had the most exhausting night of my life and wanted only to pass out, but the word $2 pitcher changed my mind, so I got dressed and went to Sports Bar with Casey.

What happened that night was a miracle. On 40 hours of no sleep, Casey and I won the beer pong tournament held at Sports Bar every Thursday and received a $50 bar tap to share. It was a magical moment and we hugged each other, celebrating like we just won the NBA finals. Casey and I spend the rest of the night getting obliterated, drinking shot after shot and smoking blunt after blunt until the sun came up.

I stumbled into my room at 6 am, ready to pass out, when I had to vomit. After barfing up my small intestine, I realized that I had locked myself out of my room. Standing outside in the hallway wearing nothing but my boxers, I began frantically knocking on my RA's door, hoping that she'd be awake to let me in.

Tiffany, (the overweight Puerto Rican RA) was delighted to wake up to me stumbling around in my underwear, and expressed how happy she was by having an emotional outburst. She looked at me like I was the most pathetic excuse for a man she had ever seen, before beginning to scream at me. When she was done yelling, she shot me a look of disgust and said, "I can't believe you're in college," before letting me into my room and walking away (muttering curse words under her breath in Spanish).

I pulled two additional all-nighters. One was when I had to complete a paper on violence in Grand Theft Auto III for a Comparative Literature class. The other one was when I had to finish a take home final for my Nazi Cinema class.

I finished off the semester with a 2.6 GPA. Although mediocre by most people's standards, considering where I came from, a 2.6 felt like making deans list.

This semester brought me out of my shell. I went from being a socially awkward retard who couldn't get laid to save his life, to maintaining a 3-girl rotation for the better part of a semester. I had transformed my personality and had the swagger to prove it, the swagger of a socially confident guy that people wanted to be around.

Last year I was in a cocoon, an emotionally nurturing environment with less than 300 kids, and here I am now, succeeding at a major university with over 10,000 students. After all the obstacles I had endured and overcame, I considered successfully completing my first year of college to be a huge accomplishment. So many people, including myself, doubted whether or not I would make it at Binghamton, and I had just proven everybody wrong. I went home for the summer feeling very proud of myself, like I could do anything I set my mind to. And I was ready to take on the whole world.

***

As for Nicole, we patched things up. I wanted to stop thinking about her and told myself over and over that she wasn't worth it. My pride kept telling me to cut that bitch out of my life. But what has listening to my pride gotten me other than meaningless sex and superficial relationships?

Fuck my pride!!! I missed her. I missed having someone to talk to, someone to spend time with, someone who I actually felt safe around. Especially after what happened with Mary, I didn't even care about fucking anymore. I was tired of having empty sex and wanted something meaningful, if it meant having to wait, than so be it.

Nicole and I started taking walks together now that the weather was warm. There was a grassy hill on the outskirts of campus where we would go to watch the stars and lie down next to each other. As we lay their looking up at the sky, I felt as though we were immersed in each other, isolated in our own little world, together in a bubble that nobody could pop.

***

Nicole and I got into a fight the day before she went home. She wanted to say goodbye to me before leaving. But I was already at Sports Bar with my friend Ralph (who I knew from playing basketball) when she texted me.

I had just finished my last final and wanted to get fucked up. Casey smoked me up on a couple of bowls and I was high as a kite. We played Mario Kart afterwards and I was transfixed by all the pretty colors in the game.

I picked up an ounce before I left, because I needed weed for the summer. Ralph called me while I was walking back to my room and invited me to Sports Bar for "Beer Olympics." Beer Olympics were held every Tuesday and have been compared to the decathlon of drinking games. Beerpong, Flipcup, Quarters, and Boat races were among the many events held to determine who would be crowned champion of drinking games.

Before I go any further, let me explain that as much as I liked getting high, I hated being high around large groups of people, so I decided to get as drunk as possible in order to forget about being high. Ralph, however, had a different agenda and wanted to spend the night hitting on girls. Unfortunately, Ralph had lower standards than me and I went to high school with a bunch of zoo creatures. So while Ralph was hitting on hippos and walruses, I was at the bar getting blackout drunk.

In the midst of drinking myself into a coma, I received a text message from Nicole, saying that she was leaving tomorrow and wanted to see me before she left.

We agreed to meet at 1:30, since the bars closed at 1. But I was late to meet her, because I spent close to a half-hour throwing up in the bathroom.

It didn't take a rocket scientist to realize that I was a drunken mess, especially after Nicole saw me walk face first into a tree. She was pissed, and couldn't believe that she would have to spend her last night in Binghamton taking care of a drunken idiot. I wish I could tell you what Nicole was doing or how she was acting. But I couldn't. I was fucking wasted. All I know is that she wasn't happy. Who would be? You meet a guy that you care about, have a rollercoaster ride of a semester with, and this is how it ends, with him unable to walk straight or speak to you in complete sentences?

Nicole deserved a proper goodbye, not this. But how was I to know that she was leaving tomorrow? She didn't tell me anything until I was already wasted at Sports Bar. Had I known she was going home, I would've never gone out and spent the entire night with her instead.

Not like it matters now. I'm wrecked and Nicole's disappointed. So lets at least go to sleep with our arms around each other. That's all I really wanted to do anyway. Sleep. I was drained and exhausted, wanting only Nicole, because lying in bed with her made everything ok.

Instead of waking up to Nicole, I woke up naked next to a large pile of vomit. This was not good. Why was she gone? Who did this? Nicole couldn't have thrown up on the bed. "Oh, shit. Nicole's going to be pissed," I thought. For once I was right. If I thought she was angry last night. Well that sent her over the edge. I went to her room and it took over an hour for her to open the door. "Man this was bad; I must have really fucked up." I thought, nervously waiting outside.

I needed answers and wasn't leaving until I got them. We just undressed and went to sleep, right? So than why was my bed covered in vomit? I thought I did all my peuking before meeting Nicole.

Apparently not! When Nicole finally came to the door, she told me that I threw up in the middle of trying to go down on her. "Whaat??

That's bullshit!! Who the hell throws up while trying to eat some pussy? Besides, her vagina smells like cinnamon. Wait. Did I really?? No, I couldn't have. I wouldn't throw up on Nicole no matter how drunk I was. Would I?"

But I did and she wanted nothing to do with me. I was stunned and felt a combination of shock, disgust, and embarrassment with myself. Yet, no matter how bad I felt or how many times I apologized, the damage was done and Nicole wasn't hearing it. She kicked me out of her room, saying that she needed "time to think" about whether or not we should continue seeing each other.

I thought I had fucked up what could have been a beautiful relationship. Until Nicole texted me a few days after I got home, saying that she missed me, and that her parents were out of town for the weekend. She invited me to her house on Long Island and that was when we took our relationship to the next level, as she gave me head for the first time.

OH MY GOD!!! Nicole could suck a dick. Before going down on me, she said that this was her first time. But if that were the case, than this girl was a fucking natural; kissing the shaft, licking the head, taking the whole thing in her mouth like a pro.

Dammmnn!! That was probably one of the best blowjobs I had ever received in my life and I felt as though I were in a porno video. Nicole was that good; and as I lay spent in her arms, I couldn't help but wonder whether or not that she had done this before.

"Nobody's that good the first time they suck dick! Nobody!" I thought to myself. "Had Nicole been playing me all along? Was she really as innocent as she claimed? What if she used to be a huge slut in high school and was using sex as a weapon in order to string me along and trick me into being her boyfriend? What if she 's still a slut and is only a prude to me while fucking other dudes on the side?"

Nah, these are just crazy thoughts. "Nicole's a nice girl who respects herself. She wouldn't lie to me. Would she? No. She had big lips. Of course she's going to give good head. Who knows? Maybe she just watches a lot of porn or has a huge dildo in her room that she practices on. Yeah. That's probably it. I mean, just because she sucks a good dick doesn't mean she sucked a lot of dick in the past. Right?"

"Sasha this is ridiculous. After all this time, not only did you finally get what you wanted, but it also happened to be amazing, and you're complaining? The girl that you want to be with just sucked your dick, so stop filling your head with nonsense. Just look at it as a sign of things to come, that you're going to be in for an awesome semester when you go back to school next fall."

And besides, I had Christina. Yeah, that's right, you heard it correctly. Christina. We still continued seeing each other when I came back to the city and our relationship hadn't changed a bit. Great sex and emotional intimacy, that's what we shared together. Yet why did it feel like something was wrong?

I thought I loved her. After all, she was a beautiful girl with a caring personality. So why was that no longer enough? Was it because I was in college, surrounded by beautiful girls who wanted to fuck me? Was it because college made me realize that all pretty girls have nice personalities if you hit it right? Or was it because I wanted to be with Nicole? Who knows? All I know is that I no longer wanted to commit to Christina.

Although I no longer wanted Christina to be my girlfriend, I was petrified of losing her. Always there for me, she was my safety net, the only consistent thing in my life, the one person I could turn to when things were bad, and I'd have been a fool to let her go.

Don't get me wrong. I'd be happy if we wound up together. But if something better came along, I would've pounced at the opportunity and left Christina in the dust. I didn't love her. At least not in the way I thought I did during my freshman year. No, I was with her out of co-dependency, because I needed to feel cared for.

Retard Camp

I got a job, as a general bunk counselor at a special needs camp in upstate New York. The camp serviced both children and adults with a wide range of disabilities ranging from ADHD, OCD, Depression, Bipolar disorder, Autism, Mental Retardation, and many more.

The high functioning campers, those with ADHD, OCD, Depression, etc. were similar to myself, perhaps needing a little more guidance than I did in order to successfully function in mainstream society. Many of these kids had the potential to go to college and hold down a 9-5 job if given proper support.

The lower functioning campers however, those with Autism and Mental Retardation, were a different story. Many of them were unable to dress themselves, shower, or use the bathroom without assistance. Some of them couldn't even talk. Picture that for a second.

I changed my first diaper at camp. He was a 45-year old man with a mustache. Fuck! I could barely change my own diaper and here I was changing someone old enough to be my father. Weird.

Imagine going through life completely unable to take care of yourself, knowing that you will never, no matter what you do or how hard you try, become a fully functional independent adult. That for as long as you live, you're going to have to depend on other people to meet each and every single one of your basic needs.

You will die a virgin. You will never experience a woman's touch, what it feels like to kiss someone, have a woman hold your hand or put her head on your shoulder. Just imagine that. Going through life without loving human contact? Because that's what many of my campers were faced with.

Speaking of women, I turned over a new leaf in terms of how I looked at and treated them. Well, at least I tried to while I was at camp. No. Wait. Fuck that shit. I turned over a new leaf in terms of how I looked at and treated people as a whole.

Since I've been in college, I felt the need to put on a false image of cockiness and bravado in order to be socially accepted, to get girls, to have people want to be around me. But at camp it was totally different. It takes a special kind of person to spend their summer working at a camp filled with disabled people; someone loving, caring, understanding, and most importantly non-judgmental. My co-counselors weren't regular people. No they were angels, and the only thing that mattered to them was whether or not you were a good human being.

The people I worked with inspired me to be a better person. I had this really cynical view of the world, believing that you needed to behave like a total asshole in order to succeed, but working at camp changed my mindset, because I realized how subjective success was. You could have all the money in the world and fuck the hottest bitches, but if your "closest friends" care about nothing aside from your superficial image, than how successful are you really? Whereas on the contrary, you could be some "nobody" working a minimum wage job and living in your parent's basement, but if your surrounded by people that genuinely love and care about you, well, than to me you're a success.

So yeah, I stopped caring about how I presented myself to other people. And the only thing that mattered was whether or not I gave these kids (and adults) the best summer they could have. I mellowed out, stopped drinking so much, stopped judging people and jumping to conclusions about them based on first impressions.

Hell, I even started respecting women. No, really I did. The girls at camp were nothing like the girls I went to school with. Binghamton girls were fucking shallow pieces of garbage; manipulative sluts that cared only about money, fashion, social status, getting drunk, and sucking dick. But the girls at camp were different. They were sweet, caring, nurturing and maternal; everything I wanted in a woman. So I started looking at women differently, because I realized that there was a whole different type of woman I'd never been exposed to.

My new attitude gave me the closest thing I'd ever had to an honest and meaningful relationship. Her name was Emily and she was beautiful. An 18-year old college student from France, tall and slender, with the ass of a music video vixen, she had long straight brown hair, soft olive skin, seductive green eyes, and a smile so infectious that it made everyone around her want to smile too. But the best thing about her was her voice. Oh that voice. It was heavenly! She had this soft, sweet, melodic French accent that made her sound so cultured and sophisticated, yet so unbelievably sexy at the same time.

We met at the creek during staff orientation week, which took place a week before the campers arrived. The creek at the edge of the woods was where everybody used to go at night to get high. The scenery surrounding the creek was beautiful, so peaceful and serene, and for miles and miles, you could see nothing but woods, water, and open space.

So that's how we met, smoking weed at the creek with the staff members after the 3rd day of orientation. I found out earlier in the day that we were going to be working together with severely autistic adults in cabin E5 and I decided to introduce myself after smoking a joint.

We hit it off instantly, both physically and emotionally, and couldn't stop touching each other from the moment we met. Emily and I spent the entire night sitting on a rock, talking and growing increasingly more attracted to each other as the night wore on.

Before camp started, I told myself that I wasn't going to hook up with anybody other than Christina or Nicole, but that plan quickly went out the window. "Emily's beautiful and I'm a horny 19-year old kid, so why not? Besides, Christina just told me that she was moving back to

Greenwich, Connecticut this morning, and Nicole's working at a sleep

away camp as well, possibly doing the same thing, so fuck it, I'm going to

see where this goes." I thought.

Even though we barely knew each other, it felt as though years of

sexual tension were pent up inside us. So when Emily and I got back to

my bunk, there was only one thing to do, and that was act on the passion

that had been brewing for what seemed an eternity. (Way to sound

poetic. Douchebag!!)

I was scared that working together would've made things awkward

between us, but that wound up being the furthest thing from the truth.

In fact, it actually brought us closer together. When I first met Emily, I

thought that she was just a gorgeous girl with a beautiful voice, but the

more I got to know her, the more I came to realize that her physical

appearance merely scratched the surface of her true beauty. Emily was a

nurturer, a loving, compassionate girl who never hesitated to put other

people before herself. Whenever one of the campers needed help with

something, she would instantly put aside whatever she was doing and

help him. If one of our campers were mad or upset, Emily knew just what

to say in order to calm him down. So patient and tolerant, our campers loved and gravitated towards her, and it made me want Emily to be the mother of my children.

I thought that spending every waking moment with Emily would've caused me to grow tired of banging her, but it turned out to be the exact opposite. Sex was amazing! Better than my wildest fantasy, unparalleled to anything I had ever experienced before. We used to have marathon sessions and would fuck for hours on end in almost every position imaginable. I fucked her from behind, fucked her in the missionary position, fucked her in a chair, fucked her in the cowgirl position, fucked her in the reverse cowgirl position, had her rub her clit while she was on top of me so that I could feel her pussy clench up, as she had orgasm after orgasm while I was inside her.

It wasn't long before Emily and I began having sex in public places. A hot summer day, it must have been close to 100 degrees outside, so Emily and I decided to go swimming at the creek in order to cool off. Making out in the water, one thing quickly lead to another, as I started fingering her while she rubbed my cock through my bathing suit. It didn't take long for the two of us to be overcome with lust, and in an unbridled frenzy of passion I took off my swim trunks, flinging them on to the shore before sliding inside her.

It was on after that! Having made love at the creek sparked an inextinguishable fire, where the urge to fuck in public places became uncontrollable. My inhibitions went out the window and it became a turn on to see how much we could get away with. We did it everywhere, on the swings, on people's front lawns, on the basketball court. Shit, I even gave her the flesh musket in our bunk while the campers were sleeping.

I was a month into camp and everything was going perfectly. Seriously, nothing could have been any better. I was having an ideal summer, surrounded by awesome people, having earth-shattering sex with a woman I felt closer and closer to with each passing day, and to top it off, my job caused me to feel a sense of personal fulfillment. When I woke up I felt as though my life had purpose, that I was leading a worth while existence, and this was something I had never experienced before.

That was until I was assigned to work with Hans. Hans was a 37-year old severely Autistic man who was fat, balding, and asked to use the bathroom every 30 seconds as part of his Autism. This guy could've just gotten back from taking a Hippo sized shit, but it made no difference, because there was nowhere Hans would rather be than on the toilet.

If taking a dump in the bathroom was his passion, than so be it. Who was I to stop him? As long as I didn't have to keep him company and watch, than whatever Hans did was fine by me.

But I did. Counselors had to watch their "kids" at all times and follow them wherever they went, even to the bathroom. In Hans's case, I had to actually go inside the stall with him, because he had a habit of trying to "eat his creation"; thinking it was chocolate.

What the fuck did I get myself into? This is not for me. No matter how good this job was making me feel about myself, keeping a grown man company and watching as he took a shit was something I just wasn't cut out for.

That could have been why I got fired. By now I had been working with Hans for a week and not once had he eaten out of the toilet. So than why, of all days, did he decide to do it when I came back from smoking a blunt at the creek during lunchtime?

Man that must have been some good weed I smoked, because I was in another dimension. "Stoned off my ass": talk about a fucking understatement, I was on Jupiter! Wait. That was another understatement. I was on planet Tatooine!!

"How come Hans has a chocolate mustache? And why does it smell funny?" I asked myself, as I stared blankly into outer space. "Oh no. Did Hans just do what I think he did?" Yep. He did. And that mustache was not made out of chocolate.

I felt like a camper. That's how high I was: which could have explained how Hans was able to run to the bathroom and sneak in a turd sandwich while I wasn't looking.

When your camper takes a crap and eats it in front of you, than maybe, just maybe, you're not meant to work with the special needs population. That's what the director thought, which probably accounts for why he fired me the next day.

Easy Living

So that was it. Camp was over and now I needed to find something to do for the rest of the summer. Luckily for me, my friend James, who I had known since I was a baby, was able to get me a job collecting signatures for the Guifford Miller Campaign Fund. The Guifford Miller Campaign Fund was a program designed to put Guifford Miller (former speaker of the New York City Council) on the ballot for mayor under the smaller class size initiative program, which campaigned to reduce classroom sizes in New York City public schools to 17 kids.

***

I went out with this kid Jermaine (who I knew from Concordia) the day before starting my new job. He lived on 79th and Columbus and we went to this bar called Timeout on 77th and Amsterdam.

For a 6'5 250 lb black guy, Jermaine couldn't hold his liquor for shit, as he was blackout drunk after a pitcher of Coors light. I couldn't believe what I was witnessing. This guy looked like Michael Strahan. And here he was passed out at the bar, unable to speak coherently, after what, one pitcher? Ridiculous.

Jermaine couldn't function and I didn't want to spend the night taking care of him, so I took him home. "Shit. What am I going to do now? It isn't even 12:30 and already the night's about to come to a close? No. It can't end like this! I refuse to allow my night to get cut short on account of someone who can't drink." I thought, as I left his apartment in disbelief.

Brother Jimmy's on 84th and Broadway had Karaoke night. "I can't sing. But fuck it. That'll all change after a few more drinks. Besides, there are some hot ass girls in the bar. And well, I hadn't gotten pussy in a

week."

"Excuse me, can I see some ID." The bouncer said, as he stepped

in front of me, blocking my path into the bar.

Me: "Sure." I said, as I casually pulled out my Michigan ID.

Bouncer: Skeptically scrutinizing my ID, studying it like a forensic scientist.

"You sure this is real?" He asked: giving me a funny look in the process.

Me: "Yeah."

Bouncer: "Alright, go ahead."

"Who was that cute girl with long brown hair and a slender physique

taking shots by herself? Who cares?" She wasn't going to be alone for

long, as I walked up to the bar and sat next to her, right when she finished

ordering a Soco Lime shot. "Yo bartender. Let me get two more of

those." I called out, just as the bartender was about to leave.

Her name was Rachel and she was a recently divorced actress, who

also happened to have a degree in French and Chemistry from Stanford

University. Now if I told her my real age, that I had just finished my

freshman year of college, she would have gotten up and walked away. So

I did what I do best, I lied. As far as she was concerned, I was a Columbia University graduate student who was working with Autistic kids in order to help pay his tuition.

About a half hour went by and it was Rachel's turn to sing. She told me to comment on her voice, asking whether or not I thought she had the tools to make it in show business.

This bitch should stick to Chemistry. She sang, "You're the One That I Want" from Greece, and if there was one word to describe her singing, it was atrocious with a capital A. She sang so badly that I would've rather anally impaled myself on top of a flagpole than hear one more note out of her.

"How did I do?" Rachel asked

Me: "Damn, your singing is almost as good as my back massages." Wow, did I really just say that? Somebody's full of shit.

Rachel: "You should let me provide you with a second opinion."

Me: "Turn around."

Rachel: As I was massaging her: "So, was going out and picking up chicks part of your major?"

Me: "Nah. My Psyc. Degree just helps me talk to supermodels in bars. It aint nothing."

Rachel: "Oh Wow. You must've really paid attention in class. Tee hee."

Me: "For sure. You know this'll feel a lot better on a bed, right?"

Rachel: "Prove it."

"You've gotta be kidding me!" Here I was in this girl's apartment, about to rip her vagina in two, and I forgot to bring a condom? Really? And she doesn't have one either? Fuck Me!!"

At least I got some brains. Rachel was still down to fuck, but I'm not dumb enough to raw dog some random skank the first night I meet her (at least not anymore), so I settled for a blowjob. After I came, Rachel asked me to go down on her, but that was out of the question, because her pussy looked like Julius Erving's Afro **(WHEN HE WAS PLAYING IN THE ABA)**.

***

By the way, the Guifford Miller Campaign Fund turned out to be the most pathetic excuse for a job I had ever seen. They paid $15 per hour and my only responsibility was to walk up to random strangers and convince them to sign a petition, which contained 20 signatures and took no more than 30 minutes to fill. I was on the clock for six hours a day, and spent the remaining five and a half hours smoking weed with James.

Saying Goodbye

Emily and I continued to keep in touch after I'd been fired. So when camp ended in late August, I let her spend a few days in my house before she went back to France.

Talk about an eventful couple of days. I hadn't had sex in a month, and my dick was like a wild beast, ready to destroy anything with two legs and a vagina.

A hot make out session ensued from the moment she walked into my apartment, and we were feeling each other up before the door even had a chance to close. "Fuck it. My bedroom's too far. Let's do it in the living room. Mom and dad are in Cape Cod and Leah (my 13 year old sister) is in The Hamptons visiting her friend Deb. It's not like anybody's going to walk in on us." At least that's what I thought.

"Oh shit, why do I hear a key turning?" I wondered, as I pounded

Emily out from behind like a jackhammer, while she knelt on the couch, pussy juice leaking on the furniture. "Mom and Dad were supposed to be in Cape Cod all week. Oh no. Leah! But wasn't she supposed to be in The Hamptons?" I asked myself.

She was and only stopped by because she forgot her wallet. So when Leah came home to the sight of us fucking each other silly, her face turned white as a ghost and she stood there frozen with her mouth open, paralyzed with both fear and disgust at what she had just walked in on. "Ewww, gross, I'm never sitting on this couch again." Leah cried out, as she ran screaming into her room. At least it wasn't mom and dad who caught us.

It got worse. The next day, Emily and I had just finished getting busy, when we decided to go out and smoke hookah on my terrace. Uneventful. Right? That was until I tried to open the door and realized we were locked out. Emily and I only planned on staying out for 20 minutes so we didn't think it was necessary to get dressed, and now the two of us were trapped on my terrace wearing nothing but our underwear. This was bad. My phone and keys were inside, Emily and I were practically naked, and we had nobody to turn to for help.

Well, there was someone. But I really didn't want to call her.

Grandma Ethel lived across the highway from us and was the only other

person in the family who had an extra set of keys to the house. She was

also 90-years old, legally blind in her right eye, and suffering from the

early stages of senile dementia.

My downstairs neighbors were playing beerpong outside so I

called out to them, asking if I could borrow one of their phones. I couldn't

believe I was actually going through with this. That I was about to call **MY**

90-YEAR OLD GRANDMOTHER to let me in to **MY** own house, because **I**

was dumb enough to lock myself onto **MY** terrace after **I** had just finished

FUCKING. My dignity had officially flown out the window!

Grandma Ethel hadn't seen me in my underwear since I was 2-

years old. And I did not want to change that (especially when I had a half-

naked girl next to me). So when grandma told me that she'd be at the

house in 20-minutes, I knew I had to think fast. Luckily, we found some

old clothes and towels drying on the terrace. Emily made one of the

towels look like a dress, while I put a shirt on, as well as another pair of

boxers over my boxers, in order to give off the appearance that I was

wearing shorts.

Fortunately for everyone involved, Grandma Ethel can't tell the difference between a dog and a squirrel, and had no idea that her "bubula" just finished impaling a bitch in the living room. Of course she didn't. Do you think my grandmother would've prattled on about her 94-year old boyfriend Irving for 45-minutes had she known I'd spent the afternoon assaulting some girl's vagina? HELL NO!!! According to her, I was still a virgin.

***

A chapter of my life was coming to a close. Emily was leaving for France tomorrow. Christina had already left for Greenwich. And it may be a very long time before I have another chance to be intimate with a woman I cared about.

This past year had been an emotional rollercoaster and I just wanted to get off. I was tired of being single, putting on a cocksure image and pretending to be something I'm not merely to hook up with random girls at the RAT; girls who at the end of the day left me feeling frustrated and disconnected with life.

I needed someone to talk to. Someone to love, nurture, care for, and support me while I tried to turn over a new leaf, and Nicole was the

only person I could see taking on that role. Even though we hadn't

spoken in over two months, I still thought about her everyday, even while

I was seeing Emily and Christina, because Nicole was the only girl I could

realistically see having a lasting relationship with.

Here was a girl I could confide in, open up to, and spend a lazy

Sunday (or Monday, or Tuesday, or any other day for that matter) lying in

bed watching movies with. Yet I hadn't spoken to her all summer long. A

million things could've happened within the past two months and I no

longer knew where we stood. For all I knew, Nicole could've lost interest

in me, found another guy, or decided that she wanted to be single.

Hopefully she wanted to make this work, because without her I would be

plunged back into the empty lifestyle I was trying to escape.

***

Emily and I spent her last day in New York lying in bed watching

movies, before I took her to the airport. Throughout the day we

reminisced about the summer, recalling memorable stories involving the

campers and us. It saddened me that in a matter of hours, Emily would

permanently disappear from my life. Yet it also dawned on me that getting to know her had been an amazing experience, and that thinking about her would always brighten up my day. Everything ended on such a good note and it made me happy that she will forever be instilled as a positive memory. So that was it. Finally her plane came and we hugged and kissed good-bye, never to see each other again.

A Spiritual Epiphany

I tripped on mushrooms for the first and last time the day before going back to school. My parents weren't home and I had ¼ of mushrooms that I picked up from Chris. Needing someone to share them with, I called my next-door neighbor and invited him over. Each of us had an 8th before going onto my terrace to blaze.

An hour later the two of us were tripping balls, having the time of our lives when I realized that everything I valued was a bunch of bullshit, that the only reason I was happy was because I was tripping on mushrooms. This drug controlled me and it made me feel powerless, like a bug that could be squashed on a whim.

I thought about my own existence and realized that I was nothing. I thought about the universe and how big it was. That compared to its infinite nature our planet was nothing more than a dot. If planet Earth was just a dot, than what did it make me? The more I thought about that question the more insignificant I felt, because in the big scheme of things I was just a particle of dust.

Why am I here? I asked myself as I waved to the tree. Am I really a lost soul who has absolutely no control over his life? Is life a gift or a curse? The beautiful planet I call home is unfortunately consumed with ugliness. Human beings are fucking retarded because they keep coming up with new ways to destroy our planet. People have the technology to live in a utopian society but choose to make nuclear weapons instead. Oil companies poison our water; corporations launch us into pointless wars, and our own government supports genocide all for the sake of making a dollar. We live in an apocalyptic age, where the entire human race can be vanquished with the push of a button. Our species is doomed to destroy itself and I'm going to live to see the end of the world.

Here we are trapped in a web of evil expertly woven by politicians and corporate businessmen, and nobody's doing a damn thing to stop it. I'm not doing a damn thing to stop it!! I live in a bubble of superficial happiness where the concerns of the world don't apply to me. How is getting drunk and hooking up with girls going to make the world a better place? It isn't!! What kind of man sees a serious problem and does absolutely nothing to stop it? Not the kind of man I want to be!!!

The bottom line is that this shit has to stop once and for all. My eyes are open and I am no longer in the dark. Our planets fucked and I'm going to save it or die trying! I am going to be an instrument of change and in order to do that I have to become a fucking machine. From now on I am going to get excellent grades, learn a bunch of martial arts, read a ton of books, and learn how to shoot a gun. My life has a purpose and that purpose is to be the psychologist of congressmen and expose government corruption through their visits to my office. The weight of the world lies on my shoulders and I have to be strong enough to carry it.

PART 3

JUST WATCH IT ALL UNRAVEL

The end of the summer caused me to feel like an image on display. On the surface, I looked like a cool kid who was headed in the right direction, but I felt as though my life was falling apart. Tripping on mushrooms made me seriously question the purpose of my existence and I felt like nothing more than a waste of space. Last semester, I lived to get drunk and bone bitches, so that I could make fun of them in my journal, but now I looked for a deeper purpose in life. I wanted to improve myself, to be a better man and lead a positive existence. I craved stability and needed a girlfriend to support me while I tried to change my ways. Christina and Emily were gone so I looked for Nicole to fill that void. We may have had a tumultuous relationship, but that's because I was a self-centered asshole. I was a new man now. Yeah, that's right. I was mature and ready to take her seriously.

133

I envisioned a quiet semester, where I would concentrate exclusively on school, the gym, and Nicole, but that was not to be. I moved into Seneca Hall, which was in College in the Woods, CIW for short. Instead of a nice quiet life free of distractions, I ended up living in a 5-person suit where the concept of privacy was non-existent. CIW was known for its rampant drinking and drug use, so any hope of productivity was pretty much thrown out the window.

To make matters worse, I had two roommates instead of one. Jeff, Jack, Ron, and Sean were my four suitemates. I lived in the triple with Ron and Sean. Ron and Sean kept to themselves so it was as though they didn't exist. Jack and Jeff lived in the double. Jack was a tall, gangly, redheaded sophomore from New Paltz who played guitar and smoked a lot of weed, while Jeff was a jr. transfer student from Suffolk Community College who looked like he was 12 and tried really hard to impress people. Nearly everything that came out of his mouth was meant to either brag about all the people he knew or insinuate how much pussy he got. If that wasn't off putting enough, it became apparent after 5 minutes of talking to him that 90% of what came out of his mouth was complete bullshit and should have been predacessed by: "I wish."

We went to a party at the AXP house since Jeff supposedly grew up with a bunch of the brothers. However, nobody in the frat had any idea who he was and we were promptly turned away from the party. We wound up getting wasted at Sports Bar by ourselves.

Jack and I spent the following day smoking weed and playing Super Nintendo. As we sat on the couch, playing Mario World in a drugged stupor, I realized that this semester was going to be very different from the last.

Something wasn't clicking. My swag and confidence were gone, replaced by social anxiety and confusion. Feeling like a robot, scared and incapable of human interaction, all I wanted was to be by myself, alone with only my thoughts. But how was I going to do that in a suite full of people?

What the fuck was I doing? Here I was spewing out all this bullshit about transforming my mind and body into a machine, yet I'm getting high instead. After all this talk about turning my life around and changing for the better, I'm still doing the same thing that I did yesterday, the day before, and the day before that. What happened to being productive? Granted, classes hadn't started yet. But still, this was an awful way to start the semester, especially if I planned on exposing

government corruption after graduation.

8/27/05

Right now I feel like I'm stuck in a maze, trapped on another

planet in a scary, foreign environment from which there seems to be no

escape. My mind's in a fog and I need Nicole to help me think straight.

She has no idea how important she is to me. I know she thinks I'm just

some kind of player who only wants to get drunk and bang girls, but that

isn't true. I need her. She's the only person in Binghamton who makes me

feel safe, the only one I feel comfortable talking to, and I'd be totally lost

without her.

I'm just too scared to admit, both to her and to myself, that she's

the only person I want to interact with. That she's my escape from life and

the only time I can cope with reality is when we are together.

The world's a scary place but when I'm with you it's soothing and

comforting. Together the two of us are in a bubble, insulated from the

rest of the world, and I want to stay there forever.

Without you I'm all alone. A drunk, high mess, that's all I am when we're not together. I need someone like you, classy and ladylike who doesn't smoke or drink, to support and spend time with me so that I can turn into the man I want to become. I know that's a lot to ask, for you to single handedly transform me into another person but please try, because I can't do this without you.

I saw Nicole the next day and I knew what I had to do. She wasn't going to wait around forever. No, Nicole was a beautiful girl who plenty of guys wanted to be with. And the longer I postponed asking her out, the more likely she was to move on and leave me hanging, filled with regret over not having had the balls to commit to her.

We met outside the University Union and took a walk to the soccer field. There was a tree about 30 yards from one of the goalposts and we lay down beside it. As we feverishly made out in the grass, I realized there was no better moment than now to tell Nicole how I felt. I looked into her eyes and told her how beautiful she was, that there was no other girl on the planet I'd rather be with than her. She looked at me and smiled, asking with a look of concern and pressing vulnerability if I was sure. I told her that I wasn't sure of anything, except for how badly I wanted to be with her, and that the only time I felt like a whole person was when we were together. Nicole then pulled my head toward her and gave me a long passionate kiss on the mouth. I asked if that was a yes and she smiled, nodded her head, and kissed me again several more times.

It was getting dark so we decided to head back to my suite. The suite was empty and I was grateful for this rare occurrence, as a steamy make out session ensued on my bed. I took her shirt off and lightly caressed her breasts, before kissing down her neck and softly sucking her tits, biting her nipples ever so gently.

Just as Nicole's tits were in my mouth, Sean walked in on us and I immediately jumped on top of her, using my body as a protective shield. Oblivious to the fact that I had a half naked girl in my room, Sean sat down at his computer and started playing backyard baseball. I tried to get his attention, by repeatedly calling his name and motioning for him to get out of the room, but to no avail, as inning after inning seemed to go by without notice. Finally, after the fourth inning of backyard baseball ended, I screamed at the top of my lungs for him to get the fuck out of my room, before he finally got the picture and left.

By now, Nicole had grown uncomfortable and got dressed, so we watched TV in the common room until she left. Fucking Sean!! At that moment, venomous hatred flowed through my veins and I wanted nothing more than to kill him.

9/7/05

All the pain, insecurity, suffering I felt is going to come out again. I thought it was over but its far from over. Far from over/. I worked in a camp and it was a maturing experience. I realized that I need to maintain my focus but sometimes its just too hard. Nonetheless I have to keep on keeping on.

Nicole can't ever know about my emotional problems. I care about her to much to burden her with them. I just hope she knows how hard I am trying to be with her. Once the Long Island Cocktease she is now something special. I really want to be with her because I know she will like me even when I tell her about my emotional problems. But I just don't want to tell her because I want her to be happy and comfortable and telling her what I am really like can jeopardize that.

I really would like to be with her and only her but I am scared. I told her I wanted it but I am afraid that if I show my utmost commitment she will reject me and treat me like shit. Where will I be then? Where? All I really want from her right now is her love and support. I just want genuine love. Sometimes I feel like pussy will always be my only and best friend. It's always there and it likes me/

The world can never know the pain I feel. No matter what, I am cool, calm, and collected. Nobody can ever know how I really feel. There are times where I wish I were dead. Not by some random shit but I want to die a hero's death. I want to be killed in battle for a noble cause. I want to die while giving someone the chance to live. I want to make a difference but I feel that I can't and I ultimately won't. It's scary!!!!

My campers lived in the dark world. It's scary and frightening and sometimes I feel as thought I venture there. I kind of escaped but I didn't. Although on the surface, I seem alright, I still live in that dark world. I am seldom happy and when I am I get nervous that my happiness won't last. I am scared about this and I can't rely on anybody for help because I need to help myself. The most help I can get is for somebody to simply care about me and show it. It looks like that person is Nicole but I am worried that its all an illusion. Please let something in my life be real.

The Alpha guys invited me to play poker at the house. Nothing eventful happened. We just got wasted and smoked a lot of pot. I then went home and wrote in my journal, before going to sleep.

On the surface, everything was great. I got along with my suitemates, was doing well in school, had a group of friends, a girlfriend, a nice body, and a frat that wanted me to pledge. However, despite how good everything seemed, I was miserable. I was uncomfortable in my own skin and felt disconnected from everyone around me. Everything I had accumulated was the result of putting on an image, a fraudulent image of bullshit where I pretended to be "the man" in order to gain acceptance, and it was only a matter of time before my foundation collapsed.

Perhaps the fakest and most unfulfilling part of my life was my relationship with Nicole. Both of us were extremely busy with school, and rushing was taking up all of my time, that simply being able to see each other became a huge obstacle in it of itself. On the oft chance that we did hang out, it was next to impossible for us to be alone since both of us lived in suites. We spent so little time together that not only did it feel as though I didn't even have a girlfriend, but I got way more pussy back when I was single.

Rush Week

The Alpha guys called me for more rush events and seemed really interested in getting me to pledge. Greek life at Binghamton had very little perks attached to it and I initially had no desire to join a frat. It wasn't until after I tripped on shrooms that I began to seriously consider pledging. My trip made me feel like an insect and I had this overpowering need to be a part of something, regardless of how stupid it was. I wanted to make a difference and be a force for good, but felt that I couldn't do it on my own. I wanted to make as many connections as possible and use those connections to implement positive social changes. I wanted to change the system and felt as though the best way to do that was from within. With my new connections, I would be one step closer to my dream job of counseling politicians and exposing their corruption.

9/10/05

Even if people think that I am dead, I am alive and kickin it. The only reason I would be dead is if Nicole asked for the author of the journal and then the author may be dead but only after a long fight and very intenst fight and argument. They want to make the chicks look sexy to a dying man because it's the last thing ta=he may see next to monz, baby I love you and would never let the bar tenders kill you by poisoning your drink so that the economy could somehow be boosted. Shit I'm drunk cause that passage is madd incoherent. Good entry. I have no idea what the fuck I just talked about. Nobody does, even if what they are talking about has clear benefits, they don't know all o the detriment=ndtge.

All I've been thinking about lately is being with her. It makes me feel like a dick because I said that this on espn and because the four corners teasssssssssssssssssssssssss

Man was I fucked up or what? I went to a rush event and one of the brothers asked if I was dead, because he hadn't seen me out in months. After that, my mind simply went black.

I had it bad for Nicole and spent every waking moment of every day thinking about her. Everywhere I went, be it class, the gym, the bar, my room, or anywhere else, all I thought about was when I would see her next. She was the most beautiful girl in the world to me, and whenever I heard a love song on the radio or saw a romantic movie, all I wanted to do was lie in bed and hold her.

9/14/05

Wine tasting Wednesday, dats wats up. No class Thursday I get madd wasted tonight. Got the box wine in my right hand and a blunt in da left. No pressure I can just chill with madd liquor and some weed nothing to it. Everything seems madd groovy. I got shit in order, my frat, my friends, and my girl. It seems like the puzzle pieces are starting to fall together. No joke, I take Nicole seriously. I wouldn't cheat on her unless she gave me blue balls for like month or som shit like that. I mean yo my balls would have 2 look like Dr. Manhattan from Watchmen for me to think about cheatin know wat im sayin. Cause yo I really care about her and I would rather be with her and trust her than get madd ass. Yo cause getting madd ass has it's consequences. Everybody's like having a girl makes you deal with madd bullshit but you know what, being single makes you deal with bullshit too. I mean it's FUCKING nice to have stability in my life. That's what my life needed. Everything is falling together. You don't even know how good it feels to take a shower and not be afraid of finding a bunch of big red pimples on your dick. I feel so clean and so pure and I want to stay with her to maintain that feeling. No joke, even if I get potential to get madd ass I wouldn't do it I would stay with Nicole provided my balls don't look like Dr. Manhattan. Cause yo if she tries to use sex as a weapon I can just fuck other girls like that so if she tries that shit the bitch is cut. In all honesty I think she appreciates what I try to do

for her at least I hope she does. Loook here's the plan, don't take shit

from her cause if she loves you she won't try to kill you. And by kill I mean

kill me spiritually cause way back in the day I had madd bitches kill me

spiritually which was probably the cause for this journal in the first place.

Shit I'm on fucking page 108 right now this is quite the book. I'm starting

to remember my adjustment, the moose and penis breath shit were all

part of my adjustment to college. I was so confused and upset that I had

to take my anger out in this journal. In many cases I find it beautiful

because I express myself at my purest. I fucking love people, I want to

saave the planet. No joke I'm gonna be the next Spider Man I'm gonna be

Super Psychologist Man. For real I want to be the psychologist of

congressmen so that I can expose corruption through their visits to my

office. Anyway, I think I'm bout to pass out so peace.

Nicole was miserable and felt that our relationship was nothing more

than a title. In a way she was right. For someone who liked a girl as much

as I liked Nicole, I barely gave her the time of day. All I wanted to do was

be with her, yet I would go days on end without so much as making a

phone call or sending a text message. I mean shit; I hadn't even so much

as taken her out on a date since we've been together. Who cares that all I wanted to do was make her happy? What were my intentions worth

when I wasn't doing a goddamn thing for her? Good intentions aside, I

was a shitty boy friend whom Nicole had every right to be pissed off at.

9/15/05

Yo Ruben's a bitch. How you gonna say I only wanna be in this frat so

I can get drunk and fuck bitches? Do you know who I am? Do you realize

its easier to get laid than buy testbooks? Man I don't need you, I get way

more pussy than you just by walking into the RAT muthafucka. Actually

that's a lie. Ruben gets a lot of pussy. Watever, he's still a bitch!

Nicole might break up with me. Fuck that, I know she wants to

make it work just as much as I do. I mean I need her, I need something

meaningful and that's what she is. Look she was upset that we haven't

seen or spoken to each other much during this week but there was a lot of

shit on my mind. It feels like she loves me and sees me as special. When I

fuck her, we're gonna fall in love and it's going to be one of the most

amazing experiences of my life. Tomorrow I'm gonna go talk to her and

tell her how I feel and show that I care about her. She is all I think about,

in class, at the bar, everywhere all I think about is NICOLE. Nothing

happened tonight I played beer pong and lost in the first round. Fucking

Physics!! I want her, if this were to end I would be really upset no matter what I did to forget about her. It just wouldn't happen.

I couldn't get into Sports Bar and asked this guy Ruben (one of the brothers) to lend me his ID. Ruben used to always lend me his ID last semester so I didn't think it was a problem. That's why I was surprised when he said no and hung up on me. It wasn't until I went back to the house and found out Sports Bar got raided, that I understood why he did what he did.

Here I was playing beer pong, thinking everything was ok, when Ruben came out of nowhere and pulled me aside. We went into his room, where he gave me an hour-long lecture on the importance of brotherhood and what it meant to be an Alpha, that there was more to it than getting drunk and slamming bitches. He accused me of "using him to get into Sports Bar" and claimed that I wanted to pledge for all the wrong reasons. Ruben than called me a selfish asshole, saying that if it were up to him I wouldn't come close to getting a bid.

Nicole and I made up the next day. I needed Nicole and couldn't bear to lose her. She was the glue holding my house of cards together and the only time I felt safe was in her arms.

Nicole had no idea how important she was too me, because I never told her anything. She had no idea what I was going through, how I fragile I was, or how badly I needed her, because I was too scared to open up. As far as she was concerned, I was an inconsiderate douchebag who treated her like nothing more than a common whore.

I really wanted to be a good boyfriend to Nicole. She was a goddess to me and deserved to be treated as such. Unfortunately, I didn't have a fucking clue how to conduct myself in a relationship. See when it came to women, I was an emotional retard who had absolutely no idea what to do aside from sex. So although I wanted nothing more than to make Nicole happy, I just didn't know how.

It killed me that she wasn't happy and I needed to make things right. Beneath the constant fighting and bickering, this girl really cared about me, and I knew that breaking up was the last thing she wanted to do. So when I apologized and promised to treat her better, she was quick to forgive me and our relationship was saved (at least at that point).

9/16/05

Yo I fucking blew it. And I was so fucking close too. Why does this kind of shit always happen to me? What kind of animals don't have toilet paper in their bathroom? I mean shit I had to take a shit. Like this is my

faultx. Honestly yo I don't even wanna write right now..

Shortly after leaving Nicole's room, I received a text-message from Rambo, inviting me to a rush event where the brothers would treat us to dinner. At dinner, Kenny (one of the other rushes) told us about the first time he jerked off. He was in 6th grade gym class doing bicycle kicks, when all of a sudden some white shit popped out of his dick. Not knowing what it was except for the fact that it felt really good, he ran to the bathroom and spent an hour doing bicycle kicks in the stall, before ejaculating on the floor and going back to class. That's how Kenny jerked off for the rest of the week.

After dinner, all of us went back to the house and played beerpong in the basement. I was having the time of my life, getting drunk with all of my new brothers, when all of a sudden I had to take a humungous shit. It felt like a horse was about to burst out of my asshole at any minute and there was not a damn thing I could do about it. Faster than a speeding bullet, I scurried up the stairs and wound up in Ruben's bathroom, where my asshole unearthed an explosion more powerful than a locomotive.

After annihilating Ruben's toilet, I looked over my shoulder for some much-needed toilet paper, when to my shock and dismay there was not a single sheet of paper in sight. There's no way in hell I was rejoining the party covered in shit and I would have wiped my ass with anything.

That's when I noticed his New York Yankees bath towel. Well, if my luck couldn't have been any worse, Ruben opened the door and caught me red (or shall I say brown) handed vigorously wiping my ass with his bath towel.

Ruben lost his mind and slammed my head against the wall, as I sat helplessly on the toilet. Luckily, Ruben wasn't very strong so I got up and was about to start fighting, when Rambo and few of the brothers heard the noise and broke us up. They asked what the ruckus was, when Ruben showed them his doo-doo covered bath towel.

Rambo was dumbfounded, unable to utter a response, and spent the next 5 minutes standing in the doorway with his mouth hanging open in disbelief, before asking why Derek Jeter was covered in shit? "Because I needed something to wipe my ass with and it was the first thing I saw." I innocently explained. Rambo then gave me 30-seconds to leave the house before all of the brothers beat the shit out of me (no pun intended). Needless to say, I didn't get a bid.

You've Gotta Be Kidding Me

Nicole came over the next day and god knows I needed to see her. After what happened last night, I felt so alone and wanted nothing other than to hold her body close to mine. I also really wanted some pussy. It had been over 2 weeks since I'd ejaculated and I was in desperate need of relief. Unfortunately, Nicole wasn't in the mood, saying that it was "too early in the day."

"Are you kidding me? After everything I'd gone through, couldn't I at least bust a nut? Is that so much to ask from my own girlfriend? Especially when I'm saving up all my sexual energy for you? Really Nicole? How much of a fucking cunt can you be? We're almost never alone. You should want to pounce on me at every opportunity. The fact that you can withhold sex (or sexual activities since you're still a virgin) from me, considering the circumstances of our relationship, means either a) you're not attracted to me, b) you're hooking up with someone else, c) you're using sex to control me, or d) all of the above. You know what. Don't even answer that Nicole. Just get the fuck out of my room. We're

Done!!"

I had class an hour later and it was one of the hardest classes I've

ever had to sit through, because my mind was clouded with bullshit.

"What the hell is wrong with me?" I thought. Not only did I just burn a

huge bridge with a frat that was practically begging me to pledge, but I

also happened to lose my girlfriend on account of her refusing to suck my

dick. Rejection, I felt it from all angles and I hated it. What happened

with the Alpha's made me feel worthless enough as it is, and the fact that

Nicole treated me like garbage compounded it ten fold. "Nicole's a

fucking bitch for treating me like this, yet why did I like her so much when

she made me feel like shit?" Maybe it's because that's how I viewed

myself, which could explain why I put so much effort into such a miserable

relationship.

When I came back from class, I found out that Ron and Sean were

moving out. The next day, some Asian kid named Tommy came up to the

suite and said that he was going to be my new roommate. I was furious

because I hated living in a triple. However, I didn't have a choice in the

matter, since the dorms were overcrowded and I would've gotten stuck with two new roommates no matter what. At least Tommy seemed like a nice kid. So I figured living with him wouldn't be that bad.

Juan was also having roommate problems. His roommate would sit at his computer and play World of Warcraft for days on end, while blasting techno music well into the night. This drove Juan crazy and he was desperate for another place to live, so I allowed him to move in with me.

***

I smoked a blunt in the woods with my friend Jason a few days after breaking up with Nicole. Jason and I met freshman year because he was really good friends with Kevin (my roommate last semester), and was actually living with him in Onieda Hall (also in CIW). Jason was really into poker and accumulated over $30,000 by freshman year. However, last semester he lost almost all of his winnings and started smoking weed on a daily basis.

Jason was a really complicated guy. Whenever this kid would go out, throngs of drunken freshman girls would literally throw themselves at him. But unlike me, he wouldn't take advantage of it. At first, I thought that Jason didn't have game, lacked confidence, or was secretly gay, but now I realize that he was looking for something deeper. Seeing him turn down all these hoes was cool and I admired him for refusing to "eat out of the garbage can."

After smoking with Jason, it was clear that he wanted more than to lead the same empty existence as I, but like me, had no idea how to escape the cave of darkness that we were trapped in. Jason and I were two lost souls who wanted the same thing (a sense of purpose), yet were too caught up in the bullshit lifestyle of going out and putting on an image that achieving a sense of purpose became unattainable.

The fact that I could relate to him on such a personal level further reiterated how meaningless my party centered lifestyle was. I was so confused about where I was headed, but at least there was someone just as confused as me.

9/23/05

I just wanna do my best but it seems to go unnoticed. At least by those who I want to notice me. I fuck up with Alpha and the day after Nicole and I got into a fight and before you know if poof we broke up. Nicole and I broke up over bullshit. You know what it was about the sex. Not getting a bid made me feel like shit, is it so wrong for me to get my dick sucked by my <u>girlfriend</u>? Who would've thought 5 pm was too early? What a fucking cunt I finger her all the time without asking for anything and she can't give me head once after I had a really shitty day? What the fuck??? We're going out, we should be passed that shit! I'm not fucking 12, she should do more than kiss me when I am in a relationship with her especially when I'm actually turning down ass and trying to be a <u>faithful</u> boyfriend. I got more ass when I was single for fucks sake. What the hell does that say? Fuck!! Try and be a good guy and people just shit all over you. Compound that with not getting a bid and Nicole's fucking out the door. I don't need this shit. Anyway I'm not gonna date a girl who isn't attracted to me. All I wanted was to feel attracted by my own girlfriend. That's not too much to ask. Never did Nicole say thank you for the effort your trying to put into the relationship. I mean no girl's like hey I never realized the meaning behind what you do I know you really like me because of what you try to do for me. I never heard it aside from Christina *and Emily implied it but I'm not sure I trusted them. Does anybody know how upset I get trying to do my best? Nobody's like hey let me give you a hug for whatever you're trying to do because you believe its right. Nah, nobody cares about anything other than themselves!!*

I went to a party on Chapin Street and I ran into this girl Pam I met during the summer. She was a fucking cunt too. She sucked this guy Joey's dick without even knowing him and Joey was only 15. I brought a gram of weed with me and offered to smoke Pam up and the first thing this stupid bitch asked me was if it was free? What kind of grimy ass bitch asks that question first? Fucking bitch she deserves to be treated like shit. That's what I did and sure enough she was all over my cock. The more of a dick I was to her the more she wanted me. I didn't hook up with her because Jeff liked her and once again I decided to be a good guy and pass her off to him. She tried to hook up with me and I said "get away from me bitch go talk to Jeff". Well I did the right thing and rejected her but once again being a good guy totally fucked me. Instead of thanking me for swinging a bitch in his direction, Jeff accused me of trying to steal his girl and bitched at me for talking shit to her.

Honestly, my life is a mess I don't care so what does it matter. All this shit I'm talking about compared to the real shit that's going on in the world. I think I'm really done going out at least for while, forget it if I have bitches or not the important thing is that I stay focused on what's important which is school and the gym. Let's see if I can function with those two things as my goals. Honestly I proved that I can get laid and do that shit if I wanna but what I really want is inner peace. If through someway I want to get it because I'm a tortured motherfucker.

Ralph (see page 76) threw a house party over the summer. That's where I initially met Pam. We didn't say two words to each other and I wouldn't have remembered her if she hadn't sucked a 15-year old kids dick in the bathroom. So when I saw Pam propped up against the wall drinking a beer and smoking a cigarette, I couldn't help but shake my head in disbelief.

Pam had the reputation amongst Ralph's friends for being a mega slut and I decided that she would be the perfect girl to help me get over Nicole. I walked up to her and told her that she looked familiar. Pam claimed to have recognized me from Ralph's party and thought I was cute. She gave me her number within 30 seconds of us talking, saying that we should smoke sometime. I said: "why not now?" And pulled out a gram

of chronic.

Her face lit up like a Christmas tree and than she did the

unthinkable. Instead of saying: "yeah sure I'd like to smoke," or: "no, I

don't feel like smoking now, lets smoke some other time." The first thing

she said was: "is it was free?"

"Have some etiquette bitch!" I thought, amazed how someone

could have the balls to speak this way to a complete stranger. I talked to

this floozie for what, 30-seconds, and already she's trying to smoke my

weed? "Where's your sense of moral character?"

Pam had the manners of a hooker. So that's how I treated her.

And that's how she fell in love. The more of a dick I was, the more she

wanted to fuck me, and I had this bitch hanging from my nut sack all night

long.

I could have torn Pam's vagina into a million pieces. But I found

out that Jeff had a serious crush on her so I restrained myself. The kid

was borderline obsessed, instant messaging her everyday, spending hours

upon hours on the phone talking about absolutely nothing. He had it bad.

And when he confronted me at the party, telling me that Pam was the one he had it bad for, I immediately backed off. Pam was nothing more than a common slut to me, whereas Jeff was in love, so I decided to be a Good Samaritan and pass her off to him.

The more I ignored Pam, the hornier she got. I told her several times that I wasn't interested and that she should talk to Jeff instead. That didn't work! All it did was make her want me more. Once I stopped giving her the time of day, I could not get Pam to stop following me. She became this parasite that wouldn't go away, and I couldn't so much as turn around without that bitch lurking behind me.

Jeff saw all of this and was pissed. I was trying to do the right thing by blowing her off, but unfortunately Jeff didn't see it that way. To him it looked like I was trying to fuck his girl, and nothing I said could convince him otherwise.

Jeff gave Pam a guitar lesson the next day. "How much of a fucking tool-bag can you be? You don't give that type of girl a guitar lesson (especially when she spent the night hitting on your suitemate). No, you whip out your dick and smack her in the face with it. That's what I would've done." This girl didn't deserve to swallow my cum. And there was Jeff, spending time with her like a jackass. Did he not understand that giving her a guitar lesson wouldn't get him laid? That if he just offered Pam a bag of weed, his cock would've been down her throat within 5-minutes.

Despite claiming to be a ladies man, Jeff was very naive when it came to women. He was what you would call the "quintessential nice guy", the type of guy Cosmopolitan tells girls they should be with. He was the kind of guy who would take a girl out to a five star restaurant and than sit through a 3-hour ballet with her; the kind of guy who spends hours on end talking on the phone with a girl he likes; the kind of guy a girl would never date but would want her daughter to marry; the kind of guy who would fall in love with a girl but could never be more than a friend to her; the definition of pussy whipped, able to be controlled by nothing more than a hug or a smile; the kind of guy who's been abused in every relationship he has ever been in; the kind of guy who would offer her his heart on a plate, only for it to get trampled on.

Here was Jeff, trying so hard to be with a girl who had absolutely no interest in him, putting forth all this effort for some disgusting whore he had gotten nowhere with, whereas I could've fucked that same girl within 30-seconds of talking to her. The fact that I could've slammed her out so easily simply by behaving like an asshole completely undermined Jeff's efforts, and he resented me for that.

Jeff was what you would call a hater and quickly transformed into a humongous asshole. We used to get along, but now he began to nitpick everything I did and made me feel as though my mom moved in with me to college. "Sasha, pick your shit up off the floor. Clean the bathroom. Make your bed. You should study more. Stop drinking so much, women are people." This is what came out of his mouth on a regular basis.

If undertaking the role of my mother wasn't bad enough, Jeff tried to force me out of the suite by turning me into a pariah. He talked about me behind my back, telling the guys on our floor I was impossible to live with and telling the girls that I was a scumbag who had no respect for women. Even though I never liked or respected him, Jeff was still my friend; and it boggled my mind that he was willing to ruin our friendship on account of some dumb slut who didn't want to fuck him.

I was reaching a point of frustration with the semester. I really wanted to make a difference, but had no clue how to go about it and was fucking up at everything I did. Burnt bridges, ruined friendships, and dysfunctional relationships; that was my semester in a nutshell. All I wanted to do was study and workout, but instead I smoked weed everyday and got blackout drunk three plus nights a week, which could explain why 98.7% of the girls in my life were complete pieces of shit.

Nicole's the only girl I knew at Binghamton who's worth treating with respect. Talk about a depressing statement. It basically says that every girl I meet will do nothing but cause me problems if I ever get close to her, that I have to constantly keep my guard up and maintain this bullshit image for the next god knows how many years, so that I can have what, empty balls and an ego boost? No thanks!

All I wanted was a real friend, someone to open up to, someone who recognized and cared about my existence, but instead all I had were superficial relationships centered on getting wasted.

9/24/05

*So today marks the day that my 23 day not busting streak has come to an end. In a way it's kinda sad and kinda relieving. I had a girl and didn't bust from **ANYTHING** for 23 days. Shows what an idiot I was for being in a relationship. It was good and all but I'm sad to see it end. Of all the girls it had to be Mary. Like it was an end to a chapter or something or the start of something I was trying to suppress but gave up* on. I want this journal to represent my life, each a series of entries divided up into chapters. I want to see the personal phases I go through. Very few people would think I lived in a dark world. Only after reading the entire journal they would think, wow this kid has issues. I guess it may teach people that drinking actually is bad because you will lead a dark life. Or maybe it shows that I could lead a dark life and by finding something to give me light I could escape from the darkness. People will buy this journal because they will realize that its written by someone who is legitimately crazy. Just the words drunk journal will elicit curiosity.

I want a black girl. I got the jungle fever. I'll write a conversation I had with tits. TITS MCGEE, TITORAMA, I fucked her on the couch tonight. And I put the condoms in the garbage. Well it was after Juan yelled at me for leaving it in the sink, but still. I got up and threw it away which is a step up from last year. Fcucking I have a 3 semester streak of leaving condoms in all the wrong places in my room. But at least I got better. First semester I left a used condom on my floor for about 2 weeks. Second semester went down to 2 days, and now I'm down to leaving condoms only in the sink just once. That's a serious improvement.

No more fucking in the common room, fuck the girl in your room.

You fucking girls is a private matter. This journal is a breach of privacy.

That is not funny.

That night I went out with these kids Brian, Jay, and Katzenberg.

***

I met them with Juan at an AXP party about three weeks ago.
Juan and I overheard them talking about smoking weed and playing
Smash Brothers. We were intrigued and joined in their conversation. I
was really drunk so I don't remember what we talked about. All I
remembered was that that Katzenberg looked like Brick Tamlin from
Anchorman and all of his friends kept telling us that he wasn't funny.

I liked these guys from the moment I met them. They were my
kind of guys, dudes who didn't give a fuck about anything other than
getting drunk, playing videogames, and having a good time. It didn't
matter where they were, whom they were with, or what day it was. As
long as there was weed, alcohol and a Nintendo 64, these guys were
guaranteed to have a blast.

***

We never got to hang out again so I decided to give them a call.
All of us went to sports bar and spent the night cracking jokes while
sharing pitchers. I saw Tara and she gave me the finger. So I gave her a
toenail clipper that was in my pocket. They asked me why I gave her a
toenail clipper, and I told them about how she used to clip my toenails
last semester after jerking me off against her ass. Tara must have
overheard our conversation, because shortly after I said this, she walked
up to me and punched me square in the nose while holding the toenail
clipper in her right hand.

Damn that bitch hit hard. She had to have been a boxer or
something, because that shit fucking hurt. Yeah, I know she hit me in the
nose with a toenail clipper. But still, Tara could pack a punch.

My nose was gushing blood and everybody was laughing at me for
getting my ass whopped by a bitch. But fuck them. It didn't change the
fact that I turned her ass into a cum dumpster last semester. Besides,
she's a girl. It's not like I can hit her back. You know what. It didn't even
matter, because losing all that blood was only going to make me drunker.

Later that night I ran into Mary and boy was I happy to see her.
Maybe it was the alcohol flowing through my veins, or the low cut, extra

tight blouse she was wearing, or the fact that I hadn't busted off in over

three weeks, but this girl's tits looked bigger than ever. I mean shit; they

were popping out like a couple of water balloons, water balloons I wanted

to burst all over.

Mary was on the dance floor, shaking her ass and trying her very

best not to fall on it, when I approached her. "Sasssshh!! What are you

doooing?" Mary slurred in a drawn out whiny voice that sounded like an

awful mixture of Fran Drescher and Wendy Williams, as I grinded against

her. "You know what I'm doing." I replied, softly kissing up and down her

neck while simultaneously caressing her body. "But Sassssh, we haven't

hooked up in moonnnths. You can't just ignore me and expect me to

have sex with you. I'm not that kind of girl Sasshhh." Mary said, in a

pathetic attempt to sound proper and ladylike. "C'mon, you know how

good this feels. You know how badly you want it." I whispered, softly

kissing Mary on the mouth, biting her lower lip and causing her body to

tremble. "Sasssshhhhh, what kind of girl do you think I aaaammm?"

responded Mary, failing miserably at pretending to be a person of class

that respected herself. "The kind of girl that misses having my huge cock

inside of her," I said, in a soft, seductive voice. "Now lets get the fuck

outta here."

166

There is nothing like waking up to the sight of your roommate impaling a bitch in your living room. Just ask Juan. See, Mary and I wound up fucking on the couch out of consideration for my suitemates, since they were all sleeping by the time we got back to CIW. So when Juan woke up to use the bathroom, he didn't really expect to see Mary on top of me with her 36DDs in my mouth.

Shock, admiration, and disgust are three of the many words to describe how Juan felt after seeing Mary getting "power drilled" on our couch. On one hand, Juan was happy to see me get over Nicole by pounding out a chick with humongous tits, but on the other hand, he didn't want to see me do it on OUR COUCH, the same couch that we watched Sports Center and played NBA JAM on.

"Hurry up and finish, I have to take a hippo sized shit." Juan bellowed from next door, since walking in on us had prevented him from going to the bathroom as he'd initially planned. "Have a little patience. Can't you see I'm in the middle of something?" I retorted, in a mixture of English and unintelligible gibberish. "I'm giving you two minutes. Otherwise I'm taking a dump all over your bed and wiping my ass with your blanket."

Juan sounded serious and I was about to cum. After going 23 days without jerking off, my stamina was non-existent and I would've blown my load regardless of whether or not he threatened to defecate on my bed, which is what I did, coming so hard I could've written my full name (Alexander Phillip Mountain Dew Protein Strenger I) in semen all across Mary's chest.

Getting Back Together

Fucking Mary was like going 23 days without water and than quenching my thirst by drinking out of the toilet bowl. Instead of feeling relieved, I just felt like shit.

What the hell did I just do? I was holding out for Nicole, because I wanted all of my passion to be directed towards her, since that's what she deserved. So what if I had to wait in order to have sex with her? Weren't all good things worth waiting for? Way to hold out for nothing!

I was tired of drinking dirty water contaminated in shit. I wanted something pure and meaningful; someone to hold and have an intimate conversation with, someone to tell me that everything's going to be ok.

Mary couldn't do that. Mary couldn't do shit. That bitch was nothing more than a human cum receptacle. Mary wouldn't make me forget about Nicole. She'll just make me think about her more, because sleeping with her will serve as a nagging reminder of what I've lost. Fuck! I dated Nicole to avoid fucking girls like Mary. Now that she was gone, I'd have given everything to hold her and hear her voice again. For the good of my soul, I needed to salvage our relationship.

We met by the lecture hall and took a walk, making our way to the track where we found a spot of grass to sit down on. A chilly fall night, I offered my sweater to her but she adamantly refused, coldly insisting that she was fine. Nicole didn't want to be here. She was visibly upset and looked at me with these icy, sad, green eyes that appeared worn out from crying, and even though I planned out an entire speech that would've made her fall back into my arms, Nicole's scornful demeanor prevented the words from forming.

"Why did you bring me here if you have nothing to say?" Nicole said, after I had just spent the past 10 minutes aimlessly staring off into space.

Me: "Because I have 1,000,000 things to say. I just don't know where to begin. I want to apologize and say I'm sorry, but I don't know how. There are so many ways to tell you how sorry I am and how bad I feel, that I just don't know how to phrase it."

Nicole: "But Sasha, we're always fighting over the same thing. Like, I feel that all you want to do is hook up in your room and nothing else."

Me: "Baby, that's not true. I just want to be close to you. Really. That's all I want and I don't know what else to do. If that's what you really think, I'm sorry. But I just wanna be with you."

Nicole: Rolling her eyes in disbelief. "Oh please, do you really expect me to believe that shit. You're just using me for sex and that's it. How stupid do you think I am?"

Me: Are you kidding me? We haven't even had sex yet!!! It should be pretty clear after all this time that I want something more with you, that I actually like you and want us to have a meaningful relationship. I care about you so much Nicole. You have no fucking idea! And if I've been trying this hard to sleep with you, its only because I think it'll bring us closer.

I know this sounds like a bunch of bullsht, but its not. I think about you non-stop, wherever I am, all I think about is when I can see you next. Baby I'm nothing without you, and the only time I feel safe is when we're together."

Nicole: "Really? You never told me any of this. You never tell me anything. How am I supposed to know how you feel if you don't communicate? I'm not a mind reader Sasha." Nicole was slowly letting her guard down.

Me: I placed my hand on her leg. "Look, I know I haven't been completely straight with you, but that's only because communicating how I feel is scary. I have issues babe. 90% of the time, I'm frightened, miserable, and emotionally overwhelmed. And I don't wanna burden you with my shit. I just want to make you happy."

Nicole: She reached over and grabbed my hand, tightly holding it in both of hers. "Sasha, your not the only one that has problems. I have problems too. But in order for this relationship to work, we have to tell each other about how we feel. And if you really want to know how I feel, the truth is that I really like you a lot, and I know that you really like me too, but I just don't think it's enough anymore. We're not in a healthy relationship. All we do is fight, and make up, than fight some more, and make up again. And I'm sick of it!"

Me: "But that's what love is."

Sensing the right moment, I leaned in to kiss her and when she kissed back, I felt like my body was going to melt. Picture an electrical tingling sensation. Now compound it with how it feels to hold someone you love and care about, someone whose presence instantly puts you at ease, someone who when they touch you, causes all of your problems to disappear. Only than can you begin to understand how it felt to kiss Nicole again.

We fell asleep together, covered only by the warmth of our own bodies. As Nicole lay draped across me like a blanket, I could've sworn that I never felt closer to anyone in my life. Entangled together, it felt as though we were the same person, immersed in our own little world where nobody existed except for us. That's when I said: "I Love You."

Losing Control

Nicole and I shared a beautiful moment but that moment was not worth the miserable semester I was having. I felt so depressed and worthless, randomly on the brink of tears for no reason whatsoever. I would sit in class, or my room, or be at the gym, or even at the bar, when all of a sudden my eyes would swell up and I'd have an uncontrollable urge to start sobbing.

Something was wrong. I felt like a defective human being whose brain didn't work properly, but was too self-conscience to confide in anybody, so I didn't. Instead, I withdrew and crawled into a hole, cutting off contact with the outside world until I could recharge my image.

Reunited

I saw Christina over Roshashana break. We continued to stay in touch after she moved back to Connecticut, but lost contact once I started dating Nicole. So when she called me out of the blue, saying that she got a consulting job in Brooklyn, I was fucking ecstatic. Sure I had gotten back together with Nicole, but our relationship was by no means stable. I didn't want to cheat and under ordinary circumstances I probably wouldn't have, but Christina was no ordinary girl. We had history, a very powerful connection, and I wanted to make sure it was still there, so I spent the weekend having sex and drinking wine in her upper west side apartment.

Christina and I had a fun weekend but the connection no longer existed. Yes, I liked spending time with her. And yes, I loved having sex with her. Yet for some inexplicable reason, I just didn't want to be her boyfriend. Christina was the ideal girl to be in a relationship with and I had the opportunity to be with her, but I chose to say with Nicole instead.

I Need A Break

I spent the rest of the week blazing with Chris and Toby. And that's when I realized how much time I wasted drinking and getting high. The more I drank and smoked, the guiltier I felt for drinking and smoking. So I decided to take a break.

I was losing sight of myself and felt like a complete waste of space. All I did was party, having no other interests other than smoking weed or blackout drinking. Getting wasted was all I knew and I became concerned with how limited I was.

Going out was the basis of my social life, feeling like a chore instead of a fun activity. No longer partying on my own volition, I only drank because I didn't feel comfortable doing anything else. "How could I have a meaningful relationship if I can't function outside of a bar? I couldn't!! And Nicole was going to leave me if I didn't change."

10/3/05

I know what hell is. You know how people say that hell is burning in a lake of fire because you succumbed to your vices. Well to me that's a bunch of bullshit. I think what hell truly is you have to spend all of eternity succumbing to your vices. Say you were an alcoholic. Well you would have to get drunk all day every day until the end of time. No friends, no pussy, nothing except you and a bottle of alcohol forever. You're going to be hung over but you can't eat or drink water. All you can do is drink and feel more and more like shit everyday because there is no end. Say you're a womanizer and fucked a lot of women. Well you spend the rest of eternity having sex until it becomes mundane and ordinary and all pleasure is lost from it. Picture this: you're fucking tired because you've been having sex all day with no end in sight. Not only that but the anticipation of sex and the feeling after sex are gone. No spitting game, no getting head, you don't even know if the girl likes it and there is no sense of accomplishment afterwards. The worst part about is that there is absolutely no connectedness because you reduced something as physically and emotionally powerful as sex to a mere motion. All the good from sex evaporates and sex becomes merely a word: SEX. You realize that it isn't fun anymore but you can't do shit because your stuck fucking for all of eternity. Say you love to fight. Imagine fighting for all of eternity. You're fighting different people for all of eternity and will have no time to rest. Eventually you'll fatigue and spend all of eternity getting the shit kicked out of you. Say you're a drug addict. Well you're going to be locked in a room with nothing but an infinite supply of your drug of choice. Just imagine spending all of eternity doing coke in a cubicle by your self. Enough said!

Now what's Heaven? Heaven is eternal and you can't achieve eternal happiness caving into desires of the flesh because such things are temporary and not everlasting. Heaven has to be spiritual because you have to be at peace with yourself and if you achieve inner peace you can be happy doing nothing. Heaven in essence has to be doing nothing because in order to do nothing and not go crazy you have to be at peace with yourself. How else to go about that than by leading a spiritual existence? That's why heaven is so exclusive because only somebody who's spiritually at peace with oneself can enjoy heaven and not go crazy from doing nothing. So in essence, heaven isn't God rewarding you for being good; rather it's your soul rewarding itself for being pure and at peace with itself.

Sobriety

10/6/05

I have decided to quit drinking. A number of factors have influenced me in making this decision. The primary reason for this newfound change has been a severe unfulfillment with my life. Ever since camp, I began to realize that there is more to drinking than drinking. In other words, drinking in itself isn't really a bad thing unless you drink to the point of alcohol poisoning or become an alcoholic. When someone drinks a liter of vodka or 20 plus beers, that's not drinking, that's stupidity. People should have enough common sense to know that such large quantities of alcohol are fatal. People hear on the news about college kids who die of alcohol poisoning and subconsciously think that all underage kids who get drunk drink to the point of alcohol poisoning. Then you have your homeless people, people who go to AA meetings, abusive drunk dads and you think: "look what alcohol does to you, its terrible." But wait, those people generally get wasted 4-plus times a week, and/or drink during the day. In essence, the point I am trying to make is that drinking only becomes a problem when it begins to have a negative effect on your day-to-day life.

How does this little tangent tie into my desire to quit drinking? Although I don't have a drinking problem or anything against drinking, I do believe that drinking is preventing me from doing something more important. I feel that the time I spend smoking and drinking is distracting me from doing things that could make me a lot better off in the long run. I want to start lifting and playing ball regularly, and feel that I'd make greater improvements in both categories if I didn't have to contend with multiple hangovers. I want to improve my grades, because I am capable of being more than a C + student. I want to learn MMA and turn myself into a beast. I want to actually follow through on an idea that I have.

Imagine if I spent my free time following my passion instead of getting wrecked? I'd be so happy and productive. Regardless of how little I accomplish.

Here is why I am unfulfilled with drinking. There are a million things I want to do, but instead of doing them, I'm getting blitzed. I want to achieve greatness and I hold myself to an ideal standard, but when I look in the mirror, I see a completely different person from what I aspire to be.

10/7/05

Day 2, who would have ever thought? I'm about to go see Nicole once she calls me. Speaking of which, Nicole is another reason for my newfound sobriety. She's such a nice, sweet girl unlike the piece of shit bitches I meet when I go out, who only care about money, fashion, getting drunk, and sucking cock.

*Lately I've been thinking, that if I continue doing what I'm doing, I will unfortunately end up marrying some whore I meet at a bar, or become some dirty old man who tries (and fails) to pick up chicks 20 years younger than him. Either way, if I keep this shit up, I'm going to lead an emotionally empty life. And **I REFUSE TO LET THAT HAPPEN!!!***

Today I told Tits (Mary, Penis Breath, Big Tits McGee, call her what you want. At this point she has multiple nicknames.) about how I quit drinking and couldn't comprehend it. As a matter of fact, I think she lost interest in me because of it, thus justifying the way I treated her.

These girls I meet only like me when I put off this asshole image, whereas it seems Nicole actually likes me for me. I know it sounds lame quitting because of a girl, but there's more too it. I've wanted to turn over a new leaf since I got back to school, but felt that it was impossible without support in the form of female love. A huge reason why I drank was to meet girls. I already have a girl, so what's the point of going out? I would rather spend a Friday night watching a movie with her, than at a bar trying to pull some random bitch.

Life is overwhelming and Nicole's my escape. I'm so lost and confused that all I want is for someone to hold me and tell me that everything is ok. That's how I feel when I'm with Nicole. Anyway, she just called, so I'm going to go see her now.

The suite was empty and it was just the two of us. We took advantage of this rare opportunity and immediately started making out, when Nicole suggested having sex.

I had a better chance of being attacked by a terrorist on the way to her room, than fucking Nicole that night. At least that's what I thought. So when she of all people suggested it, I was completely taken off guard.

This was the moment I had been waiting for. So than why was I so nervous? Hit by a wave of pressure, pressure to perform and not disappoint, I thought about the responsibility of being her first, how Nicole built this night up to be something special, something out of a fairy tale; and that I had to live up to an ideal standard in order for her to love me.

Not to sound like a bitch or anything, but taking a girl's virginity can be pretty fucking scary. At least to me it was. Once we did it, there was no turning back. Nicole was mine. And I started to doubt whether I was worthy of her.

What did I have to offer? I was fucking powerless, a lost little boy with no sense of purpose or direction in life. Shit, I couldn't even protect her physically. What if someone grabbed her ass in front of me and I got beaten down because I can't fight? What then? Humiliation? Nicole leaving me because she no longer thinks I'm a man? Lets face facts. I felt completely inadequate and undeserving of her, so I lied like a pussy and told Nicole that I didn't have a condom.

10/8/05

Here I am two minutes to midnight on a Saturday night. I promised myself to study for an exam but tomorrow's another day. I really should have studied, but instead I played videogames.

Regardless, despite that I need to stop drinking. Everything just seemed so overwhelming that I just needed to simplify my life. For the past couple of weeks, I've been so unhappy that I would be at the point of tears for no reason at all. That's when I felt that I needed to take a break from everything and get my head in order. It's kind of refreshing, finally having the chance to get a real clear picture of myself. Although I really didn't get much work done, I did go to the gym and actually did legs. You know what, it felt right. It just did. Like working out and not drinking is what will balance out all my negative emotions.

Honestly, I'm scared, unhappy, and completely out of my comfort zone even though things seem good on paper. You don't even understand how the thought of losing Nicole consumes me, or how terrified I am to have sex with her because I'm afraid of not being good enough. But you know what, I still have to do these things because I love her and refuse to let my fears and insecurities destroy what we havet.

Fuck that! They wont!! I will fight to the end for her and that's it. If the relationship doesn't work, than so be it; at least I'm doing my best.

Nicole came over 2 nights later and I completely blew it. My self-fulfilling prophecy about fucking up during sex came true. I put so much pressure on myself to make it perfect for her that I wasn't able to get it up. I wanted to be amazing; to blow her away and make her fall head over heals in love with me, but in the end I couldn't even perform. She told me it was ok, that we could do it another time. But her tone of voice made it clear that "next time" would never happen.

I just wanted to make her happy. But in the end I only let her down, proving to be nothing more than a huge disappointment. Nicole wanted to feel special. But how special was she if I couldn't even fuck her? She was right all along in doubting me, because I had absolutely nothing to offer.

10/13/05

Oh man, I am in a little bit of a pickle here. Where to begin? I went to see Nicole after class, when guess who I saw in the elevator? Fucking TITS!! This bitch told me to come over, and then shot me a look of disgust when I told her that I had a girlfriend.

Fucking Mary was a huge mistake!! How the hell was I supposed to know they lived in the same building? What if she tells Nicole? Worst comes to worst, its over and even if its not, she won't trust me. I would hate that, because I really want to have her trust. Fuck, its Nicole who is holding me together, because without her I am nothing. I really love her and would be heartbroken if it were to end.

Look, at least I did the right thing. Who cares if Mary tells Nicole? Yeah, I fucked her for too long and should've gotten rid of her earlier, but at least I got rid of her. If she tells Nicole, I'll just tell her the truth and hope that she trusts me. I'm in way over my head with Nicole, but I'm going to at least try and have a mature relationship with her.

Fortunately, Mary had absolutely no idea who Nicole was. Not that it mattered. This bitch didn't care enough to say anything to Nicole. All Mary wanted was dick and the fact that I wasn't fucking her simply meant there was one less cock in her vagina.

10/16/05

I stopped drinking so that I could get my life together and broaden myself as a person. Why then am I replacing alcohol with PlayStation 2? Why am I never in the library? How come I don't go to the gym anymore? How come I can't remember the last time I picked up a goddamn book? It's like there's a mental block preventing me from doing what I want to do.

I am out of my element, uncomfortable in my own skin, and trapped in a body that isn't mine. This is all too much; I feel like a caged animal, imprisoned light years away from his natural habitat. All I want to do is get my life together, but the only time I feel comfortable with myself

is when I'm wasted. Lately, I've been a nervous wreck. And this period of

sobriety has brought my inadequacies to light. My grades suck, my

suitemates think I'm a pain in the ass, and my girlfriend doesn't like me

anymore.

When I'm drunk, I morph into a completely different person. No

longer am I awkward and unsure of myself, but rather, I am a cool, calm,

and collected guy who knows what he wants and goes after it. People are

drawn to me and women want to fuck me. For once, I feel accepted.

I was living in my own head and spent the majority of my time lost

in thought. Putting on an image and maintaining this veiled mask of

confidence was so stressful that performing simple everyday chores like

taking a shower, cleaning up after myself, changing my clothes, and

remembering to flush the toilet, became insurmountable tasks. My trip on

shrooms and the events that subsequently unfolded caused me to feel

hopeless and powerless. I fell into a deep depression and allowed myself

to be consumed by personal demons.

I felt like a fucking basket case who couldn't do anything right. I

smelt like ass and looked like shit. I left dirty clothes in the common room for days on end. I ordered food and forgot to throw it away, leaving it to

rot. Our suite turned into a war zone and my room looked like Afganistan.

Everyone in the suite began to turn against me, mainly Juan. Juan and I

used to be boys. But our relationship fell apart once we started living

together. See, Juan was a very clean person, almost to the point of having

OCD, whereas I was a disgusting slob whose lifestyle would've put

barnyard animals to shame, and our differences prevented us from

coexisting. In less than a month of living together, Juan and I went from

being "best of" friends to fighting almost constantly, all because I turned

our room into a 3rd world country.

10/20/05

Just write about the world. We are so detached from people

including ourselves. We go to class, play on our computer, ps2, xbox etc,

go out and drink, do work, and even smoke.

You're in a big lecture class and don't know or care to know

anybody in it. Even in a discussion class, you just want to go to class and

get out of there. Discussions are the worst because the professor actually

keeps track of whether or not you attend. That means you have to go or else your grade goes down. This causes most people who go to class to only go to avoid punishment.

This is like what college is. The college won't educate you, you have to educate yourself. Because of the overwhelming amount of people and activities there is a good chance of you missing out on this because of the overwhelming social opportunities. But when you think about it, despite the amount of social events, how much actual socializing do you do? You just want to do what is fun or what you think looks good to others. This creates a fake image that you put off to people and prevents a lot of people from really getting to know who you are as a person. It is almost as though nobody wants to know anybody as a person.

I really shouldn't take it personally because people care too much about themselves. Most people base their friendships now on convenience or what they have to offer. People can very easily be content with becoming friends with someone just because they are neighbors or because they occupy time or because they have access to things. The problem is that many people are content with that. We care so much about our own image that we view other people as objects to get what we want.

The media has so much to do with it. Sensationalized tv makes people think that happiness is based on what you are instead of who you are. We care more about Paris Hilton than we do a fireman who put out a fire and rescued people. We only care about Paris Hilton because of her name and appearance which causes our society to value status and appearance over action.

The reason societies crumble is because their values shift from positive to negative. We value someone with wealth and power more than someone like the Fireman who saved the lives of another human. The fireman's actions not Paris Hilton's name should be celebrated because it is people like the Fireman who played a big role on our survival as a species whereas Paris Hilton is so distant from the public that she can't even relate to us. The money she has for doing nothing is hurting rather than helping our population because she is doing nothing and living like a queen when people are busting their asses to support her lifestyle.

We just want the rich to stay rich and will go to any means necessary to do so. Do you think Paris Hilton wants to give up living a life of luxury or even can? She wouldn't be able to because she is so accustomed to having her needs met that changing her life would cause tremendous trauma. Trauma is more likely to occur when you experience significant changes that alter your life. I bet that she is one of the most unhappy people because she knows subconsciously that she is living immorally but is unable to live any differently.

Being rich is probably like being a junkie, the more you get, the more you want, the more you want, the less content you are with what you have. So although Paris Hilton may lead a fantasy life, to her it is mundane rather than fantastic yet she wouldn't be able to live any other way. To her living modestly would be as big a culture shock as me living without electricity. The fact of the matter is with that said, Paris Hilton is living immorally yet she is so immersed in her wealth that she can't function without it, causing internal conflict because she is acting despite the moral repercussions. In order to avoid internal conflict as much as possible, she emotionally distances herself from people and thinks of them as a number or doesn't think of the common person at all because she just can't relate. She won't attempt to relate to the common person because she will be consumed by guilt at what she is doing to him or her.

It seems like we make most of our money by hurting other people and in order to justify it, we phrase our actions as to not think about them.

Think about it, a company puts another company out of business. The boss and even his subordinates are going to say we put Company X out of business rather than actually examine what will happen to the employees and families of the employees of Company X. In order to avoid feeling guilt, you avoid thinking about it and because we make so much of our money based on other people's suffering we just dehumanize them by becoming self absorbed and referring to people as statistics. People don't stop to say "hey if I win big in the stock market, doesn't that mean somebody also lost just as big?" If we actually examined the type of harm we our inflicting to other people by doing this, we would go crazy, so in order to avoid this we have to numb ourselves with mindless television and material posessions.

I think that there is a possibility that maybe every American feels a sense of guilt for living in America because of the Indians. I mean we took land from people who lived off of it harmoniously by manipulating them and taking advantage of their initial kindness when they gave us food and taught us how to hunt. We killed the people who helped us survive and took their land for ourselves. This is why we can't trust anybody because we know that we took advantage of people who trusted us and believe that they would do the same because we deserve it. That's why we put off this image because we don't want people to expose us, since exposure leaves you susceptible to be taken advantage of.

It's like I'm here because someone fucked over someone else somehow and whatever joy I get is due to someone else's pain. At the same time you were raised with the attitude of "do whatever it takes to make it" makes it very hard to resist temptation, and those who fail to resist it feel guilty for succumbing and avoid it by basking in the pleasures as to not think about it, and will do whatever it takes to continue their way of life which avoids guilt. They are distrustful of people because they feel that their possessions are more important to them rather than who they are, which causes them to justify using others because they too felt used.

Jason and I smoked a blunt in the woods before spending the next three hours having a marijuana-induced discussion in his room. My rant was the synopsis of that discussion.

Crashing and Burning

10/22/05

So the sobriety streak is broken and I don't know what it means. Everything is a big mess it seems. I just don't know what to do anymore I feel like I am about to crack I just can't take it anymore. Why should I

treat girls like people when they don't act like people? Girls just behave on

a much lower level than we do. Even Nicole, I feel like I have to act like I

am better than who I am just to be worthy of her. It just is too stressful. I

don't know if I can take it anymore I want to be there but I feel like I am

not good enough to hold on to her because I feel that if I get to close she

may work her shit on some other guy and then I am left with nothing.

What happens then? Exactly, pain so why should I deal with it, I am just

too emotionally unstable to deal with it. And you know what else, no

matter how nice I am to her it only gets me so far. Nobody wants a nice

guy no matter how nice you are. It almost makes me think what's the

point of this shit? Why even invest in anything emotionally when all you

will ever feel is pain, pain, pain. I don't want to feel this anymore and

maybe it is why I should leave the country. I want to live somewhere

where working at Mc Donalds is just as valued as being a doctor because

both professions require going to work. I don't believe that these types

should be frowned upon because it creates a social heirchy. Everything

and everyone should be equal because we all serve our niche to improve

the work d

When I checked facebook, Nicole's profile failed to mention us being in a relationship. Seeing the word "single" beside her relationship status stung, making it clear that Nicole was losing interest, and I snapped. "Fuck this not drinking shit, I'm getting blitzed." I said to myself, before going to the RAT with Kevin and Jason.

Going out was a bad idea. Throughout the night, I felt guilty and out of my element, like I shouldn't be here. This was wrong and I knew it. What was I doing drinking and hitting on girls when I had a girlfriend and promised myself to stay sober until I got my life in order?

I lost my mojo and felt that my ability to "mack it" had vanished. Last semester I was a master of hiding behind a phony image for the sake of getting pussy, but I no longer had that skill. My interactions felt forced and awkward instead of flowing and natural, so I gave up and sat at the bar alone while Kevin and Jason hooked up with girls on the dance floor.

10/30/05

Sobriety's wack sonn. Getting crizzunk isn't. That shits fun. Especially when your girls dressed like a ho pilot and madd dudes tryin to get in the cockpit. Fuck that shit's scary bro. Having to punch someone in the face for hitting on your girl. That's why you get blitzed. So you aint scared. But yo thank god Nicole's not a ho. Cause having to fight

someone is fucking scary.

I don't know, I can't help enjoying being drunk. It is just too much

fun sometimes losing every inhibition you have. Kind of like the Jekyll and

Hyde effect I am a completely different person when drunk. It is like I

morph into something cool, someone sure of himself, confident, attractive,

and righteous. That's why I hopped the fence at Sports Bar to prevent

Nicole from getting her shit destroyed. Man move right there kidd!

Nicole's mine bro!! I'll die for that girl sonn! Jibba Jabba.

Nicole was supposed to come out (which only happened once in a

blue moon), and was dressed as a "whore pilot." A whole bunch of guys

were going to hit on her and the thought of having to hit another man in

the face terrified me, so I went to the RAT and got obliterated with Kevin

and Jason in order to calm my nerves. After drinking enough alcohol to

intoxicate an African village, I began looking for her. But Nicole was

nowhere to be found. So I decided to try my luck at Sports Bar.

"Damn this line's long": I thought, staring hopelessly at the block

and a half of students ahead of me waiting to get into the bar. "Nicole

could be getting triple teamed in the bathroom right now and there's not a damn thing I can do about it, cause there are over 300 kids in front of me." I fretted, restlessly waiting as the line crawled at a snails pace. "You know what? Fuck it! Nicole's not getting covered in jizz (unless it's mine). Not if I can help it." And I hopped over the fence and snuck into Sports Bar, blending into the crowd before the bouncer could catch me.

Frantically searching for Nicole, I instead find Jeff, his sister, and that cunt Pam.

"Yo bro, you seen Nicole?" I asked, as Pam gyrated her ass onto my penis. "Yeah, I saw her a few minutes ago. She was heading to the RAT. You should go and find her." Jeff replied anxiously.

"Phew. Nicole wasn't getting gangbanged after all. That must mean she loves me back." I thought, breathing a sigh of relief as I made a mad dash for the RAT, running like a Cheetah in order to find my soul mate.

Mission accomplished!! I gave Nicole a long, deep, passionate kiss on the mouth. And then everything went black.

It's Over

I woke up wearing the same clothes and shoes from last night, without the slightest clue how I got home. I immediately called Nicole to see if she was ok. When she didn't pick up, I left a really creepy voice message, saying how beautiful she was and that I wanted to be with her forever. I sounded like a helpless co-dependant, which could explain why she broke up with me the next day.

We met at the University Union, where she gave me a quick kiss on the lips, before telling me to take a walk with her. We had only taken a few steps, when Nicole said she wasn't happy with the relationship and wanted to break it off.

Nicole's threatened to break up with me before, but this was different, because now she actually meant it. I could tell from her icy stare and calm demeanor this was premeditate, that she'd wanted to break up for a long time, and there wasn't a damn thing I could do or say to change her mind.

I was devastated. Even though I knew it was coming, nothing could prepare me for what she said. I was crushed, heartbroken, and ready to burst into tears, so I walked away as fast as possible because I didn't her to see me crying like a bitch. She tried to grab me, asking if we could still be friends, but I told her that would never happen since she no longer existed to me.

This was my fault. I had a chance to be with her but I blew it. My insecurities got the best of me and now our relationship was over. I guess it goes to show that not every love story has a happy ending.

The next morning I went to the dining hall and spent the day looking out the window. I didn't eat or go to class. I just spent hours and hours staring at a fucking window.

11/4/05

So Nicole ended it Monday and I'm kinda pissed but not at her. It was all my faulyt. I just didn't come throuhth when it counted. I mean yeah I jumped over the fence at sports bar to find her and if I saw her with another man I would have done whatever it took to keep her but when I had the chance to fuck her I just didn't come through. I don't know it's just fucking with my head to much I don't know how much more I can take. I feel like I am at the point of a mental breakdown. Tonight sucked I got no bitches so I am gonna have to keep thinking about Nicole but fuck I hate myself. This is why I understand Nicole for leaving me. How can you love a man who doesn't love himself? It just isn't possible. Not only that my suite mates don't want to live with me. It's like I can't get anything right. Let me at least drink and fuck girls to forget about my problems because they will never go away.

Girls aren't people and they sure as hell don't act like it. They only go for money and power. After going out and seeing these girls together I understand why guys beat the shit out of their wives. I mean fuck girls are fucking annoying I swear I will never treat another girl not named Nicole as a person as long as I live. I don't even care what happens to them. A part of me would give them genital herpes I don't give a fuck. **(NOTE, I DO NOT HAVE GENITAL HERPES, AT LEAST NOT YET. THANK YOU GOD!!!)** *That's just anger talking but I am very angry. How could Nicole break up with me I would jump in front of a bus for her. All I wanted when I was off my game was for her to tell me she loved me and just show her love. But she couldn't do it. I just don't klnow what to do. Thinking hurts too mucfh I will never put myse;f in that situation. I would rather be a lonely old man picking up girls than a miserable guy married to someone he hates.*

My heart had been torn to bits and I needed to get over Nicole, so I went to the RAT with Kevin in order to ease the pain of losing her, because finding another girl would've made me feel better (at least temporarily).

"Why was every girl rejecting me?" I wondered confused by how a bunch of dumb sluts could've turned into Patrick Ewing overnight. Last semester I used to bring home girls at will, but now I couldn't so much as pull a number without getting shot down in flames. What was my life coming to?

I stumbled into my room feeling lonely and dejected, wanting only to fall asleep, when Juan accidentally broke my blender. That's when shit hit the fan. Juan tried to calm me down, saying: "dude it's just a blender," but I knew for a fact that he would've had a brain aneurysm if I broke something of his so I went ape shit, springing out of bed and charging at him like a deranged beast before being restrained by Jack and Jeff.

All Alone

Although Juan and I didn't come to blows, the damage was done. Our friendship was ruined and I completely alienated myself from the entire suite. Losing my girlfriend and being abandoned by my suitemates was a lot to deal with, especially over the course of a week, leaving me emotionally overwhelmed and alone. I was falling apart, feeling as though

I were watching my life unravel in slow motion, and I needed someone to save me, so in act of desperation I reached out to Christina.

Christina wanted absolutely nothing to do with me. We hadn't spoken in over a

Month and I had ignored all of her phone calls and text messages since spending the weekend together. She accused me of using her for sex and treating her like nothing more than a prostitute. Christina than went on to say that she deserved better, that since I've known her I had done nothing but put her through shit, and after all I put her through I didn't even have the decency to return a phone call.

Christina was livid and there was nothing I could say to pacify her. So while she ripped me a new asshole, I told her that she was really sexy when she got mad. That's when she started flirting with me. As we flirted back and forth, Christina would periodically question why she was talking to me, but would just as quickly go back to flirting. So even though she was still mad at me, I knew that we would eventually make up.

11/6/05

So I just got back and the funniest shit happened. I just got out of the cab and 4 drunk kids jumped into the cab and jacked it. Some madd gangsta shit happened right before my eyes. An entire block of people saw it and everybody cracked up laughing. This is ridiculous, I witnessed a car jacking. I thought this type of shit only happens in NWA Compton. But yo these kids are morons. If they get caught that's grand theft auto and Tyrone is gonna be comin for their asshole every night for 10 years straight.

Yo I hooked up with some girl tonight. She was such a fuckign whore but man I just wanted to rip that ass up. She had the hugest tits and the fatest ass goddammmm!!! I didn't even get her name I just walked up to her and started dancing with her and next thing you know I'm hooking up with her. She told me she was a virgin. Yeah Right!!! And I'm the President of the United States. Well I will be once my journal comes out and makes millions of dollars but that's not the point. How many virgins give their dance partners a handjob when they don't know the mutherfucker? If she's a virgin than my penis looks like the Incredible Hulk. Wait, she may in fact be a virgin then.

My suitemates had a long talk with me during the week, expressing their desire for me to move out. They saw me as a loud, obnoxious, drunken mess and were sick of it. They gave me until the end of the semester to find a new place to live.

These guys were fucking assholes! So what if I was a loud, obnoxious, drunken mess? I'm a sophomore in college. If there was a time to behave like a drunken asshole, than here it is. That's what college is for. Why go to college if not to get drunk and fuck bitches? That's the only good thing about school. Everything else is bullshit. "Study hard and get good grades." Why? So you can be a slave in corporate America and acquire a bunch of useless material possessions, while your slut wife cheats on you and takes half your money: because that's what'll happen if you go through the system like a mindless drone. It's either that or being broke, bouncing around from job to job and never getting settled. Doesn't sound like much of a future either way, so fuck it, I'm getting wasted, because what else is their to do?

Trying To Regroup

11/9/05

I think I may have just discovered the key to personal happiness. The key is to be completely comfortable with yourself at your most basic because that is what you really are. I heard my friends talking about getting rich and vacationing in South Beach and fucking madd bitches and how it was indicative of the dream. They also said that when they were older they would fine the right woman and settle down. That's all well and good but what happens when you lose the money and power. What are you left with if not for your own inner feelings. What happens is you lose your inner feelings when success catches up to you because you concentrate on external factors rather than internal factors. The problem is that internal factors should be more stable than external factors. The best way to learn about your internal factors is through finding out what makes you happy when people are not around you. If you can find out what makes you happy when alone, you find out what makes you happy most of the time since most of your life is spent alone.

Solitude is the best company because it's what you spend the bulk of you life in regardless of how popular you are. Despite the hours allotted in a day, the most time you spend on earth is alone by yourself. If you live by what you genuinely believe at your most pure, despite the external consequences, I believe that you will have the happiest and most rewarding live ever. Internal happiness is the most treasured of all the happiness because no matter what, you will be happy because your happiness is based on how you view yourself deep down.

It's like if I had nothing on the surface, would I still be somebody? The answer is only if you have a positive interpretation about yourself. The key to doing this is to do what gives you inner peace even if it sacrifices external factors. It is like risking it all for a cause and even if you fail you succeeded because you risked your life for the cause.

How could you be unhappy when you know that courage and selflessness are part of your personality? If you can do that, then obviously these aspects aren't even part of your personality. That would mean that your better than who ever spoke up for you and eventually you have to speak for yourself or else risk exploitation.

That was the night Jason and I came up with the "Amanda line". Actually, Jason came up with the Amanda line and dared me to use it on someone at Sports Bar. Before I go any further, the Amanda line had to be the worst pick up line man had ever created. Here's how it goes. I walk up to a random girl and say "Yo Amanda what's good?" She responds by saying: "I'm not Amanda, what the fuck are you talking about"? I than say "of course your name's Amanda. Amanda's a really hot name and you're really hot, it's science. I'm premed." That's when she walks away.

I would have had better luck walking up to a girl saying: "Hi my name is Sasha and I'm a convicted sex offender who molests children," than uttering out that nonsense. However, Jason said he would buy me drinks and smoke me up, if I used that line on at least 5 girls, so I swallowed my pride and did it.

True to his word, Jason got me drunk and smoked me up on a three gram blunt when we got back to campus. We then went to his room and played NBA Jam with Kevin, where the three of us had an insanely deep conversation about life and our lack of purpose in it.

11/11/05

So tonight I playted beer pong and almost won. I was so close, we won the first two rounds on the final cup, each coming back from behind. The third round we won it when it was a tie game at 4 cups a piece, my partner and I hit a shot a piece to put it away. The next round was a thriller. We were playing two Alpha guys, the guys who didn't give me a bid caused I used a bathtowel as toilet paper. I was really determined to beat these guys and throughout the game, they were leading. They already sunk 6 cups when we only sunk four and we made key shots and forced the re- rack. We then missed, and they hit a shot to make it a 4-3 game. Then Jay was up and it was an exciting thriller and he hit the cup tying the game. Then it was my turn and I took a while to brace myself and prepared and fired for a cup and low and behold got the final cup, thus sealing the game and advancing myself to the next round. That was big. I wiped my ass with your bath towel! Fucking fagits!! We came through when it counted and made it to the finals. The finals came and it was neck and neck the entire way. For once we were outplaying them the entire way. Then it was about 6-4 us and I accidentally knocked over two cups. The ultimate choke job. No matter, we still made it to the final cup and Jay was up. He missed the shot. It was my turn and I made it. Pumping my fists in escalation I thought I just sealed the win. But they still had a chance and I forgot to realize that. The first guy missed his cup and it was all up to the second guy. The game was in his hands. He was about to shoot and I did whatever in my power to distract him. No matter what I did, he remained unfased and sunk the last cup sending the game into OT. In Ot it was a tie game, we went shot for shot until the final cup. They sunk it and both Jay and I had the ball rim out on our cups. Losing that way hurt, but if there is a way to lose that is the way. We played our asses off and did more than hold our own. That's more than a lot of people can do and if I can do that throughout my life, I am on the right track to success.

Jason and I went to Sports Bar for the beer pong tournament, where the winner received a $50 bar tab. We made it to the finals, losing by a hare, and I was beside myself with disappointment. Nothing was working out for me this semester and it would have been nice to win at something, even if it was just a pointless competition.

11/18/05

I'm debating whether or not to call up Tits. I want to get laid. It's been a while, like over a month. I want it but I also turned her down. What if she isn't interested? I can't get rejected by her but I need my confidence back. She is the type of girl that I just cannot chase. It is a matter of principle but I am so horny. FUCK!!! Hmmmmm, what to do? Alright, look at it this way. The embarrassment you would feel by getting rejected by her would be worse than the pleasure you would get by fucking her. Problem solved, I'm jerking off.

Right now I'm just reading what I wrote and remembering my past. I look at myself now and realize that I am different from my mentality last year. I don't know if its good though. What made me happy felt so wrong so I changed it or at least tried. The problem is that I haven't found a replacement. I've just become depressed because I lost whatever superficial happiness I had. Pussy made everything go away for a short while but I know that using that as a sedative is a serious problem. It is not a source of self esteem. The real source of self esteem is being at piece with oneself. What I need is spiritual help because other people don't make me happy. Even when I felt like I belonged I wasn't happy. This is what lead to the change. I wanna do yoga, martial arts, box and read the bible, Koran, and Torah and a whole bunch of other spiritual books. What makes me mad is that instead of doing these things I engage myself in a pattern of self destructive behavior such as looking at porn, smoking weed, playing videogames, or getting drunk. I need an environment where spiritual enlightenment is more convenient than superficial enjoyment.

Nicole broke up with me almost 3 weeks ago and it hurts but at the same time I know it's not the real issue. I wasn't happy with her because I wasn't happy with myself. I felt that my happiness was in her control which in turn made me even more depressed. Just being in her company makes me wanna cry or hurt somebody. I've seen her the past 3 days in a row and just ignored her. I know it seems like I am mad at her but in all honesty I harbor no feelings of resentment towards her. It's just that talking to her serves as a constant reminder that I let her down and that I let myself down for not being able to make her happy. I can't handle it and that's just it!!!

Lately I've just felt downright pathetic. I don't even want to be around people because I just want to be alone and be depressed. However, I'm stuck in a suite in which I serve as an inconvenience to those who live with me. I can't wait to go home and collect myself and emotionally regroup.

11/19/05

Tonight sucked major hard core balls. We had to take care of madd drunk people. First we had to make sure these two drunk girls we went back with got home safely cutting our night by two hours. Then we get back to Jay's room and there are two guys acroos the hall who are madd drunk and they're throwing up in the toilet and we had to take care of them. After that, we had to walk these two drunk bitches home in the freezing cold. Fuck, it sucked.

You know what, one of the girls had some real emotional problems. I really want to help her or at least talk to her and give her a hug or something. She's a sad girl who just needs a little love and then she'll be alright. I understand the whole trying to put on an act for other people and I really don't want to hook up with her I just want to be her friend and make it so that she is happy.

I went to the RAT with Jason and we ran into this girl Kristen who was stalking him. Kristen was with her roommate and all of us had a scorpion bowl. By the time we finished the scorpion bowl, these girls were completely wasted (not down to fuck wasted, more like throwing up on themselves and stumbling into walls wasted, where if you slept with them you're going to prison for rape), so we decided it would be a good idea to take them home.

When we got back to CIW, Kristen broke down crying and started talking about all of her emotional baggage. As Kristen sobbed uncontrollably, two of Jason's friends from across the hall began violently peuking in the bathroom. Jason wanted to make sure they were ok, so we spent the rest of the night taking care of them. Once they felt better, we walked Kristen and her roommate back to their dorm. I then jerked off and went to sleep.

11/20/05

It seems like I can't get anything right. Tonight I went out these kids Ned, Sam, and Phil from the 2nd floor of my building who I played basketball with. They're pretty chill kids and it was overall a fun night. This kid Sam hooked up with some gross monster last week and we busted his balls about him hooking up with downs syndrome bitches. Then there's the legend, NO GAME NED who aint had pussy since pussy had him. This kid apparently has no game but he's a good kid. He got me into sports bar after I waited a good half hour and got rejected by all three bouncers. I can't even rip on him because of that anymore.

So anyway, you're wondering why tonight sucked. I am in sports bar and I decide to lay down the Amanda line. I went up to this bitch and said yo Amanda whats good, your hot, its science. She looked at me like I was retarded but danced with me anyway because she's a stupid bitch who wants cock. So anyway, I dance with this bitch who's name is Becca but for future reference her name is Psycho Mac Lunatic. We're hooking up and after a while I'm like lets bounce and she seems down but at the last minute changes her mind. I hate the fact that she goes out with other

people. Fuck. Anyway we go back to dancing and then the bar is about to

close and she is gonna go back and I am like where are you staying? It

happens to be that she is only two minutes away from me so I am like

swing by my room. She asks why and I tell her to get to know each other

better. She asks what it means I am like you know what it means

Amanda. After that she started to cry and just peaced me and it was it. I

couldn't even get a number after all of that. I was just so pissed off that I

lost everything I earned because of a stupid joke. Fucking psychotic bitch!!

I mean yo she isn't even that hot and im drunk right now but yo I fucking

hate the Amanda line. THAT LINE IS NOTHING BUT TROUBLE!

I met Ned, Sam, and Phil about a month ago. We were playing

basketball at the CIW courts a few days after Halloween. As the four of us

played 2 on 2, Sam and Phil kept making fun of Ned for being a virgin. I

chimed in because I wanted to feel included, making statements such as:

"it's ok Ned, I used to think pussy was some kind of cat too,"

and: "I was a virgin until Uncle Fred began to notice me." So that's how

we became friends, because I helped make fun of a kid who was on his

way to becoming the 40-year old virgin.

Becca poked me on facebook the next day and I was dumb enough to respond to it. We talked online and I was going to go smoke with her, but I smoked with Jason instead.

Jason and I finished smoking a joint in the wood, when he asked if I had any more weed. I told him I did, but was going to smoke with Becca later. Intrigued, Jason asked who Becca was, so I told him about the classy young lady that fell for the "Amanda line."

Jason shook his head and laughed. He then called me an asshole, lecturing me on why choosing the company of a raving lunatic over one of your best friend was messed up.

At first I thought Jason just wanted to smoke my pot, but the more I listened to him, the more I realized he was right. Here I was denying weed to one of my best friends on campus, someone who I regularly smoke and have deep conversations with, one of the few people at Binghamton who actually gives a shit about me, why? So I can try and fuck some girl who belongs in a straight jacket.

Jason and I walked along a grassy hill on the outskirts of campus passing around a joint, when I realized I have a tendency to jump to conclusions without thinking things through. I thought about the girls in my journal, how I automatically assume women are all pieces of shit because of Lauren (pg 13-16) and Sandra (pg. 58, 59).

That's pretty ridiculous when you think about it, to look down upon an entire gender based on your relationship with two **individual people.** It made me think, maybe some of the girls I've talked shit about in my journal were actually nice people, and that being narrow minded prevented me from appreciating them.

A few days later, I bummed a cigarette off of this girl outside the student union. That one cigarette lead to a two hour-long conversation, and after we finished talking I felt like we had known each other for years. We exchanged numbers and spoke on a daily basis, but never found time to see each other during the semester, since finals were around the corner. Her name was Lisa and I was enamored.

Thanksgiving

11/22/05

Well tonight is my first ever entry at home away from school. A very good day, home for thanksgiving break, first I saw Chris and then I saw Christina. Chris and I hit up a hookah bar and split a pitcher which was a lot of fun. We caught up on things and just joked about the different girls we had fucked in the past.

After that I met up with Christina and we went out to eat. Anyway, I thought we were going to see a movie but she decides after a pitcher of wine to rent one instead. There was one condition that there would be no sex. Well, we get back to her apartment with no movie and lie down on the bed and just start kissing. One thing led to another and before you knew it well lets just say so much for not having sex.

It was quite an enjoyable experience and Christina told me never to hurt her again which I said I would never hurt you baby. It kind of bothers me a little but I just won?t hurt her because maybe I will even just stay with her. If I choose not to I will really think it through and only leave her if I am 100 percent sure of my decision. This is someone who genuinly cares about me even when I am on my D game. I can?t treat that type of girl like shit. She deserves to be treated with respect. Good times though, she will still be someone I can fuck over winter break. She is still more than that because she is a genuine good friend. I feel better being in her company and fucking her on top of that just adds to it.

On to another topic, I am having a very productive college experience. Despite all that's happenned, college has been very enriching. Everyday I learn something new and knowledge is the most important thing you can get from any type of environment. When I compare myself to who I was in highschool I see a completely different person who I am proud of. Looking at myself in the mirror makes me feel good because of all of the knowledge I gained from being at Binghamton. It?s not so much book knowledge but people knowledge. My social skills have improved by leaps and bounds and I have a more objective way of looking at other people. I know that I am in the right place I?ve gained a better understanding of the world I am living in.

Sure enough, Christina and I made up. It took a while, and although she was initially apprehensive about seeing me again, I could tell that she still had feelings for me. I just had to be patient and wait for her guard to drop.

Getting back together with Christina was wrong because I did it for all the wrong reasons. Rather than be with her out of love, I was instead with her out of loneliness, desperation, and fear. I was alone in a frightening environment, detached from and misunderstood by everyone around me, and Christina was the only one who I could relate to. She was my escape, my cocoon to protect me for when life got too overwhelming, and I needed that. This girl provided me with the love I so desperately craved, and that love would never go away.

11/25/05

Yo Ray got knocked the fuckk out and I knokkled over a table and hit a pregnant woman. Whats a pregnant woman doing in a bar? Is this bitch retarded do you not udnerstand that drinking alcohol while you have a kid in you just doesn't mix? That's a fucked up situation when you got pregnant bitches getting drunk and 9 months later a retard comes out. Congratulations now your kids autistic and my tax dollars are gonna be paying for him to be in special ed. Way to go!!!

I got reunited with some high school friends. This kid Ray (from high school) called me to go out, and when I got to his apartment I found these two kids, Manny and Carl, who used to go to Summit with us.

***

Actually, I got in touch with Manny and Carl over the summer because I had a take home final for a history class and called them for help, since they were living together and had concentrations in History at NYU. After talking to Manny and Carl, I suggested hanging out with them when I got home for break.

Carl and Manny were like the odd couple and couldn't have been more different from each other, both in appearance and personality. Carl was a slightly built, mild mannered guy who reminded me of Michael Cera, while Manny was a fat, obnoxious, intellectual snob who looked and acted like Comic Book Guy from The Simpsons.

We used to frequent this bar called Jesse's on 181st and Broadway. The bar was a dump, sticky floor, dim lighting, and perhaps most importantly, a limited number of girls that could pass themselves off as human beings, but they didn't check ID's and none of us were 21, so we had to make due with the circumstances. Besides, they had Karaoke.

***

Our reunion that night was epic. Before going to Jesse's, all of us played a game called "drunk bullshit" at Ray's apartment. Drunk bullshit is played exactly the same as the card game "bullshit," but if you get caught "bullshitting" you have to take a shot. (Note. If you don't know what the game "bullshit" is, look it up online. I am too lazy to explain it in my book.)

When four guys with borderline alcoholism play a game like "drunk bullshit", the result is never good. By the time we arrived at Jesse's, all of us were completely wrecked (especially Ray, since he kept on losing), and had no idea which way was up, what time it is, where we were, or who the President of the United States was.

It was karaoke night and all of us were having a ball, singing and drinking to our hearts content, when Ray knocked over a table and hit a pregnant woman, falling on his face after giving me a drunken high five.

The bouncer promptly threw us out of the bar and Ray was livid. He got in the bouncers face, standing over him and incoherently mumbling something along the lines of: "Fuck You I'm not going anywhere, why don't you make me leave and kick that bitch out while your at it? What's a pregnant woman doing in a bar anyway? Fucking Pussy, I'll fuck you up!" The bouncer accepted his challenge, throwing a titanic right hand that caught Ray right on the button, dropping him to the floor instantly.

The Final Straw

12/3/05

I feel like I'm not performing at the level that I should be. I'm not playing up to my potential and I can't explain it. There seems to be a multitude of reasons. Letting down Nicole, being unhappy with where I live, not getting a bid, tripping on shrooms in the summer, different perspectives on life, and just generally feeling out of place are all playing major roles in my inability to swing bitches at my expected level. I'm so upset with things I can barely talk to people normally. How could you expect me to Mack it to girls? I can't, at least not right now. I need to get back to that level and in order to do this I need to get my general confidence up. That is by improving in other facets of life.

I went to two house parties which were decent at best. However, I felt very awkward and uncomfortable at both of them. Usually I feel happier coming back from parties but tonight I don't feel any different. I have been feeling so disconnected from people that I can't even enjoy their company which is taking away from my enjoyment at parties and making my social interactions seem awkward.

I really just need time alone. It's like a necessity. Tonight is going to be my last night of going out this semester. The reason being is that since I am in such a bad state, I feel awkward when I go out which is influencing how I talk to people. This in turn is influencing how other people feel about me which will lead to people not wanting to do anything with me when I am in the mood to go out and have a good time.

Jeff lost his laptop the day before he had to submit an important paper and was certain that I had something to do with it. According to him, I was the only person in the suite the night his laptop vanished, and was therefore somehow involved.

What Jeff failed to realize, however, was that he had a tendency to leave his laptop in the common room for days on end without locking the door to our suite. Anybody in the building could've taken Jeff's laptop, because valuable items (such as computers) tend to "grow legs and walk away" when left unsupervised for prolonged periods of time. Jeff conveniently overlooked this tidbit of common sense and filed a police report, citing me as the prime suspect for the disappearance of his laptop.

A police officer came to my room and took me in for questioning. After being interrogated for an hour, I was released from the precinct and not charged with anything due to insufficient evidence against me.

I didn't realize how bad my living situation had become until I'd left the police station. Jeff and I didn't get along by any means, but I would never steal anything of his, and the fact that he was so quick to accuse me of something so serious made me realize that the tension between us was far greater than I originally thought. I no longer felt safe living in the suite, so I cleaned out my room and moved in with Kevin and Jason for the remainder of the semester.

12/9/05

WOW, that's all I have to say. Is this really happening? Shits really a lot worse than I thought it was. I'm moving out of my suite and the kid I am supposed to be rooming with called me and said that he didn't want to live with me. I asked him why and it's because of what he heard about me. He wouldn't even want to give me a chance. That can't be good. I bet at least half the floor told him stuff about me because they don't want me there also.

Am I that really that kid who nobody wants to live with, that's fucking bad. It's like inescapable. Is their something wrong with me? Either that or I'm just an asshole. Fuck. It's not even in my control and it frustrates the hell out of me. Putting on an image is really stressful and I don't wanna do it anymore. I mean nothing's working out for me so why even try? I got a 2.5 gpa and everyone thinks I'm an asshole. I'm not going to amount to shit so I may as well just go into my shell and stay their. As much as I try to deny it the bottom line is that I just don't belong and never will. At least my parents are proud of me but that won't last because with the way things are going I don't know how much longer I can stay here? I just have to exercise self control that's all.

Next semester regardless of where I live I'll just continue doing my best which is all I can do. Enough being down on your self, the bottom line is that I'm in a madd good school and that's something to be happy about. It could be a lot worse and I should quit acting like a little bitch and do something about my situation if it bothers me that much. Things seem overwhelming because of finals, moving out and my overall relationship with my suitemates. All I need to do is go home for break, relax, and just get my head together. This could all just be a bad mental state I'm in and if it persists things will only get worse. Feelings influence actions so if I feel good about myself and am in a good state of mind everything else will just take care of itself. People who will judge me based on what I can't control aren't even worth the time of day. I just have to remember that.

I got a new roommate. His name was Erick and he lived on the first floor of Cayuga (the building next to mine). Erick and I had never met but we had a lot of the same friends. Well, these "so called friends" must have told him some not very pleasant things about me, because I received a phone call from Erick saying that he refused to live with me, and would do whatever was in his power to prevent us from rooming together.

When I told the RD (resident director) of my building about Erick, he assigned me to another room on the 3rd floor of my building. I was to move into room 3G with this kid Alan, who had a single because his roommate dropped out after the 2nd week of school. Alan enjoyed living in a single and had absolutely no desire for a roommate, especially after I told him about my current living situation. He was cool, polite, and respectful when we met, but it was pretty fucking clear that he didn't want me to live with him.

12/13/05

Yo all this time I've been calling Mary a bitch and saying all this degrading ass shit about her but the truth is that she isn't so bad. As a matter of fact she's actually pretty cool. So much emotional shit has been happening to me this semester and maybe it was too much too keep inside or maybe I'm madd fucked up right now but I took the mask off and she

listened. She cared what I had to say and was madd comforting and

nurturing and that meant a lot. Now I feel better and less overwhelmed

cause she was there to listen. All this time I've been calling her a bitch but

she's anything but that! I mean there's a real person behind those

humongous tits and maybe I should get to know her. Not like I wanna be

her man or anything like that but who knows maybe we could have a

really intimate friendship or something like that.

At least the semester ended on somewhat of a good note. It was the last day before I was supposed to go home for winter break and I went out with Sam, Phil, and Ned. We went to this bar called Uncle Tony's where they had 75-cent mugs, and all of us got wrecked. We spent the night singing songs, drinking cheap bear and taking shots. Finally, I actually felt alive.

Just when I thought the night couldn't get any better, I ran into Mary right when the bar was about to close. I could not have picked a better night to stumble into her. This past semester sucked the life out of me, and I needed to get laid for the sake of my emotional well being. No, scratch that. After all I'd gone through, I just needed loving human contact and I didn't care whom it was from.

For the first time since I brought her home from the RAT, we had a real conversation, and to my surprise, Mary turned out to be a very nice girl. Maybe it was because I was really high and drunk, or maybe it was because I just needed someone to talk to, but I opened up to her, pouring out my soul and revealing everything as I removed the false mask of confidence I so expertly tried to hide behind.

As I exposed myself for nothing more than a frightened child, Mary didn't judge or look down upon me, she just held me in her arms and told me that everything was going to be ok. So caring and nurturing in my time of need, I now saw her in a different light. No longer some skank I met at the RAT, Mary was now a person with feelings, and that's how she deserved to be treated.

Winter Break

1/6/06

My first day time entry, it's 3 pm and I'm at Christina's house. She's asleep after a rough day. A good day though. We smoked a j in the bathtub and had a couple of margaritas. After that we watched Happy Gilmore but we didn't finish. Now she's asleep cause I put that ass to sleep son. STOP!! I CAN'T TALK ABOUT HER LIKE THAT. I love the girl so lets keep it respectful. I can't believed that she once thougt I was in NYU grad school. Crazy! It's still pretty amazing that she still talks to me considering everything. I really should hold on to her and not let her slip away. I'm actually able to be around her for long periods of time, by which I mean days and not only that but I can just completely be myself. Still, I'm not sure I want a relationship right now. Not that I really want to sleep around but I just want everything to be simple. Being with Nicole caused so much stress and I know Christina is a lot different but it's not them, it's just that I am not emotionally ready for a relationship. Still she is so good to me, after all the shit that's happenned she's there. Anyway, yo she's awake now so I'll continue this later.

Christina's roommate was away for the weekend, so both of us spent it in bed together, having sex and getting high. As we lay naked in the bathtub passing a joint between us, Christina suggested spending the weekend in Disney World. I looked at her like she was crazy: thinking to myself, "is she serious? How in the hell can she pick up and go to Florida out of the blue when she has a full time job in New York? Besides, its not like I could afford a weekend in

Florida anyway, since I didn't have money or a job," so I dismissed

her idea as ludicrous. Christina, however, wouldn't give up,

explaining that she could find a cheap flight online, pay for most of

the trip (since she made close to six figures annually), and that if we

left right away she would be back in New York without having to

miss a day of work, since it was Saturday.

After smoking more weed and thinking her proposition

over, I realized that Christina came up with a great idea. New York

was cold this time of year and spending a weekend in Florida

seemed very appealing, so we spent the next 2 hours trying to find a

flight. Unfortunately the flights were obscenely expensive, since we

tried to book our reservation at the last minute, so we ended up

staying in New York. However, this did not deter Christina on her

quest for paradise, as she ended up getting two tickets for Valentines

Day weekend.

1/19/06

What a fuckin night. I went out with my boys Chris and David

Feinberg. Feinberg is a closet homosexual and by homosexual I mean

homosexual. He is really gay I hope he comes out of the closet and gets

the ass fucking he wants. One day he will be in the steamroom at new

york sports club getting his asshole ripped in 2 by a large black man

named Tyreese. Anyway, Feinberg got plastered and we had to take him

out of bar none and then another bar wouldn't serve him because he was

that wasted. This bitch with my name was beating the shit outta him with

a pool cue, her fist, and bottle of cold bud light. It was funny she asked if

he was a virgin. Nah he aint a virgin, somebody had to have pounded his

asshole out on the low. He couldn't even get into a cab for fucks sake but

whatever. Fucking this kid threw up on my jacket and a table and I had to

clean that shit. Whatever, fuck that I did way worse shit when I was drunk

so its cool. Besides he had a fun night which is what he needs with all the

work he does in school. I'm all about stress relief. We got him in a cab

and me and Chris decided to get a few more beers. The hookah bar was

closed that sucked so we went to this bar on 13th and 2nd. We were chillin

with a Guiness and three bud lights each when the bar tender took our

drinks which were full 15 minutes before closing time. I got pissed off so I

tried to take an empty bottle and smash the windows. Unfortunately the

bartrender caught me and got 4 of her boys from Ireland to try and beat

the shit out of me like I stole their Lucky Charms. I emphasize try because they were a bunch of pussies who couldn't do shit against one wasted kid. The only damage they caused was damage I inflicted upon myself when I smashed a beer bottle on one of those fucking guys heads and cut my hand up. Fuck them. Fucking fagits trying to fight someone who can barely walk and u still cant fuck me up. The bartender she was a piece of shit for dating one of those guys. I swear I would rape her and not even care. If anything I would be happy and after I raped the shit out of her and ripped that bitch a new one I would beat the shit out of her with a baseball bat and her boyfriend wouldn't do shit because he could barely do anything with four of his friends. Fuck those pussies, these muthafauckas tried to jump me and nothing happenned. I went out like a man swinging with a beer in my hand. What more can I ask for? I held my own against four guys and I feel good about myself. I am proud. If I can fight four guys and do alright then I am a man bottom line. That is worth more than money or sex or whatever. The knowledge that I have the will to do my best despite the circumstances is pricelsss which is why tonight was deemed most pleasant despite four pussy ass mutha fuckas trying to beat my ass.

Up until that night, I had never been in a serious fight. I grew up in a very safe neighborhood and went to a really small private school, so

I'd never been in a situation where I had to prove myself on a physical level. Because I was never tested as a kid, I had this humungous fear of being physically humiliated and made to look like a pussy. Having held my own against four grown men who tried to beat the shit out me made me feel like anything but that, and it couldn't have come at a better time.

PART 4

PUTTING THE PIECES BACK TOGETHER

1/21/06

First night back at school. It was pretty chill my new roommate seems cool and the kids on the floor seem cool too. I had a solid ten drinks in the triple room on the floor. We watched basketball and I got to know the people on my floor. Taylor showed me the throw up tally and things are looking up. I will win the competition.

The guys on my floor were the polar opposites of my suitemates from last semester. They were cool. Down to earth dudes who just wanted to get drunk and fuck chicks, they instantly made me feel at home.

Let me introduce you to them. Taylor, Jon and Tim lived in the triple next to us. Doug and Leroy lived next door to us in the other room. Matt and Tony lived across the hall, along with Tom Murphy who lived next door to them. Scott and Ahmed lived next to Tom on the other side.

There was also a suite full of girls on the far left corner of the floor. Our RA was this girl named Sarah who liked to get wasted with us.

So yeah, my new floor mates seemed like a chill cast of characters, and when Taylor showed me the throw-up tally hanging in the bathroom, I knew I was in for a fun semester.

1/22/06

I just finally realized, this is not the place for me. Two nights ago I realized what it is I really want to do. I want to be a fireman. It sounds childish but listen. There is nothing bad about it. Every other profession has a dark side to it. I don't see that as a fireman. I'm putting my life on the line so that other people can live and I don't see any corruption in the fire department. This could be the alcohol and the weed talking but that's the most noble thing I could ever think of doing as a profession. Even as a psychologist or a special ed teacher, I would be buying into a system where I can't cure the people I work with completely because the people above me want them sick. If they weren't sick there would be no business. As a fireman, you could say the same thing but fires are accidental. Not only that, but I really don't care if I live or die. I don't want to die with a bad soul but if I felt that I had a clean slate, death wouldn't faze me.

Being a fireman would almost ensure that I die with a clean slate provided I died on the job. How could you not be at piece fighting a fire?

Tonight I went out with my new floor mates. I guess it was fun. I ran into Mary at this Sorority party. I hooked up with her for a while, long enough for them to leave me. Not that it mattered, I got a cab and went downtown. I couldn't get into sports bar so I went to the Rat instead and ran into Mary instead. We went back and I fucked her but it woke me up to something. Remember how I felt I had a connection with her. It wasn't true. There will never be one with her. I realized that I always have to be on my a game around her and not just her, every other girl in Binghamton. This goes even for the nice girls. She said she came and I believe her cause im madd good but I didn't finidsh which sucked. We smoked with her and her room mate and her best friend and she didn't want to finish. I think I did something weird but I don't know what it was. It was probably nothing but the fact that I think this means that my relationships with the people are vapid and fake. The only real relationship I have with anyone other than my family is Christina and here I am betraying her to have sex with Mary. Not that she is bad but Christina deserves better than what I am doing to her. I am going to talk to her and tell her how I feel and what is going through my mind. If she still loves me than she will be mine forever. I know now that I am worthy of her love. Since the bar fight I

realized that I am capable of putting myself on the line for Amanda for

real. If she were to do the same for me I would take a bullet, get hit by a

bus, do anything, die for her. Fighting those four guys had no effect on

me. I really don't care risking myself physically. If anything it makes me

feel good. This guy at the rat was being a dick when I was dancing with

Mary. He tried to dance all up on me so I pushed him off. I would have

killed him and not even cared if he so much as talked to me after pulling

that stunt. I like this newfound attitude I can't smoke anymore because I

want to keep it. From now on if got forbid Christina doesn't work out, I

will never mess around with another girl who smokes weed.

I don't usually do this but an interesting turn of events occurred. I

met this girl her name was Laura tonight and she was chillin when I got

back from fucking Mary. I was writing and reading my journal when she

just flat out asked me to come to her room. Unsure at first, soon after I

decided to go on up there. We fooled around for madd long. But this girl

kinda bothered me. Like first she was on top of me for maddd long and

wouldn't let me in and finally when I went in I was so horny I just busted

one right there. Not to mention I fucked another girl before and didn't

cum. There is only so much a man can take. Anyway, I tried to play it off *and I think I did ok by saying that I didn't think we should fuck since we barely know each other. What really bothered me was that after I was done fingering her my hands were covered in blood. I really hope I don't have any diseases but I'm not sure. Tomorrow first thing I'm going to the health center. I'm asking questions bottom line. I got 2 girls in one night I should be happy but instead I'm terrified. If I get a disease my life is over, no more Christina and once that happens every ounce of purity I once had will have evaporated. Please God if you are listening, let this girl not have any diseases. Please. I will be forever indebted to you if I didn't get a disease from this girl. I won't even give her a nickname!!*

By this point, I was completely disillusioned with Binghamton and felt as though I were only in college because it was the socially acceptable thing to do. Dissatisfied with my major and unsure of my future, I felt as though I had nothing substantial to pride myself on. Lack of identity made me question why I was even in school to begin with and I started to think that maybe I'd be better off doing something else, like being a firefighter.

On a more positive note, I didn't have any disgusting red pimples on my cock when I awoke the next morning. As a precaution, I went to the health center and got tested, because everyone should get tested, especially when they bang some random slut who happens to be on her period and conveniently forgets to tell you.

Luckily everything came out negative, and true to my word I never gave that bitch a nickname, despite the fact that there were so many I could've come up with. Oh, and I never called her back, because I have a learning disability and forgot. Yeah. That was the reason.

1/27/06

Tonight was a good night. I went to sports bar but I couldn't play beer pong. No matter, I introduced people to fingers. Everyone liked it cause it got them wasted. Hopefully shit will continue being good. Anyway, I met this girl Ali who Kevin stole her virginity. Whatever, she cried over him and although she seemed genuinely upset I still took my boys side. She hooked up with this kid who is tight with my boy so I told this girl bottom line that my boy was 4 times the man the other kid was despite how much of a dick he supposedly was. Whatever girls like dick that's why there girls it's science. Yo, I showed the people on the floor my journal and now they know about the Moose but it's all good cause they don't know the moose. I don't even know the moose. I need to bang out 3 more girls cause if I bang out 5 girls in a month I'm getting a gold chain bottom line. Scott just hit Ahmed in the head with a ruler while he was

sleeping and Ahmed is going to kill him. Too bad Ahmed is too drunk to

turn. He's gonna get a concussion and I'm gonna laugh at him. Yo with

his wiefbeater he looks like an angry Puerto Rican guy chasing his wife

around with house wit a bat cause she didn't have dinner ready by 6

oclock. Damn that's racist, I didn't mean that.

Scott invited me out with his friends to play beerpong, but we got to Sports Bar late and played this game called fingers instead. Here's how fingers works. You put about a quarter of a beer inside of a cup, and everyone playing puts his or her finger on the outside of the cup. Each person takes turns and has to guess how many fingers are left on the cup, with everyone having the option of leaving their finger on or taking their finger off of the cup. Whoever guesses correctly gets eliminated, and the last person remaining has to chug the beer.

Needless to say, all of us got wasted, and I got even more wasted when the entire floor came out to join us. Taylor offered to go shot for shot with me, and we spent the rest of the night taking shots together until neither of us could walk straight nor speak coherently.

On my way out of the bar, I met this girl Ali, who Kevin (my roommate freshman year) used to fuck last semester. Supposedly Kevin took her virginity, and Ali consequently got attached to his cock inside of her. However, being in a relationship with her was the last thing he wanted, since she wasn't pretty, funny, intelligent, or interesting to talk to. Oh, and she also happened to be an emotional train wreck? Yeah, all I had to do was mention Kevin's name, for Ali to start crying hysterically, telling me how much she loved him and that he broke her heart in a million pieces.

Even though I could tell that Ali was a raving lunatic within 5 minutes of talking to her, the fact of the matter was that I was too drunk to care, so I got her number as I hopped into a cab. When I told Kevin about my encounter with Ali, he cracked up laughing, telling me to change my phone number once I hit it, because that girl was a stage 5 clinger.

Either at the bar, in the cab, or when we got back to my room, I began to ramble on about how I was writing a future Pulitzer Prize winning novel. My floor mates were intrigued and asked to read it. While I was showcasing my journal, we heard Ahmed chasing after Scott, screaming at the top of his lungs that he was going to rip his arms off and feed it to him. Ahmed was a beast and had the body of an action figure, so he probably would have succeeded had he not been too drunk to turn, repeatedly hitting his head against the wall as he was running FULL FORCE.

1/28/06

I'm drunk. No shit it's an entry in my drunk journal. Tonight kind of sucked. I blew it with Lisa (see page 154) cause I acted like a bitch. She was at a party I was at and I ran into her. Things went well for like 30 seconds and I asked her to dance and she just said she was going to have a cigarette. Fuck, I blew it. She was with a friend who had a man so I don't know if it was my fault. All I know is that I got to stop putting myself in stressful situations. Keep it simple, that's the plan. Whatever man fuck that bitch, I blew it just put it in the loss column. I mean cmon Jordan can't hit em all but I feel like Shawn Bradley. After that I went to this Bar Boca Joes which is a townie bar. It was kinda funny there were girls old enough to be my mom. Yo that MILF shit is hot. I gotta bang a 40 year old. That's college goal # 123 b.

Lisa called me and said she was going to a Delta Chi party, so I agreed to meet up with her. However, when we finally ran into each other, she practically ignored me, treating me as though I didn't exist. Eventually she just ditched me, going outside for a cigarette never to return.

I was upset. Lisa was a girl who I felt a connection with and could see myself liking, but after that night I felt as though our connection was only a figment of my imagination.

Just as Lisa rejected me, I ran into none other than Brian, Jay, and Katzenberg, whom I hadn't seen since the last time I fucked Mary in the common room (see page 117-121). Seeing these guys made me feel a lot better, and I quickly drowned my sorrows by getting blitzed with them.

I had to wake up at 8:30 am to attend a training seminar for an internship program working with Autistic children. Drinking was a really bad idea, as I slept through the entire seminar and was caught red handed snoring during one of the presentations. I failed the performance exam and wasn't able to participate in the program. Shocking!

Lisa apologized for "being shady" the other night and we agreed to hangout again. Talk about a crazy bitch. The girl was a nut job. She talked to me as though I were reading her profile for an ad in a dating service. This is pretty much what happened. "My name's Lisa. I like music, the color pink, being happy, and going on facebook. Now what do you like? Oh by the way you should join a frat." Hanging out with her was

so bad, that **I ACTUALLY DITCHED HER TO GO TO CLASS!!**

1/31/05

Quick question, how many Tuesday January 31st are there? About

one in 1,000. Exactly, point taken, lets drink. It's like a national holiday

hahaha. Anyway, I went out with this kid Vinit and we played beerpong at

the rat and lost in the first round by one cup. DIL baby u want me 2 be in a

frat, I'l start my own frat BITch!! That's not the story though. The real

story is that he got wasted and had to go to the hospital to get tested for

alcohol poisoning. Truth is he was just drunk but either way he had to go

so I went with him. I really didn't want to go I just wanted to pass out in

my room but he's my friend so I felt I had to. Anyway, he was fine and I

sat in a hospital room for two hours just so some dumb cops and ER

people had to conduct an emergency procedure. Fuck the Cops. My boy

was aight I would have taken care of him. But no they can't believe

whitey.

That was the first night I went out with Vinit. Vinit looked like

Apu Nahasapeemapetilon from the Simpsons and sounded like the

Notorious BIG. I met Vinit last semester, playing basketball outside the

Mountainview courts. Talk about a fucking character. Every other phrase that came out of his mouth was: "yo yo, check it check it, that's what's up," and while we were playing he would jump 40 inches in the air and do 360-degree dunks that seemingly defied the laws of Physics.

Unfortunately Vinit and I didn't talk since our encounter at Mountainview, but recognized each other playing basketball in the gym. After playing a few games together, Vinit told me about the frat he was starting.

It was called DIL, which stood for Determined Independent Leaders, and the purpose of the frat was to bring people of different races and religions together. He asked if I wanted to be a founding father and I was on board immediately. It didn't matter what the frat stood for. I just thought it would be really cool to start my own frat, so I jumped at the opportunity.

I asked if he had plans that night, because I wanted to get drunk. Actually, that's a lie. I needed to get drunk, especially after hanging out with Lisa earlier in the day.

Vinit had a Biology exam the next day but said that he'd rather go to the bar than study, so both of us immediately left the gym in order to pre-game in my room.

I wanted to get to the RAT in time for the beerpong tournament (held every Tuesday), so we needed to hurry, and we took at least 5 shots of Jose Quervo in 15 minutes before catching a cab and going downtown.

We lost in the first round and went next door to JT's for 10-cent Tuesdays. (Note. The concept of 10-cent Tuesday is pretty self-explanatory. A beer costs 10 cents.) Not surprisingly, we were wasted, especially Vinit, and he'd thrown up twice by the time we left the bar, in addition to vomiting three more times during the cab ride back to campus.

"How much peuking can one man do?" I thought to myself, as Vinit regurgitated his large intestine outside Lecture Hall 2. And why is a cop talking to him? More importantly, why did Vinit just tell the cop he was at Sports Bar?

What a fucking retard!! All this kid had to do was say something along the lines of: "Sorry officer, I had a bad case of food poisoning, and was about to go to bed after spending the night studying Physics in the library. Oh by the way, I'm standing outside Lecture Hall 2. Thanks for your concern." But nooo! He had to tell the cop he was at Sports Bar waiting for a cab, which is why Vinit was now on his way to the hospital in order to get tested for alcohol poisoning.

DIL never materialized, because we spent more time smoking weed than actually putting our idea into practice, although we did make t-shirts in order to give off the appearance that DIL was a real fraternity.

2/3/06

Fuckin A I got a bitch sleeping in my bed as I write. Mutha fuka! I didn't fuck her but whatever, fuck I didn't even bust one from that bithc but who givess a fuck. I fingered that bitch and she was loving it that's watz really good. I spent 120 at Sports Bar pops is gonna be pissed. Whatever, poppa Strenger is the reason I am enjoying college. I got on the express train no doubt kid. Fuck. Nvr mind I wouldn't wanna, tonight was just a practice round. FUckin this bitch is beneath me so I really couldn't care less. I just know I got skillz. That's right I spelt it with a Z cause I'm black from the waist down. This girl is fuckin passed out and we lost at beerpong. If we won, I would have an X Box 360 instead of a 5 sleeping in my room. What is better??? This is an interpretive journal.

It's like 8 am, why the fuck am I up and why am I still drunk? Yea so werd, so this bitch jerked me off last night. It was aight. Still she wasn't that great, I would rather have a 360. But we can't have everything we want. This girl just needs a healthy does of enthusiasm. Like the enthusiasm she showed when I was fingering her. Boy was she loving it no doubt I have that effect on people. I call it the Strenger effect.

Right now I feel like I completed a cycle. 2 of my good boy's friends got with her. One got her when he was like 12 so he is the official trendsetter. The other got with her last year but didn't bang her so he is the guy who warmed her up. My boy took her virginity like we took land from the Indians so he is the guy who broke her in. And I'm the one who hooked up with her last thus rounding out the cycle and making me the closer. Call me Mariano mutherfucker!!!

I see why No Game Ned has no game. It's not like he has no game, it's just he has no game. But it's not really his fault. These girls just don't take him seriously cause of madd factors. Like, he is 6'3 and 120 and everyone fucks with him so it's hard for a bitch to give him a chance and take him seriously. He isn't terrible, I mean back in my heyday of spitting anti-game I was way worse so I feel his cause. Yo, straight up, I'll give the kid private lessons on how to swing bitches for like 30 and hour I'm not

kidding. Seriously, he is a good kid I like him. I would have his back in an

instant if shit went down. And cause he's madd cool, I will only charge

him 25 and hour for a lesson.

Earlier in the day, I went to Phil, Sam, and Ned's suite to play

videogames. After playing a couple games of NFL Street, Phil told me

about the co-ed beerpong tournament at Sports Bar, where the winner

won an X-Box 360. I really wanted that X-Box, but the problem was that I

had nobody to call, since I didn't believe in having female friends unless I

was busting a nut from them.

Then I remembered Ali. I knew she was a complete whack job,

but I had no plans of hooking up with her. I just wanted someone to play

beerpong with in order to have a chance at wining an X-Box 360. So Ali

and I, along with Phil and his girlfriend Bailey (whom everybody called

Balls, because she looked like a man and most like likely peed standing up)

got into a cab and went to Sports Bar.

I had absolutely no cash on me, so Phil paid for my cab ride along

with my entry fee into the tournament, and in return I offered to buy

everybody drinks with my credit card.

Big Mistake!! I ended up buying 8 pitchers, along with 16 Jager bombs, and when the bill came I found out that I'd spent $120 (the cost of almost 2 hours with a hooker) on alcohol.

In the midst of drinking ourselves retarded, Ali and I began hooking up at the bar. At this point, everything was a blur, and the next thing I remember was bringing Ali back to CIW, where I spent almost an hour eating her pussy like a Scooby Snack **WITH MY DOOR OPEN**, while she screamed for seconds.

2/4/06

To make matters worse, who do I run into but Nicole? That brought back a lot of heartache as I felt sick to my stomach so I go outside and have a cigerette without talking to her. All I thought about was that I blew it with her and that talking would only give me the illusion of standing a chance when I already knew I was fucked. My blunder caused her to make up her mind about me and after that I would never get another chance to reededm myself to her. It was as though she really hated me aside from the sex. She never loved me she was just torn by and unable to handle sexual pleasure. I just wanted to love her and have her to love me back. It was as though nothing we said mattered to each other but we were just so drawn to each other. Having a girl like Nicole was the nicest ideal anyone could aspire to have and by that I mean that the idea and image she generated of herself were more appealing than her actual personality but I was to blind to her self proclaimed ideal that I thought I loved her.

She kind of treated me like shit. Always upset or mad at me when all we needed to do was fuck and everything would have been ok. That's all it is. I realized that guys and girls will get along with each other if the sex is great. I don't have anything in common with most of the girls I get wth. I probably wouldn't even say hi to them otherwise. It was like that's what they all were.

That's what Mary is but the truth is that at the time Im uncomfortable around girls that I hadn't fucked or weren't avidly trying to fuck. When I fucked up I got scared. I was terrified all along and shouldn't have brought her into a situation where I would be week in. That's what's great about Mary. She lets me stay in my shallow comfort zone and allow me my moments of fake happiness. That's why I loathed her. I felt she gave me a girl to loath and treat like shit to compensate for failing to get laid in the past. I hated that I always had to be sexy for her yet I loved her because she let me loath her and treat her like a piece of garbage. Everytime she was around I felt like I had to put on a switch like I was the man because I couldn't stop fucking her. She was my reliable safety net and kept my emotions in balance. Mary was my Mariano Rivera, always there in the 9th inning. Eventually I have to ween myself off of this kind of girl because it creates a false happiness that I can't ascribe to.

They think I'm a tough confident muscular guy who's an object of desire when in fact I am nothing. The false happinese was great. Anyway, I'm on a ramble right now so I'll get back on point. The point is that I was too pissed off and upset with myself not her to talk to her so I was instead a pussy and walked away without even trying to attain the supposed love of my life. I felt that somehow this love was false and that maybe it's better not persuing because what if I continued fucking up and being exposed for the bumbling idiot that I was. I never let myself go for her even though I claimed to but at the end was it worth it? Who knows maybe Ali isn't so bad.

I was supposed to go to Sports Bar with Phil, Sam, and Ned, but they left without me because I was taking a shit in the bathroom and didn't hear them leaving.

Instead I went out with Bailey and her girlfriends. She introduced me to her friend Elena, who looked like the Lochness Monster, but by then I didn't care, because I'd spent the past two hours pre-gaming in the suite.

I even came close to hooking up with her. Yeah, I was on the dance floor about to make out with Nessie herself, when I saw Nicole out of the corner of my eye.

I couldn't go through with this. To go from Nicole to a fucking creature, it was gross. Seeing her at the bar reminded me of what I had lost, that I could've been in a beautiful relationship had I not fucked everything up.

All I wanted was to hold Nicole and tell her how much I loved and missed her, but I couldn't, because even though she was so close, it felt as though Nicole were light years away from me.

2/5/06

Every girl I get with makes me more convinced that I should stay with Christina. Some fucking weird shit happened tonight. First, I went over to see the express train bitch and she didn't even remember what happened. I mean I still fucked her but yo she just layd their like a Lincoln Log. And to think I thought crazy girls would be good in the sack. Well apparently not.

Either way I've done with that bitch she's crazy and yo if she aint' even fun

2 slamout than wats the point?

Then I go see my boy Ralph. It took me 30 minutes at least to find

his place which I finally did. We hit up a party at this girl's house and this

kid disappears for a good hour. The door finally opens and the girls comes

out and he is looking madd dejected. Than he just disappears never to be

seen again. So I'm thinking either a) he busted in a minute b) he couldn't

get it up or c) this bitch rejected him. I am gonna have to go with b cause

if he came in 2 seconds it would have lasted 2 seconds and if it were c he is

smart enough not to bringing a girl in it. Now I'm at sports bar and the

fucking express train bitch just hugs me while I'm talking to a bunch of

girls. I don't want be a dick, I really don't so I hang out with her for a little.

Anyway, I ask her to go back with me which is stupid cause she's a Lincoln

log. Either way she said no so I said peace. Than she kept following me

and asking what the relationship meant to me. What relationship? You're

some ho that I ate out with my door open. C'mon you know what it was. I

just told her to ask me when she was sober and I walked away never to

hopefully see her again.

It didn't take a rocket scientist to realize that Ali was out of her goddamn mind. The fact that three of my friends took turns riding her like an express train was merely a glimpse into her emotional instability. Ali did not belong in an institute of higher learning, and would have probably fit in better had she been in a different kind of institution.

This girl looked like she was on the verge of a mental breakdown, one bad break up away from slitting her wrists and taking a bath, so I decided to let her down gently. We met by the union, where I told her she was a great girl, but that I wasn't interested in having anything more than a "casual friendship." Ali didn't take this very well and started crying hysterically, saying that she loved me and couldn't believe I would do this to her after she was willing to give her entire heart to me. **SCARY!!**

Florida

Christina and I followed through on our plan to spend Valentines Day weekend in Florida. We were originally supposed to meet at Port Authority and go out to dinner, before catching our flight the next day. However, I had other plans in store. I wanted to do something romantic for her since it was Valentines Day, but in order to follow through on my plan I had to get into the city much earlier than she expected.

I got into the city at noon (six hours before we were supposed to meet) and immediately went to the store, where I bought a bouquet of roses. I then took the train uptown to her apartment and rang the doorbell, hoping her roommate would answer the door so that I could make Christina a bathtub full of roses.

Unfortunately her roommate wasn't home, so I had to resort to plan B. I picked up some superglue from the hardware store down the block and then went up onto the roof, where I spent the next 3 hours super gluing the roses to say I LOVE YOU on the concrete floor, before using the remaining roses to create a trail on her staircase.

I called Christina when I finished, telling her that my bus broke down and to just wait for me at her apartment. Right as she walked in the door, I called out her name on the top of my lungs. She looked at me with total surprise and I told her to go up to the roof. Her jaw dropped upon seeing my romantic gesture, and she pulled me close to her, kissing me several times on the mouth before dragging me into her bedroom, where we made love all night before going to sleep in each other's arms.

We checked into a Best Western 5 miles from Universal Studios. The motel had a king size bed, cable TV, and a swimming pool. After christening the bed, we took a cab to the Islands of Adventure, where we went on the Incredible Hulk ride. The Hulk consists of being strapped to a seat and going from 0-60 mph in a matter of seconds. It wasn't the fastest ride I've been on, but it was fast enough to knock over the green Yankees hat I was wearing. Being a Red Sox fan, Christina was very amused by this and couldn't stop laughing at me the entire day. We then went on the dueling dragons ride and Dr. Doom's free fall, before going back to the hotel, buying a bottle of wine and going swimming, christening the pool because the lifeguard was no longer on duty.

We woke up bright and early the next day, had sex, and than got ready for a full day of adventure. The first thing Christina wanted to go was go shopping, where as I wanted to play games, but since she paid for most of the trip, I had no choice but to go shopping and watch her buy things that she would never have any practical use for. After going shopping, we went on the Spider Man, Storm Acceleration ride and than to the lost continent, where we experienced "Poseideons Fury". We than got lunch somewhere and explored the Island before having dinner at Margaritaville. After dinner we went on the Jurassic Park ride, where Christina clutched onto me like a frightened child because she was afraid of animatronic robots.

When we went back to the motel, Christina recommended that I get some studying done before we had sex again, since she didn't want to be responsible for me failing my exam. **HA!** I barely had a chance to open my textbook before Christina sat on my lap and told me how cute I looked trying to study. Yeah, like that was going to help me get any work done. Please, I had a better chance of pooping out Gummy Bears than accomplishing anything with a hot girl grinding her ass onto me, so I gave up and threw my books on the floor, taking a very extensive study break.

Our weekend in paradise was over and we had to go back to New York and resume our normal lives. In the airport I almost lost my boarding pass and Christina flipped out, ranting about how I was still a child and that she could never be with anybody who didn't even have his basic shit together.

"Who the hell are you to yell at me?" I asked myself, silently questioning Christina as she berated me in front of the entire airport. "Not only are you embarrassing me by carrying on like a lunatic in a public place, but you also happened to strike a nerve, preying on an insecurity you knew I had. Was that necessary? Did you really need to make me feel bad about myself, especially when I didn't mean to do anything wrong? It's not like I said 'hey, today looks like a great day to forget my boarding pass and piss off Christina.' No, it was an accident, and for you to yell at me on account of a careless mistake is just plain mean." I thought, wishing I'd said this out loud instead of playing it cool and pretending that her words had no effect on me.

Resuming The Shit Show

2/17/06

I am wasted as a muthafucka. MuthaFUCKA!!!!! I'm so drunk, I had like 12 drinks before coming and I had like 6 or 7 more drinks at the bar. So tonight I stole some bitches cell phone but I didn't mean to. It's just that the express train bitch had a guy who was being a cock sucker and I didn't want him to go back with her cause he was such a douche. So I took her phone in order to cockblock the kid. Fuck that, he was being a dick from the get go. Threatening to beat my ass with 2 of his boys to impress some girl who's vagina smells like Sea World and than backing away like a lil biznatch when my boys stepped in. Whatever, I asked the bitch for her phone so she wouldn't go back with that cock sucker and when I saw her with him I refused to give the girl her phone back. Who the fuck cares??? SHE IS NOT A PERSON!!!!!! I have to make decisions for her and I don't even want her, she is a Lincoln log. FUCK!!!! That's it bottom line, I'm gonna give the bitch her phone and tell her once and for all that she is forbidden from talking to me ever again bottom line!!!

Not only that, this bitch Elena said I tried to fuck her. It wasn't true, I didn't even try making out with her. I tell you what, I would rather stick my dick in a pencil sharpener than fuck that stupid cunt bottom line. So I told her friend what happened and I also told her what I thought about her and she slapped me. Fuck her, she should have a train run on her. I wouldn't stop them, she aint human. I mean she is kinda human so she's been upgraded to CHIMPANZEE status. That is it, I'm out, no more arguing about a Chimp named Balls.

Tony and Matt made punch in their room with a mixture of Bartons Vodka, Keystone Light, various fruit juices, and Death. The entire floor spent the night pre- gaming in their room before going out to Sports Bar.

Man was I drunk! One minute I'm pregaming in Tony and Matt's room, the next minute I'm waiting in line at Sports Bar, without a clue as to how I got there. "And I have 5 missed calls from Ali! Why the fuck is bitch calling me when I cut her off weeks ago?" I wondered, as I stood outside drunk, puzzled, and slightly afraid. "Whatever, maybe if I ignore her she'll go away."

Wrong! By now I had lost the guys on my floor and was in the middle of an exciting game of fingers with Phil and Sam, when lo and behold, look who decided to show up. Yeah, that's right, Ali, aka the #5 Lincoln Log Express Train, accompanied by three of her guy friends, who threatened to beat the shit out of me for no reason other than to impress her.

Talk about a pathetic display of masculinity. These guys looked like they belonged on the set of "The Brady Bunch", the type of guys who thought that playing Street Fighter II resembled a real fight, so it came as no surprise that they ran away like a bunch of pansies once Phil and Sam stepped in to get my back.

Crisis averted! Well, at least I thought it was before Ali came back and started talking to me, apologizing profusely for her friends and begging me like a dog to take her back. "Take you back? Really? I never wanted you to begin with. The only reason I hooked up with you is because I spent $120 at Sports Bar and was shit-faced drunk. Besides, do you seriously think I'm going to want to be with you after you just pulled a stunt like that? You must be delusional!"

Some girls just can't take a hint, which was probably why Ali continued following me even after I had just shot her down in the middle of Sports Bar. Wow, this was annoying. I just wanted to get drunk and fuck bitches, but I couldn't, because this emotionally unstable nutcase was latching onto me like a parasite.

All I wanted was for Ali to leave me alone, but since I had a better chance of being struck by lightening while drinking a Strawberry Daiquiri and talking to a Pink Elephant, she may as well at least go back to my room and fuck. Yeah, I know she was a Lincoln Log, but at least if we did it there would be a 20-minute period where I wouldn't have to hear her speak, so I suggested we leave the bar together.

"But what about my friends? I can't just leave them here." Ali whined. Her behavior and tone of voice indicating that she was a complete and total imbecile when it came to dealing with guys.

Me: "Are you kidding me? Those pussies just tried to beat my ass for no reason. Fuck them. Go home to a real man instead. I'm right here baby."

Ali: "But Sash, these guys are will call me every 30 seconds until I pick up my phone and go home with them. You don't know them. They're crazy."

Me: "So turn your phone off."

Ali: "I can't. You should know by now that I'm incapable of rational thought." (Note. Ali didn't really say this, but she may as well have considering how stupid she was.)

Me: "Than give me your phone. I'll give it back to you once I finish pounding you out."

Ali: "Ok."

Well, Ali must have been retarded or something, because instead of going home with me, she came back with the same three guys who threatened to beat me up, demanding that I return her phone. Fuck that bitch! I wasn't giving her shit, especially now, so I told Ali that I had absolutely no idea what she was talking about, that she was a deranged idiot, and to get away from me because I didn't have her phone. I than got into a cab and went home, leaving Ali crying outside.

The next day I realized what I did, so I walked over to her room and gave Ali back her phone. I apologized for what happened and made up an excuse about being too drunk to remember having her phone in my pocket in order to save face. I than bought her breakfast and apologized once again for how I conducted myself last night. Over breakfast, she told me that the entire hockey team heard about what happened and wanted to beat the shit out of me.

2/26/06

Tonight sucked. I got drunk and then I smoked. There were no bitches. Bitches are hard to find these days. It doesn't matter because I have Christina. Stop referring to women as bitches, it is not nice. This isn't me, it isn't me. Natural Sasha never called a woman a bitch. Its cause of all these bitches I started calling women bitches. I honestly am so upset that in order to fit in I have to call women bitches. Why are girls attracted to guys like that? I did that shit last year and had all the pussy. Now I am a lot nicer and more chilled out and I fit in less!!! What The Fuck? Honestly girls think I'm weird because I tried to be their friend instead of fuck them. What does that say? It makes me cry sometimes, I'm serious. It made me feel like being a drunk asshole is the best I can be as a person and that is very depressing. If that's the case, I would rather try to improve myself and my situation with a chance for making things worse by going out of my comfort zone than settle for being just that kid who's fun to get drunk with and nothing more. This is my away message:"Get on the #5 Lincoln Log Express Train. People don't have a clue as to what I'm talking about and I plan on keeping it that way. Only the few and the proud know of the legendary #5 Lincoln Log Express Train and it's real that's all I gotta say. It's madd real son werd". Now you know I'm gone. The End.

I went to a party at the Hockey House and could count on one hand the amount of girls that were there. The party was a complete sausage fest and it reminded of prison, minus the part about getting fucked in the ass everyday. Oh, and just for the record, nobody laid a finger on me, because none of the hockey players knew who Ali was.

3/4/06

Tonight was fun. I busted out the Amanda line. I walked up to bitches with my boys and said YO Amanda what's good? She said I'm not Amanda and I said yeah you are Amanda is a hot name, your really hot, its science. Bottom line. I'm Premed. This one bitch went for it. She was 28 and a mother of 3. She wanted my cock no doubt kid. Yeah I got this bitches number but I wont fuck her because 3 kids equals a pussy as big as the Atlantic Ocean. Fuck long voyages.

Yeah I went up to girls and acted like a complete dick and said my name was Jeff Watson. This kid was my suite mate from last semester. He is a faggot. This is the kid who got mad at me for swinging a bitch in his direction. Fucking kid, he should be shot. I was in the cab and there was this girl who was at a stripper show at a frat party so I said that I just busted one right there cause I'm Jeff Watson. Fuck that kid.

I went to Flashbacks aka Boca Joes. Speaking of Flashbacks I got a story to tell about a bitch I met over the summer. Her name was Rachel and she was an actress. She was 26, hot and recently divorced. I told her I just finished school and I was madd smooth. Anyway, I brought her back and her pussy was so hairy it was like Macy Gray or DR. J. She had the Julius vag. Disgusting, I would rather eat my own shit than eat that bitch's pussy fro. Bottom line I'm out.

Juan and I made up that night. We saw each other at Boca Joes and drunkenly hugged it out, before apologizing for our actions that drove us away from each other. After that we hit on a bunch of girls, where I used the Amanda line and made a complete ass of myself.

I was so frustrated with women and how I felt I needed to act in order to get them, that when you combined that with my own personal insecurities, my sex drive was pretty much out the window, therefore causing me to have absolutely no problem acting like a moron for other people's amusement. By the way, the woman who I thought wanted my cock ended up giving me the wrong phone number. What a surprise.

I had a paper due next week for my politics of gender and sexuality class and went on an Adderall bender for three consecutive days, in which I didn't sleep, in order finish it. I've pulled all-nighters before, but never like this, and by day three I looked like a crackhead, twitching, coughing, shaking, and unable to stand up straight. I even had a conversation with my taste buds during class, and for some reason they reminded me of the Smurfs.

Later that night, Alan and Taylor took me to Walmart to get cold medication, and I was so out of it that I couldn't pay for my medication without the cashier thinking I was high on crystal meth.

Even with over 100 mg of Adderall in my system, I still failed to hand in my paper on time and had to e-mail it to my professor, who gave me an A-. Despite my grade, the fact that I took so long to complete a six-page paper was just plain embarrassing. (And to think I'm writing a book.)

Aside from getting me sick, my Adderall bender had a few other unwanted side effects. I saw Christina over spring break and my body was so drained that I turned into a minuteman who couldn't last more than 30 seconds without busting all over himself. We had sex at least 10 times over break, yet I wouldn't be surprised if those 10 times totaled less than a half-hour. My confidence was shot and I stopped wanting to see Christina for fear of making this a habit.

3/25/06

It's 12:30 and I'm wasted and I'm so happy right now. Uconn just hit a shot to send the game to OT. UCOnn was my National Championship pick and they're still alive. Yo son I'm in it to wint it knw wat im sayin.. I want that TV muthafucka. Aight UCOnn is my national championship pick and I want UCONN to win so that shit can go my way. UCONN's up by 3 now now yea baby yea. Up by 4, Washington called TO, hopefully UCONN will win. I need this. I do. Hilton needs to hit this. YES. UCONN up by 5.

No wASHINGTOn STOle it but UCOnn stole it back. YEAAAA. I am HAPPY.

Williams hit two and UCONN won. I am so happy. This is better than sex!

If UCONN beats George Mason, they go final four and they become closer

to the national championship. I am this close to that TV. UCONN won.

YEAJHHH baby, I want that tv muthherfucker.

It was March Madness and I entered a contest on facebook where I predicted the outcome of each game. The winner won a 27-inch plasma screen TV. After that game I was in 2nd place, and three of my final four picks were still in the elite 8. I was very optimistic about winning a TV.

3/26/06

So I had a bad basketball day. I'm basically done in terms of

getting the tv. Why did Memphis and Texas have to lose on the same

day? Not fair. Whatever. I went out, got drunk and chilled with good

friends. It was a fun night. I ran into girls I knew too. Some girl gave me

her number but let me tell you some weird ass shit. I think it would be cool

to have a female friend without an ulterior motive to fuck. I've never

really had a friend that was a girl and I wonder what its like to be close to

a woman that I'm not fucking. Honestly, Christina's my fest friend. I know

nobody else would like me more. I saw PB, or TITS or whatever you want to call that bitch and I didn't even try to talk to her. I just don't care. I have something meaningful and I won't let it get ruined because of TITS. I hate Binghamton girls, I do. Even when I was getting them I was talking all this shit. It just goes to show that my shit talking was justified. Whatever, some bitch is probably reading my journal as I write. I tell her to go fuck herself and then I have the entire office ganging her. My life is empty, at least there is alcohol. AT least I don't even know. Im going to bed PEACE.

My floor had a holiday called 3A-L day, which took place every March 26th. The point of the holiday was very simple; you had to be shitfaced by 3:26 pm. The entire day was a blur, so I'll recount what I remember. I started drinking from the moment I woke up and didn't stop, having thrown up at least twice before 1:30. Matt punched me in the face because I wouldn't get out of his chair, since he thought I had vomit on my clothes, but he hit like my little sister so I stayed in the chair and laughed at him. He later apologized and we were friends again.

Somewhere along the line, I realized that I had to meet Vinit and talk about DIL., but by then I was so drunk that I took a 4-hour nap inside the lecture hall instead. After my afternoon nap, I went back to the room and continued drinking, only to fall asleep again. As I lay passed out, Scott came out of nowhere (wearing a gorilla suit) and started jumping up and down on my bed. I freaked out, screaming in terror, only to find out that everyone on the floor was laughing hysterically at my reaction.

I spent the following weekend at Christina's place in the city. She almost didn't let me come over after looking at my wasted facebook picture from 3/26 (where I was completely shit-faced in Matt's chair), and only let me in her house after I took it down.

It seemed strange that Christina was willing to deny me sex over a facebook picture, but since I'd rather fuck than argue, especially about something as stupid as facebook, I took the picture down and caved in to her demand. Although I ultimately gave in to her, Christina's actions provided me with a glimpse into her personality that I really didn't like, and I thought to myself "if this girl's going to try and control me when I'm three hours away from her and not even technically her boyfriend, than what's she going to do if we end up together?"

I fucked the shit out of Christina that weekend. No, that's an understatement. I annihilated that pussy, helping her discover parts of her vagina she didn't know existed, taking out all my frustrations on her

wet, tight, juicy, pink taco.

For a moment, I thought my dick was ruined, that my Adderall

bender had robbed me of my one and only talent, but fortunately that

wasn't the case, as the general was back and ready for battle.

Christina had to ditch me for a few hours to go shopping, so I had

to find something to do. Since I didn't want to stay in the house, I called

up Chris to play basketball. Chris told me that Toby was driving down

from Connecticut, where he was currently living with his girlfriend and her

mom.

I hadn't seen Toby in almost 2 years. Back in high school, the

three of us were inseparable, spending hours upon hours hanging out,

playing basketball and smoking weed, before Toby had a mental

breakdown and got sent away to a boarding school in Utah. His parents

told him that if he graduated from the program and received his high

school diploma, they would've bought him a house, a car, and gave him

full access to his trust fund. Unfortunately Toby never graduated,

choosing instead to leave the program on his 18th birthday in order to be with his girlfriend in Connecticut: so now his parents have nothing to do with him and Toby has neither a diploma nor a job.

Toby looked like shit, haggard, worn-out, and anorexically skinny. He went from having everything handed to him on a silver platter, to being nothing more than a bum whose sole existence consisted of sitting at home, smoking weed, eating fast food, and fucking his girlfriend. It's sad. This kids parents were millionaires, but he pissed it away and was now no better than white trash.

Rest In Peace

When I got back to campus, Manny left me a really sad message, telling me that Carl was in a coma after being hit by a car. He was in critical condition, suffering from a broken leg and swelling in his brain, after being hit by a Mercedes-Benz while running away from 5 kids who tried to rob him.

This was serious. Carl was hanging onto his life by a thread and the doctors had a grim prognosis for his future. They said that even if Carl survived, he suffered from irreparable brain damage so severe that he would be nothing more than a vegetable for the rest of his life.

I woke up the next morning to a message from Manny. Excepting the worst, I checked my voicemail, but nothing could have prepared me for what I was about to hear. Carl was dead. The news filled me with sadness, anger, but most of all shock. I couldn't believe what I was hearing. The situation was so surreal to me that I couldn't even register what had just occurred.

"How was this happening? How can someone my age be dead and how could that someone be my friend?" My mind and body went into a state of shock, followed by numbness, followed by guilt. Carl called me that weekend, asking if I was in the city, but I ignored him, choosing to hangout with Christina because I cared more about getting pussy than chilling with my friend. Maybe if I returned his call, he would've hung out with me instead of going up to Harlem, and would still be alive. But none of that mattered now. My friend was dead and there was nothing I could do about it.

In Memory of Carl Herman dated 4/6/06

Carl died Monday April 3 2006 at the age of 20 from being hit by a car. He was in a coma since Saturday April 1st after being chased into the middle of the street by a group of kids trying to mug him when a car

accidentally hit him. He suffered from a broken leg, swelling in his brain, and would have been nothing more than a zombie had he survived. Carl and I became close last summer when I started going out with him and Manny. We went to this bar called Jessie's on 181st and Broadway throughout the summer, and that summer has a special place in my heart largely because, despite how eventful other aspects of my summer were, going out with Carl gave me an opportunity to soak up these experiences and allowed me to appreciate how privileged my life actually is. Carl was one of the best human beings I ever knew. I never heard him say or do a single mean thing to anybody. Not only that, but he would also be the first person to comfort you when you were feeling down. Just being in his presence always brought joy to me despite how sad or angry I may have been before. Carl, you were a beacon of light in a world of darkness and for that the only comfort I have in your passing is that you are at peace.

The funeral was postponed for over 2 weeks, because the police ruled his death a homicide and needed to conduct an autopsy. His death made the news and the DA tried to charge his assailants with a hate crime, since Carl was white and his assailants were black. The media had a field day and the press kept hounding Manny night and day for a story.

What happened to Carl was tragic, especially because he had such a bright future ahead of him. A junior at NYU majoring in Metropolitan Studies with a concentration in History, this kid was on pace to make a huge difference in the world, and it all came to a screeching halt because 5 kids from the hood wanted money.

4/8/06 By Leroy and Alan

Alan's entry

Rose Williams "the black rose" brought her seed to class on Thursday. The battle will ensue .   yet the victor, shall be the Black Rose.

Leroy's Entry

BlaCk RoSe

Yo one time I banged this bitch and I hit her in the face when I was done with the slut. I cant believe I tricked that hoe into thinking I was rich and shit. That dumb bitch was all up in my shit..and I was like yo you stupid whore ima kick that shit outta youima teach that bitch a thing or two about dojo studies. Ima karate chop that bitch and then round house her in the face. BAM she down…now its time for me to take my

prize. Mediterranian wheat I made her the appetizer then fucked that bitch straight in the face…fuck nah I aint gonna fuck you hoe…I aint gotta condfom ya herdddddd

I stayed in that night. But Alan and Leroy went out and came back completely shit faced. They asked to write a guest entry and made a complete mockery of my journal. Before I go any further, I usually explain myself after each entry in order to avoid coming across as a complete idiot, but there was just no explaining what they wrote because it made absolutely no sense.

During the week, Vinit took me up to University Plaza, where the both of us planned on living next semester. He introduced me to this kid Greg, who was in the pre-med frat with him. Yes, you heard that correctly, Vinit, the same guy who told the cop he was at Sports Bar, when in fact he was throwing up his large intestine outside Lecture Hall 2, was going to be a doctor. Now that's frightening!

Anyway, Greg gave me a tour of the house, telling me how his frat planned on having huge parties every weekend, and that the three of us were going to "do it up big" next semester. We then had a beer and talked about moving in.

The End Of A Tumultuous Relationship

I saw Christina for the last time when I came home for Carl's funeral. However, I had no idea that this would be the last time I would ever see her.

Coincidentally, Carl's funeral was during Passover break, and on the way back from Binghamton, Christina texted me, suggesting we have a quickie before my Sedar. Having the self-control of an infant, I immediately went to her job upon getting into the city, and fucked her from behind for 2 minutes and 15 seconds while she was bent over her desk. I then showed up to my Seder two hours late.

A couple of days later, Christina finally met my parents and they took her out to dinner, before taking her to the ballet. Can you say disaster? I went to sleep midway through the performance and Christina was pissed. She looked at me with a mixture of disgust and embarrassment throughout the show, as though my presence served nothing more than to humiliate to her. I tried to put my arm around her when I woke up, but she pushed my hand away from her like I was some kind of plague.

Christina suggested we get drinks after the ballet, and after what had just transpired, I couldn't have agreed with her more. The waitress at the bar was really hot and struck up a conversation with me. That's when she blew a gasket. This girl must've had some jealousy issues I didn't know about, because she flipped the fuck out, flying into a hysterical rage where she accused me of blatantly hitting on the waitress in front of her face, before knocking over a table and storming out of the restaurant.

"Shit, this is not what I signed up for." I thought, as I chased Christina into the middle of the street in order to calm her down. Tears were streaming down her face at this point and all I could do was stare in disbelief. "Why was she so upset with me when I didn't even do anything?" I asked myself, in a state of puzzlement and confusion. "This made no sense for her to carry on like this, when I was just having a simple conversation about the Knicks."

If there's one thing I'm used to, its seeing women fly off the handle for absolutely no reason. After all, I do have a mom and sister, so I knew just how to handle the situation.

Just fire out compliments! Fire that shit out like a machine gun! Like your playing Time Crisis 3 and have to kill everyone in sight! Tell her how much you love her, how beautiful she is, how you're life isn't

complete without her in it, and do it while gazing soulfully into her eyes.

Than softly kiss her until she calms down.

That's exactly what I did and it worked to perfection. Christina

wasn't even mad by the time we got to her apartment and even

suggested having sex after we'd finished a bottle of wine on her couch.

Expecting to wake up to Christina, I instead woke up to a note

from her. It read:

Dear Sasha,

There are a million things I want to say to

you but I just cant verbalize it, so maybe this

letter will help explain how I feel. Whenever I

think of you I'm filled with mixed emotions,

unsure of whether or not to love you or hate

you. A part of me wishes we'd never met but

an equal part of me can't fathom life without you. Not a moment goes by where I don't think of you and I want nothing more than for us to be together. Unfortunately what I want and what's good for me are two completely different things, and no matter how much I want this to work out, the truth of the matter is that the differences between us are too great to overlook. I mean you're still a kid for chrissakes, how can I expect you to live up to the responsibilities of being in an adult relationship? Baby I love spending time with you, really I do but half the time that we're together I feel like I'm your mother and that's

not what I want in the long run. Maybe that's

because were just at separate stages in our

lives and like I said earlier, no matter what your

intentions are, the fact is that you're still a kid

and theirs no hiding it. I know that one day

you'll grow up but its just not fair for me to

wait for that to happen and neither is it fair

for me to force you to grow up on my

account. So although I love you to pieces I

just don't see how this relationship can ever

work out between us. I still want to bring

you to Greenwich because we had so much

fun together, but I wont do it since it will just make our inevitable goodbye harder than it needs to be. I don't want to end this but I have no choice since we could never be together, so please take this letter for what it is and know that I love you.

Love,

Christina

4/15/06

Its beginning to hit me. Carl is dead!!! There was a gathering amongst friends in honor of Carl. Friends from highschool, college, and other areas of Carl's life all came together to celebrate his life. First we had lunch and later that night, we went up to Jesse's on 181st for drinks, Kareoke, and an evening prayer/sendoff. It was a *very weird night not only because a good friend of mine is dead but also because I saw kids that I haven't spoken to in years. The kind words describing him really made me upset about the fact that dying at such a young age prevented him from continuing to spread joy to others. People were crying and hugging each other during the prayer and it made me realize what a huge difference Carl made in such little time.*

You can't fight nature but you can trust it. Everything in this world matters but nothing matters enough to dwell on it. I realized today that whatever is meant to happen does and it is beyond my control while also realizing that my actions influence certain events. Not only that, but I have a new sense of perspective on life. It's like yeah, Christina and I are fighting but it's not the end of the world. I still have a life ahead of me regardless of whether or not things work out and I'm going to whatever time I have left on this Earth to make it a better place. I'm gonna end this because I'm really tired and say that Carl 's legacy has and will continue to make me a better person.

There had to have been at least 200 people who showed up to Carl's funeral, and it was beyond amazing for me to see how that many people could care about one individual. Seeing so many people cry for him made me see firsthand what an extraordinary person and positive force he was. In less than 21 years, Carl touched so many lives, and it was tragic, because he could have done something really special with himself had he not died so young.

Christina apologized for how she acted the other night and invited me over the day after Carl's funeral. She made me this delicious steak dinner and afterwards we watched "The Graduate". As we lay in bed together with our arms around each other, it hit me how much we've been through, and that despite the obstacles we endured, Christina and I were still together. That's when I realized everything was going to be ok between us.

4/21/06

Yo I just got me some brainziti kid. Sasha you're an asshole!!! You fought with Christina tonight because she somehow found out that I hooked up with a couple of other girls. Yea, it was my fault, I was being a dick when I slipped out tongue that I hooked up with about 60 girls during my entire life. Now I did. Her name is Sherry and she's Irish so I'll call her Mrs. Potato Head. Fucking A she sucked my dick and I showed her the Strenger effect. Wow Sasha you really are an asshole. Asshole asshole

asshole asshole!!!! I may as well give you the names. Fuck that it would take too long. This girl said I was talented no joke. Hopefully I am as talented as I played and as I drive. Yo the Amanda line bitch gave me the wrong number. Whatever, fuck her she had 3 kids. The last thing I need is for 3 people to call me daddy. The night went like this, I played drunk Mario Kart for N64 in which whoever lost had to take shots. We all got wasted and didn't even go downtown. I went downtown.....on Mrs. Potato Head. Seriously, what happened to Christina? It's gonna end by the summer. Enjoy college you may as well and most of all DON'T FIGHT NATURE.

Christina and I got into a huge fight. We were talking on the phone, when she asked me how many girls I've made out up with in the past. Like an idiot, I decided to tell her the truth (for once) and revealed that my number had to have been around 60. Needless to say, Christina got really pissed off and deduced (albeit rightfully) that I wasn't completely faithful to her. She started sobbing hysterically over the phone, saying that she deserved better than to be with a man who constantly lied to and cheated on her.

Christina's been upset and mad at me before, but something was different. Usually I could calm her down by making a joke or just weathering the storm for a few minutes, but this time nothing I said could make her stop sobbing.

After talking to Christina, I had to get drunk. I was going to go to Sports Bar with Ahmed and suggested playing a Mario Kart drinking game before going out. The rules of the game were whoever didn't win had to take a shot. Ahmed was down if I could find someone else to play with; so after asking around the floor, I decided to go into the RA suite and ask this girl Sherry, who was Sarah's suitemate, if she wanted to play.

Sherry and I met on 3/26 when I was wasted out of my mind. We ran into each other a few times afterwards, but I could never remember her name because of how drunk I was when I met her. She thought it was cute that I could never remember her name and gladly agreed to play. By the time we finished playing, we were too drunk to go anywhere and it was too late to go out, so we decided to watch Anchorman in my room.

Somehow Sherry and I ended up on my bed, with her head on my chest and the room to us. She asked me what her name was and I jokingly called her by at least three fake names before making out with her. Shortly thereafter my face was buried deep in her snatch, where she sprayed me with salmon flavored pussy juice and said I was a very talented young man before swallowing my trouser snake.

I went out with Juan the following night. We had a few beers before going to open bar at the RAT, where I ran into none other than Nicole. Seeing her almost ruined my night, until I stumbled into Mary and brought her home with me, because big titties are known to cure depression. As I was leaving the bar with her, Sarah (my RA) ran into me and pulled me aside, asking how my night with Sherry went. I just smiled, shook my head, and walked out the door with Mary.

Back in my room I'm doing the usual, brutalizing her vagina like Godzilla, when all of a sudden Mary began to smell smoke. "Sashhh is there a fiiireee?" Mary asked in a whiny voice, sounding like a valley girl that just spent the past hour and a half inhaling helium from a balloon. "Nah bitch, there aint no fire. Shut the fuck up." I replied, reassuringly. "But Sashhhh, I hear a fire truccckk." Mary slurred, as she shoved her humongous tits in my face while on top of me. "I don't care, keep going. I'm about to cum. The fire can wait." I said, taking her tits out of my mouth in order to speak.

"Uhhhaahaa." I said two minutes later, removing the condom and emptying my load all over her face. "Ok. We should probably go downstairs now. After all, there could be a fire in the building." I said calmly, gathering myself and putting on a pair of Ninja Turtle boxers. "But Sasshhh, I can't go out like this." Mary whined. "Do you not understand the urgency of the situation? There's a fire in the building. Hurry the fuck up and get dressed." I said in an agitated tone of voice, like I was all of a sudden concerned about our safety. "Can I at least clean up?" Mary asked, annoyed and frustrated, as cum dribbled down her lower lip. "No can do babe. Our lives could be at risk and every second counts. Hurry up, I'm doing this for you." I said, handing Mary her shirt so that she could wipe the jizm from her face.

Downstairs in the lobby, I see my entire building congregated outside as I lazily asked the fireman what the commotion was about. "Oh, some kid was smokin' in his room and set off the alarm... maam you got a little something on your face there." The fireman said to Mary, as she gave me a dirty look and ran off. I guess that's the price you pay for trying to save someone's life.

4/23/06

I smashed beer cans on my head. What a night. Fuckin A smashing cans on my head is fun. I'm gonna do it more often and get Parkinsons. Great night I went out with Katzenberg and those muthafuckas and it was fun. I got a number which was cool I guess but it doesn't compare to the last two nights. Yea I fucked Tits last night again. FUckin bitch. There was a fire in the building and I was like keep going bitch theres no fire. Shut the fuck up. Tits aint no person. Fuck her. Fuck bitches.

I found the meaning of freedom. Freedom isn't what you can do but rather its what you can do with your limitations. Your limitations make up who you are. Your character is determined by what you do with what you can't do instead of what you just happen to do naturally or stand for naturally.

I went to a party at the Sig Ep house with Brian, Jay, and Katzenberg. At the party Brian and I played a really epic game of beerpong with two Asian guys. The game went down to the last cup, and every time they shot the ball I smashed a beer can on my head. I was really proud of my newfound ability to crush cans on my head and wasn't shy about showing it off. I had to have crushed at least 12 cans on my head by the time I went to sleep and woke up the next morning to a welt on my head the size of a grapefruit.

I now know how boxers feel after getting punched in the face for 12 rounds. Not only did it feel like I had a conjoined fetus on my head, but I could barely talk in complete sentences and felt as though I had lost at least 20 IQ points.

That night I played beerpong in the girl's suite and got wasted again. I met this guy named Terry, who had a Viagra prescription (don't ask me how), and I offered to trade Adderall for Viagra since I wanted to fuck like a superhero.

While I was walking to my room in order to get my Adderall, Alan asked me whether or not I was going to write about Sherry giving me head in my journal. Sherry overheard our conversation and immediately confronted me on it, storming into my room saying that I was nothing more than a degrading scumbag who she will never hook up with again. (Fine by me. She thought my penis was a chew toy anyway.)

After spending the weekend drinking myself into oblivion, I decided to call Christina and make things right. I guess there's only so much shit a person can take before they walk out the door, because she just wasn't having it. She de-friended me on facebook, deleted me from

AIM, and refused to answer my phone calls. Christina had enough of the

bullshit I put her through, and decided to cut me out of her life for good.

Confronting A Personal Demon

4/29/06

So many conflicting emotions. What do I want to do? What kind

of guy do I want to be? Do I make generalizations about people and put

them into categories in an attempt to gain some sort of understanding in

a lifetime of confusion? The answer to that one is yes. Ever since I can

remember my life has felt empty. Since I was a little kid through high

school, I have just never felt at peace. But whatever, I 'm madd funn to go

out with and surprisingly I get madd pussy. How do people actually k

I ran into Nicole at Sports Bar and it fucked my head up. Instead

of ignoring her like all the other times, I decided to walk up to her and

give her a hug, because truth be told, I missed her like crazy and couldn't

deny that to myself anymore. We got a drink together, and as we talked I

sensed a change in her that I didn't like. Nicole was drunk as hell, flirting

with strange men, and talking to me about all the random guys she

hooked up with. The Nicole I knew didn't drink and she certainly didn't hook up with random guys. She had respect for herself and that's why I wanted to be with her.

Unfortunately the old Nicole was dead, and there was nothing special about this new girl standing in front of me. The girl whom I had once fallen in love with was now no different from every other disgusting skank that I had degraded in my journal, and it depressed the shit out of me. I no longer wanted to interact with people, so I spent the rest of the night smoking cigarettes alone on a bench.

4/30/06

My life is empty but that's ok. I mean other people have worse lives. There are guys out there with no legs and shit and girls out there who are 400 pounds overweight. That must suck. At least I'm not like that, I'm just emotionally empty. It makes me think why the fuck am I at Binghamton? It's not like being here is really gonna help me in the long run. I may as well go to a school like Arizona or Florida and have the time of my life for 4,5, or even 6 years because I'll get the same job either way and not only that but I'll fuck hotter bitches somewhere else. Hey at least I'm not in Summit. Fuck that place was a shithole. Yo 300 kids, I should be glad I'm fucking anybody son.

Yo I blasted Scott in the face with a watergun as he slept that was fun. He got me with a Gorilla suit for like a week and now I'm gonna get him back. Fuck he has not idea what's in store for him. Tonight it's water, tomorrow its V8, Beer, Soda, and a mystery ingredient. Next week, it's smashing pots and pans next to him to wake that fool up.

Nicole and I started talking again, and I was right about there being something different about her. She wasn't the same girl I'd fallen in love with, not even close, but it didn't matter because I was still in love with her anyway.

5/6/06

There is no more sense of certainty. Going out is empty, I have no steady girl, and I don't know who my real friends are. Not to mention that I am unsure as to what the future holds for me or how I am doing in school. I don't know anything and I am alone. It's like this: I'm not sure how much I like the people I go out with but at the same time if I stay in I have no friends at all. I think what I'm gonna start doing is going to the gym on Friday and Saturday nights instead of going out. It's just so pointless. It's scary cause what I if can't function without going out and am thus forced to live this empty life?

I went out with Taylor, Ahmed, and Tony. They're cool but I just didn't feel comfortable. I ran into a few other friends and the same thing happened. Then I left Sports Bar and went to Boca Joes by myself and I still felt uncomfortable. Then I went back to Sports Bar and ran into Mary. I didn't bring her back!!! What is my life coming to? I had to put effort into it!!! She isn't worth effort!!! Finally I realized it and told her that but did I really? I actually thought that she meant no this time and her friends don't like me. It's cause I am an asshole but it really isn't. They just don't think I'm cool anymore because I was even more of an asshole last year and they loved me. This is why girls aren't people.

On another note, I think I may be friends with Nicole again. This makes things even more complicated because I don't know if a) I want her back b) I can get her back or c) I can emotionally handle being with her. If I saw her with another guy I would have just walked up to him and decked him in the face but then I realized that it's not his fault. Something like that could easily happen to me so I should act rational and not try and prove anything. Besides if she is worth liking she wouldn't go for that shit because there are enough guys out there who can kick my ass which would make my relationship with her even more shallow. I like her so much but I can't do it. Just like I eventually fucked up the Christina thing.

She eventually found out that I hooked up with a few other girls and the worst part was that I was lying to her again!!! I was really trying to be good. When I said I should just stay with Christina I did until the Sherry thing and that was because we had a big fight which ultimately ended the relationship. Now she won't return my calls FUCK. Still I couldn't have handled being in a relationship with her. Making a commitment was something I couldn't emotionally handle despite how much I wanted to be with her. It was just fucking me up too much because I am so insecure. That's why I hooked up with a couple of other girls and now I'm pussyless. I am insecure and I need a hug and that's all folks.

Ok. So I know it seems like I'm on the verge of a mental breakdown, but I just had a bad night. Yes, my life may have lacked substance and I felt emotionally empty as a result. But all in all, things weren't so bad. My life was indescribably privileged and I had not a care in the world. A typical day for me consisted of waking up at 10 am, eating, playing videogames, eating, going to class (if I felt like it), playing more videogames, eating, going to the gym, eating, smoking weed, eating, going out, eating again, and going to sleep. My biggest concern was worrying about whom to get drunk with, and when you put things into perspective, I had absolutely no right to complain about anything. Even so, there was no denying that my life lacked purpose, and the fact that I consciously led such a shallow existence was eating away at me.

At Least I Hooked Up With A Bitch

5/7/06

Tonight was a good night. Overall my life may be empty but at least I'm happy tonight. And yo I hooked up with a bitch. Who cares? Her name is random slut #961. She should be back here suckin my dick but who cares? There's always tomorrow. I'm like the BKLYN Dodgers kiddd, wait till next year. Straight up just listen to the rappers. That's my motto cause these guys know there shit. No joke, they get madd bitches so they should know madd bitches. My life is empty but girl's yo fuck bitches. Fuck bitches.

There was this Greek girl who told my friends and I that her brother died last night. That is tragic but I can't even honestly say if she's telling the truth. Is getting wasted and talking about dealing coke and trying to get free pizza a way to cope with something like that? That's what she did. It's weird. I didn't even do that with Carl but I guess it could be different. He was a great friend but he was far from my brother if you understand.

I mean what would happen if I lost my mother or sister? I have no idea what would happen. What would I do? Maybe she did lose him and if that's the case I want to talk to her and make her feel better. All I would want to do was be her friend and be someone to lean on for her. I also wanna fuck her. She was hot. Either way, it's ok because I will do my best to bring joy to others and make those around me happy and satisfied.

I spent the night pregaming and watching the NBA Playoffs with Brian, Jay, and Katzenberg, before heading out to a party at the Phi Kappa Psi house. My recollection from there on in is very foggy to say the least, although I do remember some Asian guy punching his girlfriend in the face like Mike Tyson. I was in the middle of talking to some girl who was a lot older than me; so I told her that I was a graduate TA in the Psychology department in order to impress her. Jay overheard me and decided to play along, so he asked me what was going to be on the final. I told him to read chapters 13-15 and that I expected to see him in class on Monday. Apparently she was also a graduate TA in the Psychology department and asked me whom I was working under. I told her that I was a TA for Professor Westerman, since she was my Psych stats professor and the only person in the department who's name I remembered. Coincidentally, she was also a TA for Professor Westerman and sarcastically mentioned that it was kind of funny that we've never seen each other despite working under the same professor, before promptly walking away from me.

As she walked off, I heard a loud bang and saw a petite Asian girl falling to the floor as though Iron Mike himself had hit her square in the jaw. Before you could say skullduggery, we saw 15 brothers take the guy outside and beat the living shit out of him. We then decided that it was a good time to leave the party.

Upon leaving the party, we stumbled into a cab that was filled with some of the hottest girls I had ever seen. Right when I entered the cab, I blurted out that I had just won the lottery, causing all of the girls to burst into laughter. This one girl named Stacy took a liking to me and invited me to sports bar, where we made out for hours. We were about to leave the bar together when one of her friend's cockblocked me, saying that Stacy was took drunk to think for herself and that she was going to take her home instead of me. Not wanting to come across as a rapist, I played it cool and got her number, since I assumed that I would fuck her within a week anyway[2].

After losing Stacy, we went to Rocky's for pizza, where we met the Greek girl who's brother died. She kept trying to eat our pizza and repeatedly asked if we knew anybody who wanted coke. When she left the pizza place, an 8 ball blatantly fell out of her pocket and Katzenberg picked it up. After a few seconds of deliberation, he walked up to her and said: "excuse me mamn, is this your cocaine that you dropped on the floor?" Her face lit up as though she had lost her only son and Katzenberg miraculously retrieved him. She was so appreciative that Katzenberg ended up getting his first blowjob in the back of the cab.

A Much Needed Ass Kicking

Terry paid me a surprise visit a few days later, knocking on my door at 8 am and asking for Adderall. Yeah, like I was going to give him pills after he came into my room unannounced at the crack of dawn, so Alan and I kicked him out, giving him until the count of 10 to get of our room if he didn't want the shit kicked out of him.

---

[2] I didn't fuck her :(

When Terry left, I went back to sleep, waking up an hour later to study for an exam I had the next day, when I realized my phone was missing. After unsuccessfully looking around my room for a few minutes, I jumped to the conclusion that Terry probably stole my phone, because he was pissed off about not getting Adderall, and was the only other person in the room aside from Alan.

Normally I wouldn't have cared about losing my phone, but this phone was special because it had naked pictures of Christina on it, so I had to get it back. I looked Terry up on facebook to find out where he lived, so that I could go to his room and kick the shit out of him.

When I got to Terry's room, the first thing I saw was a phone that looked identical to mine smashed on his desk in a million pieces. He wasn't there, so I waited outside for him to show up. After a few minutes, I saw him walk into his room and demanded he return my phone.

Terry tried to play coy with me, claiming to have no idea what I was taking about, but I wasn't in the mood for bullshit, giving him until the count of 5 to return my phone, before cocking my right fist back and hitting him square in the nose.

That's when a brawl ensued. Terry responded by throwing three quick punches to my face, all of which landed without doing any damage, and I promptly took him down, landing on top of Terry ready to attack.

Unfortunately, his roommate came in and broke us up before I had a chance to do anything, throwing me out of the room while Terry threatened to call the cops.

I came back to my room feeling indestructible. Although I didn't fuck Terry up, I would have if given more time to mount an offensive.

My feeling of invincibility was short lived, as I was greeted by none other than Terry shortly after returning to my room. See, I came back from the bathroom wearing nothing more than a robe and slippers, when Terry ambushed me, swinging like a madman and catching me with a flurry of punches both to the face and body. Having been caught completely off guard, I had no answer for his onslaught, and fell to the floor after receiving a right uppercut to the jaw.

I was stunned and Terry was now in full mount, beating me to a pulp, when finally a bunch of the guys from my floor pulled him off of me and broke the fight up.

When the melee cleared, everyone on the floor asked me what happened, so I told the guys about how I suspected Terry of stealing my phone. The entire floor than went up to his room to confront him, but Terry adamantly denied having anything to do with my phone, so the guys made him write down the serial number to see if it matched mine. It didn't, and I basically got the shit kicked out of me for absolutely nothing.

Summer Of Lust And Broken Dreams

My summer started out with a bang and I mean literally! My second day back I went to my sister's art show and there was a party at this guy Dave's house afterwards. I really didn't want to go because all of the kids were in high school, but had no choice since I couldn't get in touch with anybody else due to not having a phone.

Throughout the party, I felt bored and uncomfortable. I didn't want to talk to any girls because a) they were in high school and I don't want to go to jail, b) if I went to jail I would get my asshole ripped to shreds on a nightly basis, c) my sister was there and I didn't want to embarrass her by being "that creepy older guy" who hits on high school girls and, d) I would've been really embarrassed if any of these girls rejected me, so I decided to distance myself from every girl at the party and spent the night

hanging out with Leah (my sister).

That was until I met Beth. A Sr. in high school, Beth was

5'2 100 lbs with jet-black hair, a small waist, and a firm round ass

that I wanted to split open. This girl was eyeing me throughout the

party, but I thought nothing of it until she introduced herself, talking

about how she wanted to be a masseuse before I even had a chance

to get her name.

This was like taking candy from a baby, a baby with Down

syndrome. All I needed to do was challenge her to a "massage off"

and boom! 45.38 seconds later I'm fingering her in the bathroom,

making this bitch explode like a terrorist, while she just gave me

head like she's been doing it for 25 years. Can you say marketable

job skills?[3]

Too bad Beth wasn't 18 yet, because I wanted to fuck her

brains out. Whatever, I guess I just had to settle for catching brains

and getting jerked off, since I was way too pretty for prison.

---

[3] It didn't really take me 45.83 seconds to finger Beth in the
bathroom. I made that shit up. If I could really time it like that, I'd
be autistic and getting no pussy.

Beth turned 18 on Memorial Day and I gave her a birthday present she'd never forget. I knew she was in store for a happy birthday, when she greeted me wearing a schoolgirl outfit. This girl did it all, from the short plaid skirt, to the button down shirt exposing her cleavage, to the glasses, and my cock was ready to burst. We started going at it from the moment I walked into her house and spent the entire day fucking like wild animals. Beth was in heaven, and I guess penis cake is the best birthday present a girl could ask for.

This girl was amazing in bed! If I had to compare fucking Beth to anything, I wouldn't be able to, because nothing I've ever experienced has ever felt so good. Beth had the body of a model and the mind of a porn star. She wore costumes. I saw her as a schoolgirl, secretary, nurse, maid, cop, teacher, and pirate. She let me cum on her face and would then lick it off. Her petite frame allowed me to throw her around like a rag doll, and her tiny hands made me feel like Godzilla when she stroked my cock. Not only that, but she was able to literally spin her body 360 degrees while riding me. And her diminutive stature allowed me to pick her up and pound her out against the wall like King Kong. An orgasmatron,

Beth would cum in excess of 3 times per session, making me feel like the white, Jewish, version of Wesley Pipes.

Beth was fucking awesome!! Aside from being the best lay I'd ever had, she was also one of the most down to earth people I've ever met. She was extremely low maintenance and expected absolutely nothing from me, other than to fuck her right. She let me come and go as I pleased, without any kind of explanation whatsoever. There were multiple instances where my friends would invite me out while I was in her apartment, and she'd let me stay out with them all night, provided that I fucked her when I came back the next morning. Beth never made me take her out. As a matter of fact, she spent upwards of $400 on me throughout our "relationship", which, as a huge feminist, I totally supported. I also supported Beth desire to make me breakfast and give me head while I was eating it. Yeah! It's safe to say I'd found the girl of my dreams.

The problem with dream women is that they just aren't real. After only two weeks together, Beth disappeared without any kind of explanation whatsoever, never to be seen or heard from again.

Caught In A Pyramid Scheme

Shortly after Beth vanished, I got a job selling office supplies for a company called Power House Promotions and it seemed like a golden opportunity. I was to go door to door selling various office supplies, ranging from computers, printers, toners, fax machines, paper, etc. and make a 28% commission on what I sold. If I made 10 sales, or over $500 in profits for myself during the week, then I would get promoted to "team leader". As a "team leader", I had the opportunity to build a team around me, and if my team made a certain amount of money I would get promoted to assistant manager, where I would make $1,000 per week, 40% commission on all of my sales, and receive training to open up my own office. Once I opened up my own office, I would make a percentage of all of my employee's sales, plus the 40% commission I was making as an assistant manager. This job was going to make me a millionaire.

7/4/06

Who am I to be talking shit about girls? Have I brought any good to a woman's life? NO, ALL I BRING IS PAIN!!!! It's time to change that. This summer I have became a responsible working adult and it feels great. It's so great that I don't want to go back to school and revert to the Sasha of old. It's such an awesome feeling

working and being able to eventually take care of myself that I want

to take care of a woman

eventually. But I have to stop being such an asshole. I have to think

of the girl more than I think of myself. At this point in my life I have

no problem getting girls. The issue now is that I want to be worthy

of caring for the woman of my dreams. In order to do that I need to

make some changes. Aside from getting more organized, there are a

lot of

emotional things I need to work out and its extremely important that

I become comfortable with who I am as a person instead of simply

being confident in superficial things like my appearance and my

ability to spit game to girls in bars. One day I wanna bring joy to a

woman's life and maybe have a family of my own, but before I do

that I need to grow up and be a man. The question now is how?

Unfortunately, working at Power House Promotions wasn't

all that it was cracked up to be. I couldn't make a sale to save my

life, and found out the hard way that selling office supplies to

complete strangers is fucking hard. My job was entirely commission

based and I would sometimes go days on end without making a

dime. So after three weeks of slaving away at a job that paid me next to nothing, I decided to call it quits.

Broke As A Joke

7/7/06

> *Yo Manny's party's chock full of nutz kid. He rented out a hotel 4 his birfday and right now im at sausage fest 2006. How u gonna talk about respectin women wen u aint got no hoez?*

Manny turned 21 on July 7th and decided to celebrate his birthday by throwing a party in a hotel room. His party was a lot of fun, except for one small problem. Not a single girl showed up, and he rented out an entire hotel room filled with men.

There are certain guys who have a natural aptitude for attracting the opposite sex; Manny is not one of those guys. Aside from the fact that he looks like Comic Book Guy from the Simpsons, this kid had absolutely no clue how to interact with bitches. He didn't bathe, brushed his teeth "when he saw fit", and felt as though good hygiene was "overrated". His opening line for talking to a girl would be to call the bartender over and order drinks for her, and his topic of choice when conversing with the ladies was either politics or religion. This was why Manny's party was filled with men and I had to share a bed with him.

After going out with him all summer, I wasn't the least bit surprised that Manny's party turned out to be a complete and total sausage fest, so I decided to invite Chris, in order to keep me company. After killing a small bottle of Grey Goose between us, we decided to hit up this bar called The Patriot in the hope of meeting a girl. Well, the lady situation at The Patriot was just as bad as Manny's party, so Chris and I had a few pitchers of beer and stumbled back to the hotel pussyless and alone.

The following night, we went bar hopping across the village, asking every woman we came across to "show us her titties" along the way. Unfortunately, instead of seeing beautiful luscious breasts, all I saw was a $180 bar tab.

<u>You're Fired!!</u>

Manny saw firsthand how bad my financial situation was and hooked me up with a job at the Lavelle School for the Blind, where I was to work one on one with this kid named Bryan, who was blind and had cerebral palsy. The job paid $15/hr and I worked over

30 hours a week. The only catch was that Bryan was assigned to work in an animal shelter, and I am afraid of dogs.

Working at Lavelle had disaster written all over it. The dogs were fucking monsters that did nothing but bark and snarl at me the entire time I was there. I was surrounded by vicious beasts and felt paralyzed with fear whenever I went to work. The owners of the shelter could sense that I was scared shitless, and used to bring raging pit bulls within an inch of my face while I supervised Bryan, because they thought it was funny.

Bryan absolutely adored dogs, but since I was too much of a pussy to interact with the animals, I had him sit in the corner and fold newspapers by himself. I wasn't being paid $15/hr to sit on my ass and watch Ralph fold newspapers, which explained why I was "let go" three weeks into the program.

Manny was infuriated when he found out I had lost my job. He went out on a limb for me, putting his "professional reputation" on the line so that I could have work, and I completely fucked him over. After getting fired, Manny no longer wanted to have anything to do with me, and our friendship came to a close.

Alexander Stenger

The Story Of How 3 Drunk Retards Tried To Climb Onto My

Terrace

8/5/06

Tonight was a crazy crazy night. First I almost run a train on a bitch wit 2 of my boys (choooo choooo) and thatn I lose my keys and can't get into my house. I told this bitch I was the vice president of DIL and that it's a clothing company cause we got tshirts. That's all we got cause Vinit cant tie his shoes so I'm like fuck it lets make DIL a clothing company cause we got clothes. I went to his crib and saw him in an astronaut outfit and I knew it was game over. Anyway, back to the bitch. So yea I'm with Chris and Toby at a bar and this bitch invites us to her house so she can model for DIL and taste some Pickle Juice and then Toby threw up on her so no pussy for us. Its all good I dunno if I'd want that anyway. I mean it would be cool to triple team a bitch with 2 of your boys, but not having genital herpes is pretty cool too.

So now I'm locked outta the house cause I lost my keys and Toby took a shit on my neighbors front lawn. Good JOB! And I gotta figure out how to get into my house without keys right now. The 3 of us must join forces. POWER RANGERS UNITE!! Chris and I climbed onto the top of the second floor garage like ninjas but the Jack drained Toby of his ninja powers so I had to squat Toby onto the roof like the BeastMaster. Man that shit hurt. I gotta start doing legs at the gym. Than Chris helped me onto the garage. After that, Toby climbed onto the ledge of the 2nd floor terrace and both of us grabbed one of his legs and he got to my building sneaking through the bathroom window like SpiderMan to let us in. That was crazy, I felt like an action hero. Arnold watch out, I'm the new Predator! Only the sexual kind sonn!

My parents went away for the weekend and I had the house to myself, so I decided to call Chris. He told me that Toby had driven down from Connecticut in order to visit, and the 3 of us reunited to have one of the most memorable nights of my life. We started drinking from the moment they stepped foot in my apartment and didn't stop until we stumbled home at the crack of dawn.

Chris saw that I was playing NBA Jam in the living room and suggested making a drinking game out of it, where we adjust the game settings to put the clock speed on extra fast, and whoever scored the most points at the end of each quarter stayed on, while the loser had to sit out take a shot of Jack Daniels. That's when things got out of control, and all 3 of us were bombed by the time we left my apartment to go out,

especially Toby, since he hadn't played Sega Genesis since 1994.

We decided to stay local because Toby didn't have a fake ID and

the Riverdale bars don't card before midnight. On the way to the bars, I

thought it would be really funny if I started pissing on the doors of cars

that were nicer than mine, because I don't have a car. By the time all of

us arrived at the bar, I had emptied my bladder on every automobile in

the neighborhood and felt that it was time to replenish myself.

So now all three of us are at the bar, barely able to stand up

straight, but that wasn't going to stop us from drinking more. The bar was

completely dead, so the 3 of us spent the night drinking pitchers and

playing fingers in an attempt to get as drunk as humanly possible.

For the next few hours, absolutely nothing eventful happened.

That was until some random girl walked into the bar and struck up a

conversation with us. I told her that I was the Vice President of a

woman's clothing company called DIL and began making up clothing

designs off the top of my head. I told her that DIL means heart in Arabic

and began lightly tracing hearts with my finger all over her chest, ass, and

inner thigh.

312

By this point, Chris and Toby had jumped into the conversation, so I told her that Chris was in charge of marketing and that Toby was in charge of manufacturing. Chris then suggested that she model for DIL. This girl thought it was a great idea and invited us to her apartment, so that she could "show us what she's working with".

Here I was in a strange apartment, about to triple team a girl with two of my best friends, something I never thought would happen in either my wildest dreams or worst nightmares. This girl was now in her thong, on top of Toby and making out with him, while simultaneously rubbing both my cock and Chris's. I couldn't believe what was about to happen, and felt that the only thing missing from this situation was a video camera.

Boy was I right about that statement! But not in the way that you dirty minded folks reading my book think. Right when Toby and Princess Gangbang finished making out, Toby preceded to throw up on her, causing all 3 of us to be kicked out of her apartment immediately.

A part of me was mad at Toby, but a larger part of me was extremely grateful to him. Triple teaming a chick didn't rank very high on my list of things to do in life, and I was actually relieved to have gotten out of that situation unscathed.

Right as we arrived back at my apartment, I realized that I had lost my house keys somewhere during our night of misadventure. This was fucking bad!! I was locked out of my house and nobody in my family had an extra key. Toby was taking a shit on my neighbor's lawn and Chris was too busy laughing at him to be of any help whatsoever. I began flipping out and almost had a mental breakdown, when all of a sudden I remembered that the window of my terrace was unlocked. Now the questioned remained, how in the hell were 3 drunken retards going to climb 2 stories in order to get onto my terrace?

Chris and I had recognized the seriousness of the situation and had somewhat sobered up. We lit up a joint and brainstormed of a way to climb onto my terrace, while Toby lay on the grass passed out covered in shit. There was a roof covering our garage on the 2nd floor, so we decided to climb up and use the terrace on that floor to pull us up to our apartment. Chris and I made it up to the 2nd floor with ease, but still had to worry about Toby, who could barely walk, much less climb onto a roof. Toby was completely useless, but we needed him, because without a 3rd

person, there was no way that Chris or I could get onto my terrace. Since I was considerably stronger than Chris, it was my responsibility to pick Toby up and literally squat him onto my shoulders so that he could make it up to the roof. Chris volunteered to climb onto my terrace, because he was the lightest one out of all us, and I had to squat a shit covered Toby onto the roof. Chris got onto the ledge of the 2nd floor terrace, where Toby and I each grabbed one of his legs and catapulted him onto our terrace, allowing him to crawl into my house through the bathroom window.

Realizing What I Did Wrong

8/ who the fuck cares/06

I am afraid of girls. All the shit I say in my journal is entirely based on fear of getting hurt. But it's such bullshit, everything I write in here, because getting hurt is part of life. I am a real asshole who cares only about himself and how the world relates to him. The fact that I refer to women as bitches and hoes and nothing more says it all. I mean there's really no reason for me to be talking about women like that. It serves no purpose other than to give me bad energy and there's no need for that. It's not even about respecting women or any or that nonsense, what it really is about is exuding a good aura because nothing positive will ever come about from calling a woman a bitch. I wanna live a happy and positive existence but how the fuck am I gonna do that when I relate to an entire group of people so negatively? These women are my neighbors on planet earth, a part of my natural environment, and you need to respect your environment in order to be spiritually at peace. Even beyond everything I just said, life is way to short to waste it being negative.

I see now why I fucked up with Nicole. I thought it was cause I wasn't man enough for her or that she left once she saw past my image of bullshit, but its way beyond all that. Nicole left me because I didn't get it until now. See the reason things didn't work out with her is cause of this fucked up attitude I have. Bitch this, bitch that, you can never treat a girl right if you think like that. I thought I treated you like princess but that's only cause I'm comparing you to girls like Mary who I've treated like garbage and you're way, way, way above that. I mean I treat homeless people in the street better than I treat those kinds of girls because I give them food, so the fact that I treat you like a princess compared to how I treat Mary says nothing, because everyone's a princess compared to how I treat girls like that.

But I see the light and I'm gonna do whatever it takes to show you that I'm a changed man. I want you back! I miss the way your hair smells, the way you look at me, and how your body feels cuddled up to mine. You're an angel, a goddess, and I'm gonna do something to show how much I love you, I don't know what it is yet, but it's gonna be beautiful.

I saw Jason for the first time in 9 months (see part 3). Jason had wanted to study finance, but didn't have the grades to get into the School of Management at Binghamton, so he decided to transfer to SUNY Albany last semester.

We hadn't spoken to each other since he left, and I decided to give him a call to see how he was doing. We ended up hanging out and smoking a blunt on my terrace, when out of the blue he asked me if I still talked to Nicole. I told him that Nicole and I had a falling out, that we had barely spoken since breaking up.

Jason asked why we stopped speaking, so I told him about the pain, the pain of not being able to hold her, to kiss her, to run my hands through her hair, to know that everything was going to be ok because we were in each other's arms, and that whenever I saw her, I knew that things could never go back to the way they were between us.

The more I talked about Nicole, the more I began to miss her. I remembered our sleepovers freshman year, where we would do nothing but lie in bed and cuddle, and that all of my problems would go away whenever we lay next to each other.

Nicole meant the world to me, but she had absolutely no idea how strongly I felt about her. In my mind I treated her like a goddess, but in reality I treated her like nothing more than a hook up buddy, only treating her well by comparison to the girls I treated like shit

Even after all this time apart, I would rather lie in bed and do nothing with her than do anything else with any other girl in the entire world. Nicole was the kind of girl that I wanted to buy flowers, cook dinner for, and watch the sunset with. And I had to get her back. She needed to understand how special she was, so I decided to pour out my heart to her in the form of a handwritten letter.

Dear Nicole,

There's so much I need to tell you but I don't know where to begin. Since we fought and parted ways, I felt as if there was

something missing. I feel a gaping hole in me

that can't be shut or seared closed. I've tried

being with other women and just having a good

time with my friends, but no matter what I do

I'm always preoccupied with thoughts of

you. I miss you so much that no amount of

words can ever describe the pure loneliness I

feel when you're not around. There's so much

I want to say but I can't, because no amount

of words can ever do you justice.

I treated you badly. I didn't know any

better. My understanding of respect was

warped; you were right about that. I just

didn't know how to express how much I

appreciated and loved you, and when I got upset

with you, I behaved according to what I knew,

which was bullshit. I admit to you that I do

not know much about treating women with

respect and dignity, and it's a constant issue I

have to deal with. But obviously, the history I

have which has led me to such wrong behavior

and my wronging you does not excuse it. I

just can't do anything except tell you that I

was so wrong, and I am so sorry and I want

to do whatever is in my power to make you

happy.

I want you back. I don't know how I'll

make it better for you, but I will do what I

can. I want to be the guy who gives you soup

when you're sick and comfort you when you're

upset. I want to do things for you regardless

of whether or not I benefit from it. I want

to cook dinner for you, take long walks on the

beach, and buy you flowers. I can't guarantee

that everything will be better, but I beg of you

to not give up on me. What is most important

to me right now is that you know that I

accept that I was wrong. The responsibility

of our relationship faltering is strictly and

solely on me. And for that no amount of

words can describe how sorry I am for all the

pain I've caused you. At the darkest moments

of my day and evening, I'm sorry that you ever

knew me, because of what I did to you.

Please believe that I would never want to hurt

you.

I love you Nicole. I long for you. I

long to touch your hair, and I long to hold you

while we sleep in bed. I want to hold you and

feel that feeling when those who love each

other have found each other. I long to talk to you and to be comfortable with you, and you with me. I long for that bliss, that bliss of being yours.

And if I could have that, then no amount of being with other women would ever usurp such a special and powerful feeling. No amount of sex, drugs, or alcohol can replace a fraction of the time we spent together. Despite the worst, during the good periods, I could feel that we had something special, even if we can't admit to it or grasp what it is now. I truly believe that those moments where we fully experienced that special thing

outweighed and overshadowed all the bad that

existed.

I won't ask you of anything. I just

want you to know. Know in your heart that I

love you.

Sasha

For days on end, I waited for a reply. A phone call, a text message, something, but nothing ever came. I sat by my computer for hours, hoping she would IM me, and whenever my phone rang I jumped with excitement at the possibility of hearing her voice again. After over 2 weeks of waiting with bated breath, I finally received an e-mail from Nicole.

Dear Sasha,

I really appreciate the letter. That letter was one of the sweetest things anybody has ever sent me. I never knew you felt this strongly about me and what you wrote was beautiful, but it's just too late. I'll always care for you because we've been through a lot and had a history, but too much has happened for us to get back together. I wish I understood how you felt earlier because than maybe we could've worked things out, but right now I just want to stay single. I'm still young and so are you and I just want to go out and have fun without having to be tied down in a relationship. Don't take this the

wrong way, I care for you but I just don't

look at you the same way that you look at me.

I'm sorry.

Nicole

    Nicole had moved on with her life and it was about time I do the

same. Yes I was crushed, and yes I was heartbroken, but at least I could

take comfort in knowing that I did my best. Nicole may no longer want to

be with me, so the best I could do was take our relationship for what it

was and use it as a learning experience to make me a better person.

PART 5

FUCK IT ALL

This past year was fucking rough. I got fired from my job at a special needs camp, rejected from a Frat that I wanted to pledge, dumped by my girlfriend, made into a pariah by my suite mates, had to bury one of my good friends, got my ass kicked in front of everyone on my floor, slaved away at a job that paid me next to nothing and left me broke, got fired from my last job for being afraid of dogs, and got rejected by Nicole when I tried to get her back. Having gone through so much shit in such a short period of time left me feeling as though things weren't in my control, and that the only thing I had control over was whether or not I enjoyed myself. Being in a positive frame of mind became my sole objective, and I decided to do whatever I wanted whenever I wanted. If I didn't want to go to class, I wouldn't, and would either smoke weed, play videogames, go to the gym, or get laid instead. If I decided to go to class, but was no longer interested in what the professor had to say, I would get up and leave without any hesitation. If I had an exam, but didn't feel like studying for it, I would go out and get drunk instead. After all that had transpired, I felt as though I were unable to function in society, so I decided to have as much empty and meaningless fun as I wanted without any regard for the consequences.

Vinit ended up graduating early, so I ended up living in University Plaza with Greg (see p. 196) and this kid Paul from New Paltz. From the moment I set foot into the door, I was in love. I had my own room, equip with its own bathroom, a state of the art kitchen, common room, and a backroom with a beerpong table already set up. University Plaza was like a luxury apartment, and living their caused me to feel like a king.

Paul became my partner in crime. A 5'3 skinny kid with sandy blond hair and blue eyes, who couldn't have weighed more than 100 lbs, this guy had the ability to out drink and out smoke 300 lb offensive linemen with ease. Here was a kid who loved getting fucked up just as much as I did, and the two of us put on a shit show together. We would go out 3-4 times a week, smoke weed everyday, and play beerpong in between classes. Paul and I were the dynamic duo of alcoholism, and if getting blitzed were a videogame, both of us would've been unlockable characters.

A Vacation From Writing But Not From Drinking

9/2/06

This will be my last journal entry. It's over. The journal, it's all the same thing. I'm only a Jr. but I really don't see myself progressing in life. In fact, I think I was more well adjusted as a freshman. Drinking never brought me any satisfaction. All it did was blind me from the real issues plaguing me. I'm just at a loss for words right now. I just really don't know what to say. I guess the most I can say is I'm sorry and even that's not good enough. There are no words that can describe how much I miss Nicole. I cry myself to sleep thinking about her every night if that's any consolation. Yet no matter what, I was the one who disappointed her. Baby I'm so sorry! This book was meant to end tragically. It had tragedy written all over it unless I drastically changed my life which would never happen unless this book officially comes to an end. If this book got published, it would be a mockery of human literature and for that I want to apologize to all the great authors of my time.

Nothing eventful happened that night. At least nothing I can remember. All I remember is coming home feeling sad, hopeless, and dejected, so I decided to take a break from my journal and focus on myself.

Blue Balls and Throw Up

Just because I stopped writing in my journal doesn't mean that I stopped going out. As a matter of fact, I was going out more than ever before, and some of my craziest nights happened during my break from writing.

Two days after writing my "last entry", Paul's friend Adam, who he knew from home, ended up bringing 3 extremely hot girls over to our place. These girls were out of control, and within an hour of us drinking, they were 3-way kissing each other and licking whip-cream off each other's tits. One of them even started sucking on the tip of a beer bottle as though it were a dick.

Adam's friends wanted to get drilled, and we were just the guys to do it. Adam ended up fucking this girl Tina on our couch and Greg passed out from drinking too much, ao Paul and I ended up playing beerpong with Tina's friends, Lacy and Kim, until 5 a.m.

Talk about an x-rated game of beerpong. Whenever Paul and I had to shoot, Lacy and Kim would distract us by flashing their tits, shaking their ass, rubbing our dicks through our pants, or making out with each other. Whenever it was their turn, the girls would take prolonged breaks in order to make out with us.

This went on for over 3 hours and I was hard as a rock. Unfortunately, relief would never come, because just as Paul took Kim into his room to pound her out, Lacy began violently throwing up all over our beerpong table. My boner instantly went away and I went to sleep alone, with the bluest case of blue balls imaginable.

Not fucking Lacy was the best thing that ever happened to me. Paul and I got breakfast after he finished impaling Kim, and he told me some shit about Lacy that blew my mind away. Apparently Lacy was a huge skank. She had a boyfriend who she would cheat on with a different guy every weekend; Lacy even had a train run on her a few times (all before her 18th birthday). Yeah! That's right, Lacy was only 16, and if that weren't disturbing enough, her dad happened to be the Binghamton Chief of Police. **Good Thing I didn't Hit That!!**

<u>Sometimes Date Rape Happens To Guys</u>

The following week I got date raped. Well sort of. Adam's girlfriend from home came up to visit and brought two of her friends with her, one who was a recovering alcoholic. Why a recovering alcoholic would want to visit Binghamton of all places, where there is nothing to do but drink, is beyond me, but that's neither here nor there.

Anyway Adam, Rachel (his girlfriend), Paul, Becky, Jenna (AA girl), and I smoked a blunt in the common room before playing beerpong. Jenna just watched because she doesn't drink anymore, so the rest of us took turns playing pong and taking shots before going out to the RAT.

At the RAT, all of us shared a scorpion bowl (a gigantic bowl filled entirely with alcohol, topped off with a drop of fruit punch, in order to give off the impression that it's an actual mixed drink) except Jenna. I was now completely shitfaced and have absolutely no recollection of anything that happened past that point, except that Jenna randomly crawled into my bed and woke me up by giving me a blowjob while I was passed out drunk. Just for the record, Jenna and I hadn't spoken to each other until that point, and I would be surprised if she even knew my name.

A Lesson In Karma

I also almost went to jail. It was Roshashana break and I needed to buy weed for the long weekend/car ride back home, so I called Adam in order to pick up a baggie.

While taking out money from the ATM, I noticed that the guy who used the machine before me had forgotten to take his card out, and the machine asked if I would like to make an additional withdrawal.

Because I'm not a complete asshole and had no desire do buy anything other than pot, I only took out $20, before throwing the guys card into the garbage (so that nobody would steal his money except for me) and heading to Adam's room, where I spent the entire day taking hits from his vaporizer.

A few hours later, Adam and I were in the CIW dining hall eating everything in sight (because smoking weed all day works up an appetite), when Paul called me, suggesting we pick up a 30 rack of Keystone's at GIANT.

Since I was the only one with a chalked ID, it was up to me to wait in line and buy the beer. Not a problem. Binghamton was an economically depressed shit hole that reminded you of a bad episode of the Jerry Springer Show, and there was no way in hell that the toothless redneck behind the counter was going to reject my ID. Besides, underage

drinking is the town's primary source of income, so there was really

nothing to worry about.

Everything was going great. I was high off my ass without a care

in the world, getting my ID checked by "Cletus The Slack Jawed Yokel",

when out of the blue I was approached by the store manager, who asked

to take a second look at my ID. He examined my ID like a forensic

scientist for what seemed like an eternity, before taking it into his pocket

and asking me to follow him into his office.

Before I even had a chance to sit down, I saw a flash go off. The

manager had just taken a picture of me and gave me a lifetime ban from

every GIANT in Binghamton. "How old are you?" the manager asked,

staring me down like Wanderlei Silva, as I reclined comfortably in the

chair he laid aside for me. "I'm 26. I was born on June 8th 1980. Check

my ID". I said confidently. "So you think this is a big joke don't you?

We'll see how funny this is when I call the cops."

The manager then left his office, returning 5-minutes later

accompanied by a police officer. The first thing the cop asked me was if

I'd ever been arrested, and that's when I remembered the gram of weed I bought from Adam. The cop could've searched me whenever he wanted, and I would've gotten into some serious trouble if he had found the bag of weed in my pocket, so I decided that cooperating with him would be in my best interest. I told the officer that I just had a big exam and wanted to have a few beers in order to celebrate, that I had no intentions of hurting anybody whatsoever. The cop told me that he didn't "give a flying fuck" about what my intentions were and to "answer the goddamn question", before leading me outside.

I thought I was fucked. The cop was leading me to his car, about to arrest me and find the bag of weed, when he saw Paul and Adam standing outside their car waiting for me. He asked me if the three of us were together, and I told him that we were, but that I was the only one drinking. The cop knew I was full of shit and asked me if Binghamton University offered courses in lying to police officers. I said no, and after intensely staring me down from head to toe, he asked me for my information and let me go with nothing more than a warning.

Phew! That was a close call. And my run in with the law made me a firm believer in Karma. I had stolen $20 from someone and had gotten my fake ID taken away from me that same day. If I hadn't taken that money out of the ATM, than maybe the manager at GIANT wouldn't

have confiscated my ID and banned me from the store. But what if I had

taken out a lot more money? I had the opportunity to take out hundreds,

if not thousands of dollars, but I didn't, choosing to only take out $20 for

weed. Had I taken out a larger sum of money, I probably would've been

arrested, made to pay a huge fine, and wound up with a criminal record.

If that's not Karma, than I don't know what is.

<u>Role Model My Ass</u>

I saw Toby over Roshashana break. His girlfriend broke up with

him, so he ended up moving back in with his family due to having

nowhere else to go. Toby's mom made him join the army as a condition

for returning home, and he's working on his GED in the mean time.

I hadn't seen his mom in almost two years and boy was she happy

to see me. Giving me a tour of their new 14-room mansion in Great Neck,

before making us pancakes. Toby's mom made feel like I was part of the

family.

As we ate, she talked about how proud she was of me, and that

by going to Binghamton I was a role model for what Toby could

accomplish. **Ha!** Good one Mrs. Goldberg. If only you knew how I spent my time? That I never went to class, fucked around with random bitches (who I treated like garbage), and won't amount to shit, because I'm drinking, smoking, and fucking my way through college.

9/30/06

I thought I was done but I'm not. I can't, it wouldn't be fair to my readers. I'm not 21!!! I owe it to my readers to write an entry on my 21st birthday. Tonight was so much fun. I saw Mary last night, went home with her and smoked weed with her all day. I was talking madd shit about her throughout my journal but I realize she's madd cool. Her and her housemates are like girl versions of half baked. That's ill, I'm gonna fuck her and smoke weed all day. That's what I want my relationships to be like. I love making people happy. Thatn's my mission. Yea Yea Yea my triggays. The world is gonna end in 5 years its PHYSICS BITCH. 2001 a Space Oddsey sonn. Yo some drunk retard at the RAT is gonna one day control a nuclear bomb. Yo that's some scary shit.. How am I on page 251. Muthafuckaah. That sounded Arab. Then, I smoked with Paul). I then took the ultimate weed nap. Then I got wasted and railed an ADDY. I then had 2 scorpion bowls and a couple shots. I saw Mary again. Then I saw this bitch Pam who was the girl Jeff wanted. Jeff likes big hard rock *solid dick up his ass. I hope when I publish my journal its on the English*

Regents in 2026 one of the questions will be who likes big hard rock solid

dick up the ass and the answer will be Jeff Watson for 1 and 2/3 of a point.

He has a girl friend. Fuck her she's a bitch. I'll bang her and write about it.

She fucked some other dude on his couch in front of him last semester and

he took her back. That guy is gonna be one of those guys who marries

some bitch and she starts fucking 12 black guys at once while Jeff sits in

the corner crying and jerking off. I can't even comprehend that shit.

Guess that's what happens when you're a nice guy. You're girl gets

pounded out by the New York Knicks while you sit there and watch. But yo

I hate those guys. The nice guys not the Knicks. I'll be a Knick fan till I die.

But yo those fucking nice guys piss me off, always telling me to respect

women and shit when they haven't had pussy since pussy had them. Who

are you to talk to me about women? Let me tell you something about

women. I like having sex with them!!! Oh yea, I made out with Pam. Her

man was wating for her at home. Good Job Buddy!! Than I got a cab back

with no money and got stuck with 8 or 9 sexy ass bitches. I won the lotto

kiidddd. I made out with this blond bitch and then tore that ass up when I

got back to her crib. That sexy bitch. She had a fat asss sonnn, shit was

bubblicious if you know what I'm sayin. Than she paid for my cab cause I got my pimp cane on but its all good cause I paid that bitch back in semen. Gotta love those freshmen!!!

Vinit came up to Binghamton that weekend. And we started drinking from the moment he walked in the door. Friday night was a blur, so I'll explain what I can remember to the best of my ability. Paul, Vinit, and I had at least 10 shots of Vodka and smoked a blunt before going out, coincidentally sharing a cab with my friend Joey from home, who had just transferred to Binghamton this semester. Joey was whacked out of his mind, and spent the entire cab ride entertaining us with a story about how he got head on the dance floor at Sports Bar from some girl who looked like she could play Offensive Line for the Jets.

The next thing I remember was sharing a scorpion bowl before going to Sports Bar, where I ran into a bunch of Mary's housemates. All of us ended up taking shots together and I drunkenly told her best friend that the only reason I behaved like a dick to Mary was because she seemed to get turned on by the way I treated her, and that I was afraid she wouldn't like me if I were nice to her. Her friends said I was adorable, and brought me back to their house so that I could fuck Mary.

The next morning Mary and her housemates smoked me up on four bowls, a joint, and a blunt. The fact that they willingly smoked me up on that much weed without asking for anything in return made me see these girls in a different light.

For far too long, I thought of them as nothing more than a bunch of bitches, low class pieces of shit that deserved to be treated like garbage, when the truth of the matter was that they were just really nice girls who liked to share. Just because they slept around and liked to fuck didn't give me the right to look down on them. Besides, who was I to look down on a girl for sleeping around when I was doing the exact same thing?

Mary may not have been "relationship material", and there was no way in hell I'd ever go out with her, but she still deserved to be treated with respect. For the past year and a half, Mary has done nothing but share her pot with me, while letting me fuck her without any strings attached, and there was absolutely no reason to degrade a girl who has done nothing other than given me pleasure.

I was high as balls by the time Mary dropped me off. Paul and Vinit were watching 2001 A Space Odyssey in the common room, and Paul asked me if I wanted to smoke. "Um, Yes. You may as well have asked

whether or not the Pope was Catholic." I thought, while taking hits of his

Roor bong, before drifting off into a weed-induced slumber.

I woke up disoriented and covered in drool, to the sound of Greg

and his "frat brothers" playing beerpong. Talk about a pathetic excuse for

a frat. Two thirds of his fraternity was composed of girls, most of who

didn't believe in premarital sex. At least half of the members were

straight edge and over 75% of them were virgins, who thought that a "ho"

was some kind of gardening tool. One of them even busted out a pack of

YU-GI-OH cards while we were playing beerpong. Greg's "frat" was like a

sorority for men, and hanging out with them made me feel as though I

were at a Japanese Anime Convention instead of a party.

So anyway, Paul and I spend the night hanging out with Greg's

"forority" (cross between a fraternity and a sorority), taking enough shots

to kill a horse, before heading to Sports Bar with Vinit.

At Sports Bar, I ran into Pam, the cum guzzling slut that Jeff had a

crush on last semester, and we ended up making out until 3 a.m. I

wanted to bring her back to my place, but Pam told me that she couldn't,

because her boyfriend was waiting for her at home. Classy.

The bars were now closed and I had drank away all of my money. Paul and Vinit had already gone back to University Plaza, and I had to figure out how I was going to get home. That's when 8 or 9 of the drunkest girls I've ever seen hopped into a cab.

"Money's overrated. I just saw a bunch of hot ass bitches jump into a cab (cause they're all hot ass bitches when your wasted). I'm going in."

Before I had a chance to sit down, some blond freshman pulled me onto her lap and began making out with me. "Your cute. Can I take you home with me?" She slurred incoherently. "Sure, but only because I care about your feelings as a woman." I mumbled, just as incoherently. "Awww, your sweet. Why can't all guys be as nice as you?" She swooned, as though the man of her dreams was standing beside her, and we had sex three times once we got back to her dorm. If only I could remember her name.

10/4/06

Yo today was an ill day. Pam came over at around 3 and we spent the day having sex, getting high, and watching porno together. Fuck listen to what I just said. I WATCHED PORNO WITH A BITCH. And Yo IT WAS HER

IDEA. She wanted to watch a gangbang and than told me to call her a dirty little slut and pull her hair while we were fucking. Shit man I guess this is just living proof that girls get turned on when you degrade them. How can you even say its wrong to call a woman a bitch when she's asking you to call her that? Who knows maybe it's just her, but I'm starting to think that girls are nothing more than guys without penises. Whatever man, this shit aint my problem, its not like I'm gonna ever call that bitch again.

So anyway, I kicked Pam outta the crib and played beerpong with Paul before going to the RAT and bringing Mary back. She's asleep cause I put her to sleep with my big fat Kosher Sausage so now I'm writing in my drunken journal. That's crazy I went from being "no pussy guy" to fucking two girls in a day like its nothing. I'm a whole new man and I owe it all to you Binghamton University.

My life was a dream and a nightmare rolled into one. Here I was, living this extremely carefree existence, banging girls left and right, smoking weed all day, getting drunk every weekend, and playing Playstation in between. Don't get me wrong, I was happy. How could I not be? I was doing whatever I wanted, whenever I wanted, but there was a huge problem in that I had absolutely nothing substantial to pride

myself on. My life had no direction and I lacked a basic plan for the

future. I no longer cared about school and my grades began to plummet.

I felt that no matter what I did, I was destined for failure, so I abandoned

all hope and accepted the fact that I wouldn't amount to shit.

10/7/06

So here I am in Mary's bed again. I saw her at the RAT and went

home with her AGAIN. Now she's asleep and I'm writing my journal entry

on my stomach. If only you were Nicole.

I was having the time of my life, getting drunk and boning bitches

on the regular, but no matter how often I went out or got laid; I couldn't

hide the fact that I was lonely. Despite having a lot of friends, I had

nobody to talk to and felt as though each and every one of my

relationships were centered on partying. I was incased in a bubble of

superficial happiness, and once that bubble burst I would be left all alone.

10/11/06

I'm an auhor!!! It's official this shit is copyrighted. I'm so happy. It

doesn't matter I wrote a book. Who can say that? Oh yeah I got a 3.5 gpa; but I wrote a book so fuck you!!!!! Wait I forgot something, FUCK

YOU !!!!!!! Oh yeah, FUCK YOU!!!!!!!! Did I miss something, oh yeah, the

ad for Strenger Effect Cologne. Witout it your game

is defective. Bitch IT's Physics. Am I dead, no I'm alive and kickin it!!!

Bitch it's physics!!! Wait Fuck you!!! **BITCH IT"S PHYSICS!!!B.** *Who*

knows. The world may end but tonight was the shit. I followed my dream

of being an author. I accomplished something which is actually doing

something for myself. I wrote a journal on my own which nobody can take

away. I wrote my feelings which nobody can take away. That's

PRICELESS!!!!

Nicole, all I think about is how beautiful you are. I just want to

hold you and tell you how beautiful you are and how much I love you. If

there's one thing I wish it's that Nicole realizes how much I love her from

my journal. That's worth more than any money or endorsements I may

get from it. Baby I'm sorry I couldn't do it. I was just too scared to subject

you to the pain of my pleasure. Fuck, it was the worst mistake of my life.

My only wish is that we were still together. You have no idea how many

times I cried myself to sleep thinking about it!!!! FUCK, I'M A WORTHLESS

PIECE OF SHIT!!! LOSER!!!! You know what, It's all my fault it didn't work out and all I wanna do is spend the rest of my life making it up to you. I

HOPE YOUR HAPPY, I TRULY DO!!!!! Because the truth is that I can't stand

to see you unhappy.

I copyrighted my journal earlier in the day and went out with Paul to celebrate. Nothing crazy happened. We just played beerpong and drank a lot. But I had a great time getting drunk with my friend.

That was until I started thinking about Nicole. I missed her. I missed her touch, her kiss, her smile, her voice, and the way she smelled. I wanted her back and would have given anything in the world just to hold her again. Although I was happy on the surface, deep down I was miserable, because the girl I loved didn't love me back.

A Second Chance

10/15/06

So today could have marked a new beginning. I saw Nicole tonight

and we actually talked for real in person. Hopefully we made up and

eventually Nicole and I will be happy together. I actually told her instead

of wrote to her how I felt. When I saw her downtown I at first ignored her

but then realized that if I truly loved her, the least I would do is talk to her.

*It actually worked. She actually seemed to care about what I said and felt which really meant a lot to me. Last night I stabbed myself in the thumb with a knife. It was an accident, I was drunk and tried to stab through a bottle. I obviously had to bandage my hand and Nicole was the only one who cared enough to notice on her own. It felt as though she loved me too. I love you too!!! I could tell we loved each other or at least I hope she loves me because I'm drunk and who knows if I can tell. Every time I think of her I want to cry. Tonight was worth it. So was stabbing myself since Nicole actually cared about me? She was probably just drunk dumbass!!! That's right I spouted negativity to myself but why? You know what, we could feel the love. **There's nothing I have ever been more confident about!!!!** I'm happy, at least I got to kiss you again. If this doesn't work out, I won't take any negativity from it because at least I got to kiss you. At least we held each other for as little as we did. Everything's ok.*

After months of ignoring her, I finally worked up the courage to tell Nicole how I felt. Normally when I see her out, I would ignore her and leave the bar in order to run away from the pain, but last night was different. When I saw Nicole at the RAT last night, I knew that I couldn't run away forever, and that putting my heart on the line was the only way I could ever hope to get her back.

We went outside, sitting down in the lobby of the Holiday Inn next to the RAT. I explained to her why I wrote the letter, saying that I finally realized what I did wrong, and that if I had another chance I would do whatever it took to make her feel special. I told her how much I missed her, that my life hasn't been the same since she left. But Nicole was skeptical and didn't believe me.

When I wrote Nicole that letter, I poured out my entire heart to her, bombarding her with a torrent of powerful feelings and emotions that had seemingly come out of nowhere. She hadn't the slightest clue how much I loved her, and had absolutely no idea what to make of the letter. Nicole couldn't understand how someone who supposedly felt this strongly about her would've waited so long to write something so powerful, especially after I practically ignored her for almost an entire year. The entire thing made absolutely no sense her, and I realized that nothing I said could have ever convinced her of my sincerity, so I went for broke and leaned in to kiss her.

Nicole looked beautiful, more beautiful than I had ever imagined, and when she kissed me back, I felt like I was walking on air. Holding Nicole that night made me feel as though I were in the presence of an angel, and being in her arms made me feel safe, like someone was

watching over me. For the first time since we broke up, I was whole,

reborn, as though I were a new person, and it was all because I got to hold

Nicole like she was mine again.

10/19/06

Sasha you're an asshole!!! Oh I love Nicole but you hooked up

with two girls tonight? What are you retarded? SHIT!!! You dumbass!!!

How can you say you love her when other girls get in the way so easily.

The worst thing is that I don't know if I could handle her (much less a girl

beating) What the fuck am I talking about? I dunno, I never do. I can't

function in society and I accept it. How the fuck am I at BINGHAMTON?

Seriously!!!! AND how do I get girls? I must be really really hot because

I'm a retard and theres no way any girl would like me based on my

personality. Whatever though, I live a fantasy life I have sex without

dating. That's ILLMATIC!!!! No for real, just make people happy. That

should be your mission in life. You can't make people happy for real

because you can't function but you can make people happy for a little. Is

that bad? No!! If I make 143 people happy for 2 hours that's a lot of

happiness hours and in essence I lead a positive existence. You know what, I'm just a stupid American with superficial happiness. It's okay

cause I have NBA Jam, Madden, Basketball, the gym, alcohol, and pussy.

That was the night I met Jamie. Paul and I had gone out to Sports

Bar to play beerpong and went to the RAT once we lost. Both of us got

blitzed and I don't remember anything, except for hooking up with some

girl on the dance floor whose name or face I cannot recall, as well as

hooking up with another girl outside the Holiday Inn. That other girls

name was Jamie, and she told me I was adorable, before giving me her

number and jumping into a cab.

I broke my knee the next day. I was blackout drunk, playing an

intense game of tackle football on the grass outside University Plaza in my

slippers, when I tripped and awkwardly landed on my knee attempting to

catch a pass. Because of how drunk I was, I didn't feel any pain and

continued drinking as though nothing happened.

Brian, Jay, and Katzenberg were hosting a Mexican themed party

in their CIW suite, and that's where I met Amanda, who lived across the

hall from the guys. Amanda was beautiful. She had long straight black

hair that went just below her waist, seductively penetrating brown eyes,

olive skin, voluptuous breasts, and the waist of a runway model. More importantly she was extremely nice. I spent the entire night talking to her

and felt so comfortable in her presence, like I had known her in a past life

(if such things exist). The connection we shared was unparallel to

anything I had ever experienced, and when we finally hooked up that

night, it felt as though we had been together for years.

When I woke up, my knee had swelled to the size of a grapefruit.

I could barely move my leg, much less walk, and I asked Paul to drive me

to the hospital. Paul had gone with me to the Mexican party and had

driven us back to University Plaza twisted off his ass, which could explain

why his car was parked sideways. Anyway, the doctor told me that I had a

small hairline fracture and gave me a knee brace, a cane, and enough

vicodin to knock out an Elephant.

10/22/06u;d

Damn I'm so drunk!!!!! I dunno whats gooood!!! Just enjoy yoiur

cigerrette!!! Oh my god I keep hurting myself I stabbed myself with a

knife and broke my knee. WOWW I'm an asshole. I met people but yo I

can't remember anything. Maybe I'm an alcoholic. Damn rithg, how else

would I have a book. Sasha your wasted that's right PIMP CANE!!!!! PIMP

CANE!!!!! BITCH I'm THE JUGGERNAUT BITCH!!!! I'm a kich the shit outa you CHARLES!!! I lost my Giants hat. I wanna kill somebody. Sasha your in love. WITH NOTHING!!!! That's right you vapid dick!!! Muthafucka fuck. Theres no point in making sense. Your just funny cause you're an idiot. That's ok I accept it. Im just gonna be like YO I'm Sasha DUHHHHH!!!!!!! Why change anything, I'm a cripple, in the head. Shit!!! I'm crippled in the heart too!!! I'm just a natural born cripple!!!! OHHHHH!!!! People are hard to understand that's why theres no need to understand. If I don't get it why try? Why noy just be a little kid? It don't matter. What am I waiting for?? For the perfect girl to sweep me of my feet. Wait, that'll never happen!!! WOW I'm a dumbass I'm gonna pass out before I emberass myself futher. I LOVE LOVE!!!!!

Nicole and I had continued to talk after that night at the RAT. However, I really wasn't sure whether or not she wanted a relationship, as she was either too tired or too busy to hang out with me on a regular basis. Nicole was someone who I wanted to spend every single day with. But unfortunately, her schedule was so busy that she couldn't find the time to see me more than once a week, and that just isn't enough time to spend with someone who you want to be in an exclusive relationship with, especially when you're in college, surrounded by drugs, alcohol, and pussy. I remembered what happened the last time I committed myself to her, so I decided to keep my options open and see other girls just in case our relationship didn't work out.

Speaking of Nicole, she came over the next day and I decided to make her strawberry cheesecake with whip cream, since it was her favorite desert and I wanted to do something special for her. Actually, I had one of Greg's pledges make it, because I don't know how to cook anything other than cereal and would have probably burnt down the house had I actually tried to independently operate an oven. Either way, that's inconsequential, because it's the thought that counts, and Nicole was floored. She couldn't believe her eyes after seeing what I had made for her and leapt into my arms like an excited child, kissing me everywhere imaginable before closing the door to my room.

We spent the day lying in bed, watching movies, and eating cheesecake off each other's bodies. As we lay cuddled up to each other, covered by only a blanket, I realized that my wish had come true. After all this time apart and all of the agonizing days I spent longing for her, hoping against all odds to feel the sensation and comfort of her body next to mine, things were finally going back to the way they were. Or were they?

10/24/06

Yo I'm feelin nice right now. Nice and guilty! Yo Jamie came over and jerked me off and then we played NBA JAM. Son my dick went boomshakalaka all over face kidd. Nah but that aint right. I wanted to be with Nicole and after this talk about wanting to be with her I'm gonna blow it on the first pair of ass and titties I see (definitely some nice titties though). I mean I dunno, who knows if Nicole even wants a commitment anyway. Fuck yo a girl jerked me off what the fuck am I complaining about? and it felt good and check this, I'm not even using the word bitch right now. I don't even want that word in my vocabulary because that just spreads negativity and why be negative when you can smoke weed.

Jamie came over the next day, and to my surprise she was actually pretty fucking hot. She had long curly blond hair, beautiful C cup tits, and a body that was shaped like a coke bottle. Aside from looking like a playboy playmate, Jamie had to have been one of the coolest girls I had ever met. Not only did she jerk me off, she also happened to make me an omelet and play NBA Jam with me while I was eating it. This girl was going to be my future wife.

10/26/06

You wanna do the right thing so do it. Stay true to Nicole, the fact that I can hold her and be with her again means more than any other girl. From now on, it will be a seriously big mistake if I hooked up with another girl. The fact that anybody could respond to a letter I wrote almost a year after talking to them means something. I firsthand should know that. Nicole's the girl I think about after sex. Early on in the semester I fucked Mary and I was happy but I couldn't help but wish Nicole was the girl in bed next to me. Still, it wouldn't be right to fuck over Jamie completely. I have to chill with her 1 or 2 more times and explain my situation to her so that at least she knew I treated her with respect. At least she knew that she was a cool girl who I liked as a person. You know what, I truly hope Mary knows that. Despite all the shit I said about her in my journal, the truth is that she was nicer to me than almost anybody else I know. This is our relationship. Meet at the bar. Hook up at the bar. Go home. Fuck. Smoke weed. Fuck again. Go to sleep. Wake up. Fuck. Smoke weed. Chill and watch tv or a movie. Smoke 4 more times. Chill and smoke again. Mary drives me home and I smoke with Paul. Than we go out to the bars and get blackout drunk. Wow, weekends with Mary were the shit. I am truly truly sorry for being an asshole to you in my journal!!! You have no idea about the awful things I've written about you and I'm soooo sorry because you didn't deserve any of that. You were nothing but nice to me and I just want you to be happy and find someone who truly loves and appreciates you as a person. All I can hope for is that your happy and that you will one day find someone who truly loves and appreciates you as a person. I'm sorry that all I can see you as is my friend but know that I truly am your friend. Hopefully, you see things the same way but I understand if you don't.

I want my knee to get better so I can start doing things with Nicole. I want to show her that I'm more committed to spending time with her. I've always wanted more than to hook up in my room. Deep down I just want a real relationship. I was thinking about it and maybe I would rather go to the library and do work with Nicole than fuck Jamie and play NBA Jam. I dunno though, what if I went to the library with Nicole every day and got nothing? I think I would rather option B if that were the case. Jamie's a sex fantasy. You know what I'm thinking in ridiculous extremes which is fucking ridiculous. I'm a college student and so is Nicole. If I act like an adult who cares about her everything will be fine. However, as long as Nicole and I can be close with each other everything should be fine. Hopefully I've moved passed pressuring her and she's moved past withholding things from me. I really like her as a person and I believe that if we shared something more than we could really be together. Maybe

we've accepted each other. The one thing I can be sure of is that I really

have to try my best to get Nicole to like me because all she wants is for me

to do my best. I just have to show her that I'm trying that that shouldn't

be too hard to fuck up should it? Nicole cares. Even if she doesn't care

about what's bothering you, she still cares enough about how you feel to

ask which more than a lot of people are.

Wow, I just realized it. Nicole doesn't want me to be an image or

change my personality, she just wants me to love her. All I have to do is

show that I love her. What if that's Amanda? No, it's not!! Well maybe

Amanda is waiting for me to ask her something. Sasha are you fucking

stupid? Amanda doesn't know you well enough to have the feelings Nicole

has. Amanda doesn't see me when I'm not at my best. I dunno about that

but she didn't see me at my worst. Come to think about, neither has

Nicole. That should be a hint. Don't let these people get to know you too

well or else you'll just get fucked. Nicole knew me for 1 year and a half at

least and she's still talking to me. What more can I ask for? That's it, I've

made my decision I'm sticking with Nicole!!! Something has to be there if

you still think of me after all this time. Maybe my wish that when we were

apart all we could think about was being with each other which came true.

I know you had to have thought of me and that makes me want to be with you more. Anyway, good night.

Finding Closure

Nicole slept over a couple of nights later and I came to a profound realization about our relationship. Nicole was sick and not in the mood to fool around, so we didn't do anything other than cuddle. For the entire night, my balls were in throbbing pain, begging for a release that never came, when it hit me that I had been lying to myself about her all along. "This fucking sucks," I thought, as her body once again lay draped around mine like a blanket, teasing me mercilessly. "And as much as I love this girl, the fact of the matter is that I have needs and can't deal with this shit on a regular basis."

If one night of blue balls made me question my desire to be with Nicole, than what was our relationship really worth? When you truly love someone, you have to love him or her unconditionally, through thick and thin, through a stroke, a psychotic breakdown, a heart attack, a degenerative disease, paralysis, mental illness, dementia, and much more, and if something as insignificant as blue balls was enough for me to question how I felt about her, than maybe I didn't love Nicole as much as I thought I did. Nicole was the nicest idea anyone could've ever aspired to be with, but that was it, she was just an idea, and it hit me that I loved the idea of Nicole much more than I actually loved her.

I felt like complete shit the next morning, exhausted, confused and blue balled, so I decided to call Amanda for lunch in order to clear my head. Amanda and I became best friends after the Mexican Party, able to hangout for days and talk about almost anything. Here was a girl I felt completely uninhibited around, more so than when I chilled with Chris and Toby, and I've never been more comfortable around anybody else in my life.

Amanda could see the exhaustion on my face and invited me to take a nap in her bed for a couple of hours, which is what I did instead of going to class. I know I probably should have gone to class and learned something, especially since I had a paper due within two weeks, but none of that really mattered to me, especially when I had the chance to sleep in the same bed with a beautiful woman. Besides, its not like I would've paid attention. So I may as well cuddle with Amanda, because at least I'd feel good for the moment.

10/28/06 11:35 a.m

This is where the journal gets interesting. Here I am, this good looking guy who hooks up with his share of girls but why am I so scared of them? All I do is fuck bitches so how the fuck am I still scared of women? I look at myself in the mirror and think to myself "damm I look like an underwear model" but I still don't feel like I deserve pussy. These girls I'm hooking up with are way to good for me and even though they like me, I have nothing to be proud of because I don't bring anything to the table.

This stream of consciousness is coming out and the only way to turn a negative into a positive is to write about it. I saw Jamie and was too wasted to get it up. If there was a word to describe her aside from really hot, it would be cool. She's a cool girl. The only reason I wouldn't be able to have a platonic friendship with her would be that she's just too hot. I just wouldn't be able to keep my hands off her so I really really really hope she gives me another chance. Even if she doesn't, I learned a valuable lesson about blackout drinking. Don't do it or else your dick will stop working. That's the reason why people shouldn't smoke, drink, or do drugs. Because as much fun as these things are, eventually they will prevent you from doing things that are worthwhile and meaningful like fucking.

My definition of true happiness is having sex and playing sports. Sex and sports free your mind which make you happy and causes other people to be happy. It's only now that I truly appreciate how much fun it is to be outside and throw a football around or go to the park and play basketball. That's where the motivation to work out comes in, because the harder I work out the better I will be and the more fun I will have playing sports, plus I'll fuck better. It's not about making friends, fitting in, or putting on an image but rather it's about having fun and enjoying yourself. I want to be vibrant and full of life. Even if I tone myself down which I intend to do, what if all this takes a toll on me when I'm 45 and I can't sleep with my wife naturally or I'm fat and disgusting and can't pay the rent. That won't be me!!

From now on, I'm going to go about what I think is right. I'm not getting that drunk tonight. Blackout drinking when your emotionally unsure of yourself is a bad thing. If there's anything I learned from last year, its that. I want to make it the entire year and still have a positive relationship with my housemates.

I can't be afraid. I just have to do what's right and what would make me feel good. I have to be around people who make me feel good.

Amanda makes me feel good about myself. Even though, we've just kissed I feel happy in her presence. I would be really upset if I couldn't be friends with Amanda. I could tell that she would be really patient and understanding if I just show her I care. That's basically what I need in a girl. I need a really nice patient girl who doesn't get mad at me for doing stupid things. I want a girl who appreciates me and shows that she cares. Now am I ready for that? NOOOO!!! But I think girls like Jamie, and Amanda understand that and wont pressure me. I want a girl who supports me as I go about what makes me feel comfortable. I don't want some girl to pretend to be happy around me and act like my mother; I want a girl to actually be happy. I want a girl who makes a fuss over me while not secretly resenting me for being lazy. I want to be self reliant and sufficient while simultaneously having a girl make a fuss over me to show that she cares. I want a girl who doesn't need a lot to be happy. I just want her to need me. I just want friends who are supportive and cool with what I do. I don't want to be around people who type cast me or bitch at me. I just want to be around a chill group of people and have fun. Sometimes I think that I would just end up hurting them in the long run but I don't think I will. I just want a pressure free relationship. Why not have an easy relationship? Life has enough obstacles so why make relationships hard? Why not just chill? I'm really good at chilling and doing nothing.

I just thought myself into a positive mindset. I want to be around people who make me want to do the right thing instead of being around people who make me feel like a pussy for doing so. I know I have to grow up and be a man but I need support in the form of positive relationships. The more positive relationships I have, the easier it would be for me to assume the role of responsible adult.

Last night I ran into Nicole but check this out. She didn't call me and even when I was there she only hung out for like 5 minutes and went to sports bar. She didn't even ask me to come. Don't get me wrong, I'm not mad at her nor am I mad in general but stuff like that planted some serious doubts about being in a relationship with her. Besides, I'm past being mad at this point.. I think that I want to give Nicole a chance while at the same time giving everything else an equal chance. Nicole never told me she loved me. She said it in the way she kissed me or lay her head on my chest but its not the same as actually saying it. I would rather have a substantial life than a bunch of meaningless stories.

Chris and Toby came up for Halloween weekend and all of us got destroyed. Paul and Adam were over as well, and the 5 of us wound up taking enough shots of Jim Bean and Jose Quervo to obliterate a small village in Kuwait, while I railed enough Adderall to go into Cardiac Arrest.

Needless to say, the night was a blur, and I don't remember anything other than running into Nicole and her ditching me to go to Sports Bar, before going home with Jamie shortly afterwards, where I was too wasted to get it up.

Jamie was fucking awesome! Beautiful, smart, funny, fun to smoke pot with, knew how to cook, and most importantly loved NBA JAM just as much as I did, and I fucking blew it. I felt completely worthless when Jamie dropped me off and needed to smoke in order to cope with what just happened, so that's what I did. Chris and I smoked a bowl in my room and than spent the next couple of hours throwing a football around on the grass, when I came to a realization of what's truly important in life, which is to just be happy, and that true happiness was staring me right in the face all along. Being happy has nothing to do with money, status, or how much pussy you get, but rather, true happiness is all about enjoying the simple things in life, like being outside and chucking a football.

10/29/06 2:30 p.m

Aite yo so I banged Mary last night and hit that shit again today. Chris came through and banged her roommate while Toby slammed out the emotionally challenged bitch in the crib. Than Mary's roommate made us pancakes and they tasted like Big Foots dick son. But you cant be telling girls that shit cause its one thing to shit on a girl, but when you take a dump on her cooking, she's gonna hit you in the face with a frying pan and that aint proper know wat I'm sayin. Even if a bitch makes you food that looks, smells, and tastes like its fresh out the sewer you gotta say something like "Baby this is the most delicious thing I've ever tasted" and than you gotta eat that shit without vomiting. Speaking of vomiting, im drunk as hell right now we just played 22 cup beerpong back at the Plaza after I smoked madd weed and drank a 40. I haven't drank a 40 since high school and now I'm blackout drunk at 2 30 in the afternoon. Watever yo at least my penis works.

Mary's house was a well of pussy and we all drank amply from it. By the time we got back to University Plaza, all of us were fucked up, high, drunk, and hung over, but that did not stop us from drinking more. Toby suggested playing 22- cup beer pong and decided to put Vodka in some of the beers, which could explain why all of us were blackout drunk before 3

pm on a Sunday afternoon.

11/5/06

   So tonight sucked. It had to be one of the worst nights of my life.

Girls gone Wild was supposed to be there and instead a bunch of dudes

showed up. There was like a 10-1 guy to girl ratio. I felt like I was back at

Summit. Not only that but the bar was packed (with dudes) so I couldn't

even get a drink. I'm home and barely drunk. I'd say one of the worst

nights ever. The only positive thing I got out of this is the fact that I

appreciate the fact that every night won't be like tonight.

   Wow, so I'm reading some previous entries and wow, I sound like a

crazy person. Just looking at the shit I wrote about Nicole indicates that

something up there isn't quite right. I just flat out lied to myself in

writing!!! I dunno man, I really like Nicole but we're in college. Another

thing with Nicole is that I just don't know anything. I really want to make

her happy but I don't even know how to talk to her. I mean I know how to

spit game out but I wanna be able to talk to her without spitting game.

What makes her tick? What is she actually interested in? Do we have any of the same interests? Could she see being around me everyday? Does

she care?

In a way, I miss Christina because ever since she left I realize what

a caring girl is. You know what, it was annoying hearing her get mad if I

didn't answer her im's within 5 minutes of receiving them and it was

pretty ridiculous how worried she got over me for stupid shit, but deep

down I really liked it because it showed that she cared. I know now that I

don't want a relationship with her but hopefully down the line when I'm

more mature, I'll have the fortune of meeting another girl as caring as her.

Sex, Drugs, And Pussy

The week that followed had to have been one of the craziest,

most draining weeks of my life, so intense that breaking it down day by

day is the only way to accurately portray what I went through.

Sunday

I woke up at 9 am, making myself breakfast before railing an

Adderall and going to the Library, where I spent the next 5 hours

highlighting information for my Psycholinguistics paper. None of my

sources could be found online and each source was located in a different library book, so I decided to go into the bathroom and tear out the specific pages I needed from each book because I was too cheap and lazy to rent and carry them back to University Plaza.

When I finished studying, I saw a text message from Nicole asking me to come over. Nicole and I had barely spoken since Halloween and I thought that our relationship was all but over. However, when she texted me, all of the latent feelings that I had for her came rushing back, and there was absolutely no way that I could say no to her, so I stopped studying and immediately took a cab to her house on Seminary Street.

Nicole and I spent the night cuddled up in bed together watching movies; she even gave me a blowjob, but make no mistake about it, our relationship was by no means restored. Throughout the night there was this unspoken awkwardness between us, nothing tangible, just this feeling inside that Nicole and I had no natural chemistry.

Don't get me wrong, I loved Nicole, but no matter how attracted we were to each other, or how much we liked each other as people, the fact of the matter was that we just didn't know how to make each other click. Ever since I've known her, I've been trying to make this relationship work by attempting to build an everlasting connection with her, but no matter how hard I tried, I just couldn't do it, because it's impossible to build a connection if the connection just isn't there.

I left her house the next morning without so much as a kiss goodbye. Both of us knew that our relationship was over and it didn't bother me in the least bit, because I realized that we just weren't right for each other. As I walked out the door, I felt as though a huge weight had been lifted off my chest. A chapter of life had come to a close and I could finally go on with the rest of my life.

Monday

My mom turned 53 and I called to wish her a happy birthday right when I left Nicole's house, before going to the library to work on my Psycholinguistics paper. While I was working on my paper, I got a surprise text message from Jamie, saying that she wanted to come over and smoke. I thought that Jamie wanted nothing to do with me after my debacle on Halloween weekend, and nearly jumped out of my seat with excitement upon reading her text.

A few hours had passed and I had just finished studying, when Jamie called to say that she was running an hour late. I was no longer in the mood to study, so I smoked a bowl with Paul, before inviting Kevin over to play NBA Jam with me until she arrived.

Jamie finally came and boy did she look smoking. Wearing black leather pants that stuck to her body like glue and a tight white halter-top causing her beautiful c-cup breasts to jut out like watermelons. My jaw dropped upon seeing her and fucking the shit out of this girl became my only concern from here on in.

We lay in bed passing a joint back and forth, and I was beside myself with lust. Even watching her smoke was making my cock throb, as she blew cloud after cloud of smoke, teasing me with what she could do with her mouth.

The joint was almost dead and I had to make my move. I gave her a shottie and began softly making out with her as I released the joint from my lips. Jamie kissed back and the flick of her tongue caused me to feel this electrical tingling sensation all over my body. She then climbed on top of me and began straddling me with her clothes on. By now I was overcome with pleasure, consumed with desire, and almost past the point of no return. This girl was a fucking expert, having me on the edge before I could even take my clothes off.

Jamie had me just about ready to burst, but there was no way in hell that I was going to cum in my pants, so I unhooked her bra, rolled her over, and began rubbing her clit in an attempt to give my aching cock a rest. I slowly took my shirt off as I continued massaging her. Her pants came off just as quickly, followed by mine. Jamie than began stroking my cock, up and down, in slow maddening motions that had me squirming in ecstasy. She than placed her mouth on my thigh, kissing up my leg until she reached my kosher sausage, licking it like a lollipop.

Right as I was about to cum, Jamie got up and gently placed her firm round ass on my face. At this point I was in heaven, and began licking at her wet dripping cunt like it was a honeydew melon.

Oh my god!! I wanted to fuck this girl more than ever, but I was too lazy to get a condom, plus I was about to cum anyway, so I just did it in her mouth, unleashing blast after blast of Strenger Sauce down Jamie's throat.

Jamie and I were spent, lying naked in each other's arms, when I decided to put on a movie. We spent the next two hours smoking weed and watching Grandma's Boy, unable to move from the comfort of my bed.

I was fucking stoned out of my mind by the time Jamie left. My psycholinguistics paper was due the next day and I had barely even started it. Just as I was about to start my paper, Paul walked in the door and asked me if I wanted to smoke a bowl. Fuck it. I was already blazed out of my mind, and was probably going to fail anyway, so I gave in and spent the next few hours driving around Binghamton getting high with Paul.

Tuesday

It was 3 am by the time I got started on my paper, and I popped about 5 Adderall's in my mouth like Skittles in order to get a jump-start on my assignment. I pulled an all-nighter trying to get this paper done, but was nowhere near finished by the time I had to hand it in.

After a while, the Adderall began taking a toll on my body, making me feel lightheaded and weak, instead of focused and alert. By noon, I had passed out in my chair and lay comatose for the next six hours, before popping a few more pills and finishing up my paper.

Wednesday

After pulling another all-nighter, I had finally finished my paper at around 2pm, close to 24 hours after the due date, and spent the rest of the day doing nothing. I had another paper for my Psychological Tests class due Friday and planned to get a head start on it, but that got derailed when Mary called me to fuck.

Thursday

I woke up at around 11 am after a much needed good nights sleep. My plan was to go the library and work on my paper, which is what I did except for one thing. I didn't accomplish jack shit!! Instead, I spent the next three hours staring at the wall like a space cadet.

Amanda called and asked if I wanted to get dinner, so both of us met at the CIW dining hall. I planned on leaving right afterwards to work on my paper, really I did, but that went out the window once she invited herself back to my room.

Amanda had a magical hold on me and it didn't matter that I had a paper due the next day, or that my body was shot and dick was spent, I just couldn't say no to this girl. She had me wrapped around her little finger and could manipulate me into doing whatever she wanted without question, which is why I let her come over, despite not having the energy

to fuck.

What the hell was I going to do? My body needed to recover and

my penis didn't have the strength to go on. As breathtaking as Amanda

was, there was just no way that I could fuck her, because my cock was

only capable of so much.

There was only one thing left to do. Before beating my ass last

semester, Terry had given me a few Viagra pills in exchange for my

Adderall, and I couldn't think of a better time than now to try it.

Viagra was one hell of a drug and I had never fucked anyone like I

fucked Amanda that night. My sex drive may have flown out the window,

but that didn't matter, because Amanda and I fucked for 3 and ½ hours

straight, doing it in every position imaginable.

Exhaustion was understatement compared to how I felt by the

time we were done having sex, as I had cum inside her 4 times before

finally losing my erection. Both of us were spent, depleted, barely able to

move, and I used what little energy I had to reach over and light up the

perfectly rolled joint that lay on top of my bedroom counter, before somehow gathering the strength to walk up to my computer and put on a

mix of Bob Dylan, Dispatch, Dave Matthews, and The Postal Service.

Amanda and I lay naked, covered only by each other, immersed in

a cocoon insulating us from the rest of the world. We were drawn to each

other like magnets, connected like the pieces of a perfectly formed puzzle

and it was unparallel to anything I had ever experienced. At that

moment, I could see the two of us growing old together, and when I

looked into her eyes, I wanted nothing more than to spend the rest of my

life making love to her.

Friday

My paper was due in 6 hours and I hadn't even started it yet. I

went on another Adderall bender, railing pill after pill like Tony Montana,

but to no avail, as my paper was nowhere near complete by the time the

deadline rolled around. I emailed my professor, asking for an extension,

and he quickly responded, giving me until 3 pm the next day to hand it in.

Ten hours had just passed and I'd barely made a dent in my

paper. It looked as though I had to pull another all-nighter.

Saturday

After staying up all night and nearly emptying out my Adderall prescription, I finally handed in my paper at 2:57 pm, before collapsing in my bed and passing out, going to sleep for 18 hours straight.

Sunday

By the time the week was over I felt like a fucking Rockstar, loaded with drugs and worn out from pussy. My body had been through a war and my brain had been put through a meat grinder. Burnt-out and demolished, it would come as no surprise to me if this past week had taken off at least 5 years of my life, and after what I had just endured I now understand how Keith Richards and Mick Jagger must have felt after almost a lifetime of touring.

My grades on both of the papers I submitted were awful, so bad that my combined score barely exceeded a 50. It didn't matter though, because I had the most memorable week of my life, filled with beautiful moments that'll last me forever. Who cares that I bombed both of my papers? The everlasting memories that I gained in return were well worth the price of a failing grade.

Freedom and Empty Pleasures

11/15/06

If any girl wanted to be in a relationship with me, all I would say is

why change something that brings out the best in each other? Think

about it, you're at your best when you're fooling around. A) your fooling

around B) you fooled around and are in a good mood because 1) you just

busted one out 2) you made the girl happy 3) you get to lie around and

chill and be happy 4) your around someone else who is happy too 5) your

at your best when your happy. Therefore, why change what makes you

happy? That's the thing, I don't feel bad about hooking up with girls

because I truly believe that I'm making them happier in the process. I

want to continue doing this but I actually have to do things that make

other people happy. You know what, I would rather not get laid than get

girls who don't enjoy getting fucked by me. I don't even know what they

think of me on that. Am I really good or do I suck? How good am I and

how bad do I suck? I don't suck because Mary wouldn't have called me at

11:30 pm to fuck last Wednesday. I'm just really tired and need a break.

This week is all business

I hooked up with this girl Tess tonight. Sexy Tess!!! I was outside

when she asked me for a cigarette. I offered to roll one for her since I bought rolling tobacco. We go to the holiday inn and I end up making out

with her. She was kind of a big girl but who cares. This girl had the

monster titties, some EE type porno shits know what im saying doggs. But

yo with tits like that I don't care how big she is, bitch could be 300 lbs

looking like Tank Johnson, I'll still tittyfuck the shit outta her.

I really wanted a female friend but why? That's jus.t one less girl I

hook up with. Just be friends with girls who have boy friends. That's how

to do it. This way, you don't feel like a complete asshole for not getting

pussy. And yo, don't be an asshole!!

No Nicole or Christina. I'm free!! I can just do my thing guilt free.

This is life right here for you. Either your free and empty or trapped in a

relationship. Your happy being free but unhappy alone. What if these

girls are demons? What if Beth was secretly a demon from hell and I

failed a Satanic test? What if Mary and her housemates are devils? I saw

a picture of her and her friends and their faces looked like demon faces. I

dunno, but yo getting to know girls is probably a good thing.

Sexy Tess came over a few nights later, and boy could this girl suck a

dick? Wow!! That's all I can say, because her handiwork left me fucking

speechless. Tess was a fucking pro and not just because of her big tits and flawless technique, but also because she was an expert at keeping me on edge. Before she even took me into her mouth, this girl teased the living shit out of me, lightly flicking her tongue all over the inside of my mouth and blowing her hot breath in my ear, while simultaneously rubbing my cock through my boxers. She then took her shirt off, and glided herself lower and lower down my body, stopping briefly to press her huge tits on my throbbing cock as she let out a soft moan.

I was panting like a dog at this point and Tess had me right where she wanted, lowering herself even further, before pressing her mouth on my inner thigh, running her lips up and down the underside of my cock, as it lay trapped within the confines of my underwear. She did this for about 5 minutes, driving me crazy with her hands, mouth, and tits before finally letting my engorged cock out, giving the head a little kiss and taking me into her mouth.

As Tess licked, sucked, and kissed up and down the head, shaft, and base of my penis, I felt as though I would faint from pleasure, and it didn't take long before I was about to explode. Tess could tell that I was about to burst and stopped right before I passed the point of no return, cupping my balls and blowing on my cock as it twitched angrily with frustration. She than softly brushed her nails up and down my cock,

driving me wild, but not stimulating me enough to cum.

After what seemed like an eternity on edge, Tess unhooked her

bra, engulfing her huge tits and placing the tip of my throbbing, twitching,

pulsating dick in her mouth. That's when the volcano erupted, and it

didn't take more than 15 seconds for cum to start shooting out all over

face, tits, mouth and tongue, causing my body to tremble uncontrollably

with each blast I let out.

If there's one thing I've learned studying Psychology at SUNY

Binghamton, it's that fat Jewish girls give the best fucking head on the

planet. There's a whole theory behind it, so here it is: The Strenger Effect

Theory on why fat Jewish chicks suck cock on a world-class level.

1) According to Sigmund Freud, all fat chicks have an overwhelming

psychological need to have something in their mouth, translating

into them having a natural aptitude for giving blowjobs. No

further explanation is necessary, its pretty self explanatory, fat

people like having things in their mouth, and that includes a dick.

2) This brings me to my next point, perhaps the most basic,

underrated and overlooked of the bunch. Evolutionary Survival.

Most Jewish girls refuse to have sex if they're not in a relationship, especially if they're virgins, so they need to do something in order to keep the guy around, because if he leaves, they have nobody to reproduce with. This is where the case of Samantha Rosenberg comes into play. Samantha Rosenberg's a virgin who sees her boyfriend on average of twice a week for a month, giving him head twice a day. Samantha gives 4 blowjobs a week and there are 4 weeks in a month. Multiply 4 by 4 and Miss Rosenberg sucked 16 dicks in a month. Times that by 6 months, which is probably the amount of time it will take a virgin to fuck you (provided you spit the right game), and Sam sucked at least 96 dicks before losing her virginity.

3) Now lets say that Samantha's over 200 lbs. According to Frued's Psychosexual Stages of Development and Modern Evolutionary Theory, Sam's dick sucking total has the potential to double, if not triple, causing her to have approximately sucked between 200-300 dicks within a 6 month period, almost as much as a hooker.

4) There's an old saying that practice makes perfect, so after sucking dick 300 times, anything short of expertise is just simply inexcusable.

That my friends, is the Strenger Effect Theory on why fat Jewish chicks suck cock on a world-class level, explaining precisely why Sexy Tess sucked my dick like a champion.

11/20/06

I smoked and saw Stranger than Fiction, which it made me examine my life a little. The end was deep. Harold knew he was going to die and spent his last night on earth with the girl he loved. I want to find a girl I can spend my last night on earth with. That beats all the money, success, and pussy in the world. Hopefully I can feel that one-day and not fuck it up.

How do you know when you've found the right girl? Life is about doing what you think is most enjoyable at the moment, be it playing basketball, videogames, going out, lifting, chilling with your boys, or whatever. When you get a girl, you spend a lot less time doing these things. You become a new man; no longer able to do whatever you want whenever you want because now you're stuck spending all your time with her. By then it shouldn't matter though, because the right girl is someone you're gonna rather spend time with more than anything else in the world. Hopefully I'll be able to meet that girl once I'm ready to.

PART 6

THE PARTY'S OVER

11/24/06

WHAT THE FUCK DID I JUST DO? *Toby lay unconscious on the concrete floor of 83rd and Amsterdam Avenue with his head cracked open on the pavement. Chris was with me and we stared in horror at Toby's lifeless body knowing that his death was our fault. I just murdered one of my best friends and now my life was over. At that moment, everything I accumulated and everything that I could have potentially accomplished went out the window right before my eyes. All I could ask myself was,* **WHAT THE FUCK JUST HAPPENED?**

This can't be fucking happening right now. My worst nightmare has just come true. I'm getting pushed into the back of a police car while Toby is getting carried away on a stretcher, unconscious and bleeding from the back of his head. Fuck Man!! Please DON'T DIE ON ME TOBY!! PLEASE

DON'T DIE! IM SO SORRY!! IT WAS JUST AN ACCIDENT, MEANT TO BE A JOKE. PLEASE FOR THE LOVE OF GOD JUST DON'T GO!!! YOU'RE ONE OF MY BEST FRIENDS AND I CANT LOSE YOU RIGHT NOW!! ESPECIALLY KNOWING THAT YOUR DEATH IS MY FAULT!!!

The bars have just shut behind me and I'm cold. I can't think of a worse, colder, or emptier feeling than sitting in a jail cell wondering whether or not you just killed one of your best friends. I'm scared to death right now. I can't have this on my conscience. This is just too much. How will I ever live with myself if you die Toby? Please Live. Please.

It wasn't supposed to be like this. The 3 of us just wanted to go out, get fucked up, and hit on girls, just like any other night. Toby wasn't supposed to fall down and crack his head open on the pavement and I sure as hell didn't mean to push him that hard. I was just giving him the drunk test and I told him to put his hands on his hips before pushing him. How the fuck was I supposed to know that he was going to crack his head open and lose consciousness.

I didn't mean for this to happen but it doesn't matter because it's still my fault. If Toby dies this will haunt me for the rest of my life.

11/25/06

It's 6 am right now and I've just been transferred to a cell uptown in Harlem with a Hispanic guy who's being charged with carrying a machete in public. Fuck!! I don't want to share a cell with him and I'm sitting with my back against the wall as long as I'm here. There's a huge black guy in my cell too. He looks like Suge Knight. Man, I really hope Toby's ok because there's no way in hell I can handle jail.

I'm being transferred downtown to central bookings to see the judge. There are about 60 of us. I can't stop thinking about Toby. I really hope he's ok. I just saw an Asian guy rollerblading down the street and I envy his freedom and clear conscience. They're fingerprinting me and taking my mug shot now. I'm in a fog. This is just a bad dream, I tell myself. This is just a bad dream.

This aint no dream. This is as real as it fucking gets!! My whole life has been a dream up until now and its time to wake the fuck up.

This shit is over. I'm fucking serious this time. It's not fun anymore. I'm done drinking. I'm done partying. I'm done with all this fucking bullshit. Toby could be dead right now and it's all because of fucking alcohol. This shit would've never happened if we were sober and I swear to god, this is the last time I'm writing in this journal for as long as I live.

Wow, guys in jail pretty fucking smart. I'm listening in on a conversation about politics, spirituality and the economy, and these hardcore convicts with no formal education sound more intelligent than most of my classmates at Binghamton. Shit, they sound more intelligent than me. I guess it goes to show you that they could've easily been where I am and vice versa had they been born into a different environment.

TOBY'S ALIVE!!! I just got off the phone with his lil brother and he told me that Toby's doing fine. Nothing's wrong with him. No brain damage. No paralysis. Nothing major. Just a few superficial injuries and that's it. THANK YOU GOD!!!

Talk about a fucking close call. I can't even begin to describe how happy I am. I'm just so fucking relieved. I was a nervous wreck all day, paralyzed with fear, sweating, trembling, my heart racing a mile a minute. I thought my life was over but now that Toby's ok, I have another chance, and I'm gonna make the most of it.

I was charged with 2 counts of possession of a fake ID and given a $100 fine, along with 48 hours of community service. The judge gave me an ACD and told me that this would be dropped from my record if I stayed out of trouble for 6 months.

Visiting Toby in the hospital was the first thing I did when I got out of jail. I gave him a huge hug, so happy that he was alive and well, that I still had one of my best friends. His mom was there too and she also gave me a huge hug, telling me that she was worried sick all night, and that his dad almost had a heart attack upon hearing the news. "Wow", I thought, as she cradled me in her arms like I was one of her own, and it dawned on me at that moment how many lives I could've ruined simply by being a drunk asshole.

I spent the rest of the day in the hospital hanging out with Toby and his younger brother, laughing, cracking jokes, and just being a little kid. Toby didn't remember anything from that night and asked me how he wound up here, so I told him. I told him about the drunk test, about how he fell and cracked his head open on the pavement, about how I thought I almost killed him, and about how Chris wanted to stay but couldn't, because he was on probation for selling drugs.

As I looked up at the night sky upon leaving the hospital, I couldn't help but feel blessed, grateful that Toby had made it, because if he were to have died, god knows if I would've ever seen the stars again. It took a nearly fatal accident for me to fully appreciate how precious life truly is; that it's short, fleeting, and can be taken away at any given moment.

What happened with Toby has opened my eyes to what's truly important, and has made me extremely thankful for everything that I used to take for granted. Not everyone is lucky enough to be born into a nice neighborhood, have access to food, shelter, clothing, and education, or even have parents that love them. Just having one of these things is a godsend and the fact that I have all four makes me fortunate beyond measure.

I wanted to write my last entry on my 21st birthday, but I can't think of a better way to end this book than by having it serve as a cautionary tale. Although nothing happened to Toby or myself, there are thousands of other people all over the world who are unfortunately not so lucky, as drug and alcohol abuse remains one of the leading causes of death amongst college students. Toby could've easily been a statistic, and I could very easily be writing this book from a jail cell instead of at my computer in the comfort of my own home.

Don't go through college the way I did. That's all I'm trying to say.

This story could've ended tragically, but thankfully it didn't, as I've been given a second chance to write my own ending. However, you might not be so lucky.

Part 7

A New Beginning

ABOUT THE AUTHOR

Alexander (Sasha) Strenger is 25 years old. He lives with his parents and spends his free time playing NBA JAM and whacking it to porn. He has a very tiny penis and has been known to pee on his balls from time to time.